THE
FORD
CENTURY

THE FORD CENTURY

FORD MOTOR COMPANY AND
THE INNOVATIONS THAT SHAPED THE WORLD

RUSS BANHAM
FOREWORD BY PAUL NEWMAN

ARTISAN

New York

A TEHABI BOOK

Published by Artisan
A Division of Workman Publishing Company, Inc.
708 Broadway
New York, New York 10003
www.artisanbooks.com

Library of Congress Cataloging–in–Publication Data

Banham, Russ.
   The Ford century : Ford Motor Company and the
innovations that shaped the world / by Russ Banham ;
foreword by Paul Newman.
   p. cm.
   Includes index.
   ISBN 1-57965-201-8
   1. Ford Motor Company--History. 2. Automobile
industry and trade--United States--History. I. Title.

HD9710.U54 F5338 2002
338.7'6292'0973--dc21

                                        2002074607

Printed in Korea
Translations of this book provided by Bowne Global
Solutions, Inc.

10 9 8 7 6 5 4 3 2 1

First Edition

The Ford Century was developed by Tehabi Books
4920 Carroll Canyon Road, Suite 200
San Diego, California 92121
www.tehabi.com

TEHABI BOOKS

Tehabi Books has developed and published many award-winning books that are recognized for their strong literary and visual content. Tehabi works with national and international publishers, corporations, institutions, and nonprofit groups to identify, develop, and implement comprehensive publishing programs.

President and Publisher Chris Capen
Senior Vice President Tom Lewis
Vice President of Operations Sam Lewis
Editorial Director Nancy Cash
Sales Director Eric Pinkham
Director, Corporate Publishing Tim Connolly
Director, Trade Relations Marty Remmell
Editor Sarah Morgans
Senior Art Director Josie Delker
Production Artist Kendra Triftshauser
Copy Editor Naomi Grady
Proofreader Patricia MacDonald
Indexer Ken DellaPenta
Automotive Consultant Bob Casey

The paper used in this publication meets the minimum requirements of the American National Standard for Information Sciences—Permanence of Paper for Printed Library Materials, ANSI Z39.48-1992.

This book is printed on recycled and recyclable paper using soy ink rather than petroleum-based ink.

A LOT IN COMMON

A WINNING PASSION *From the time of his appearance in the movie* Winning, *far left, to his role as a CART team owner, Paul Newman has been linked with racecars as well as acting and philanthropy. Right: Newman (left) celebrates a victory at the Bosch Grand Prix with driver Michael Andretti in 1996. Left: Volunteers load trucks donated by Ford Motor Company with food provided by Newman's Own as part of the America's Second Harvest food distribution event on June 15, 2001.*

You'd never guess it, but Ford Motor Company and I sure have a lot in common. We've both been around for a long time, we're obsessed with cars, and we both like finding ways to use our successes to offer a helping hand—to invest back in the community.

I've had the opportunity to work with Ford on more than one occasion. Back in June of 2001, Ford Motor Company and Newman's Own partnered with America's Second Harvest to improve hunger relief food distribution to rural areas. Ford donated some trucks, and we packed them with food. The event was such a great success— many, many people benefited from it—that Ford and Newman's Own have both continued to assist America's Second Harvest with their great hunger relief efforts.

As Bill Ford once said, "A good company delivers excellent products and services. A great company does all that and strives to make the world a better place."

You betcha!

Just as Newman's Own is about more than food, Ford stands for much more than producing quality cars. When Ford Motor Company puts time, effort, and funding behind projects that reflect their social responsibility, everyone wins.

PAUL NEWMAN
MAY 2002

Paul Newman is a founder of Newman's Own food company, which donates all after-tax profits to charity. He was a contributor to the book Corporate Social Investing, *and was the inaugural speaker of a forum on philanthropy in business hosted by the Hass School of Business at the University of California at Berkeley. He has been co-owner of a CART racing team, Newman/Hass Racing, since 1983.*

CHAPTER ONE

A PART OF HISTORY

"Men make history, and not the other way around. In periods where there is no leadership, society stands still. Progress occurs when courageous, skillful leaders seize the opportunity to change things for the better."

—HARRY S. TRUMAN

❖

Straw boater in hand, Thomas Alva Edison, inventor of the lightbulb and motion pictures, sits alongside the man he encouraged to manufacture an affordable car for the masses, his good friend Henry Ford. Above: The fruit of Henry's labor, a 1912 Ford Model T.

SETTING THE PACE *Each era of history is marked by singular images that connect people to their past. Ford—the company and its automobiles— offers such indelible links, from the dawning promise of the twentieth century through the war-torn 1940s to the fast-paced vibrancy of today.*

Go anywhere in the world today—to remote regions of the planet— find a native citizen of that country and say but one word, one syllable really: Ford. No matter the language, no matter the culture, no matter the vast gulf of differences separating you, eyes will register recognition. Over the past hundred years of human progress, Ford Motor Company has transformed the course of history. The company is an inextricable part of the social, economic, and cultural heritage of many nations, a force far more revolutionary than a mere maker and seller of cars. Ford has shaped the world around us.

This epic story of a global institution begins simply, with a boy who loved to take watches apart and put them back together again. Henry Ford was born on a farm in Springwells Township (now Dearborn), Michigan, on July 30, 1863. Abraham Lincoln was president of the twenty-four states of the Union, then torn by civil war. Overseas, Charles Dickens began work on his last completed novel, Karl Marx considered his theories on socialism, and Giuseppe Verdi polished *La Forza del Destino*, his grand opera on the force of destiny.

The forces that would shape the Industrial Age were gathering the year Henry Ford was born. The open-hearth process of manufacturing steel, the vast network of pipelines transporting oil, and the crisscrossing railroads uniting a

HOME AND HEARTH *Born and reared on a middle-class American farm, Henry Ford would grow to dislike the drudgery and toil of farming. The homestead included several outbuildings, a gristmill, and sheep-shearing facilities. Right: The home in Springwells Township in which Henry, seen below at age two, was born.*

nation lay ahead. One American in five lived in a city; the United States was still a rural nation defined by agriculture and the farmers who worked the land.

Young Henry was the son of one such farmer. William Ford, an Irish immigrant from Kilmalooda, near Clonakilty, County Cork, sailed to America in 1847 to escape the famine that had devastated his country. In 1858, he bought eighty acres of farmland for $350 in Dearborn, Michigan, named for General Henry Dearborn, a hero of the Revolutionary War. Three years later, William met and married Mary Litogot, born in Wyandotte, Michigan, of an American father and English mother in 1838 or 1839, the exact date unknown. Orphaned as an infant, Mary had been adopted by Patrick and Margaret O'Hern.

William and Mary moved in with the O'Herns in a seven-room frame house in Springwells Township, ten miles west of Detroit. William helped build the unpretentious dwelling, shaded from the hot noonday sun by a large willow tree. In 1867, the O'Herns sold the house and land to the Fords. It was at this homestead that the first of their six surviving children, Henry Ford, entered the world.

His very first memory was of his father taking him and his brother John to see a bird's nest under a large oak log. He was three years old. "I remember the nest with four eggs and also the bird and hearing it sing," he wrote in 1913 on a sheet of paper accompanying his rough drawing of the scene. "I have always remembered the song."

Like other sons of farmers, young Henry had daily chores—chopping kindling, retrieving and milking cows from the pasture, and assisting in the plowing, planting, and harvesting. He disliked the arduous sunup to sundown work. "I never had any particular love for the farm," Henry once said. "It was the mother on the farm I loved."

Ford R. Bryan, a member of the extended Ford family and author of five books about the Fords, says, "Henry would do anything to get out of his chores. Once, he put molasses in the boots of his younger brothers, preventing them from getting the easiest chores that were doled out to the first boys up in the morning." Looking back at his childhood, Henry said of the farm, "Considering the results, there is too much work on the place!"

The inquisitive youngster preferred to probe the workings of mechanical objects or fix the neighbors' broken tools, wagons, and sleighs in his father's workshop. "He'd pester people to loan him their watches so he could figure out how they worked, to the point where the whole neighborhood said, 'You'd better keep an eye out for Henry Ford or he'll take your watch apart,'" Bryan says.

little more than the moralistic metaphors quoted in the McGuffey Eclectic Readers, the primers that shaped for life his resolute sense of right, wrong, honor, and integrity. Although proficient at mathematics, he never really learned to spell correctly, read freely, or express himself well in writing.

Henry would rather tempt other boys from their studies to assist him in building waterwheels and steam turbines in William's workshop or at a workbench Henry erected in the dining room. Once, like Tom Sawyer, he led a group of boys in an impromptu dam-building project on a nearby creek, which flooded a neighbor's potato patch. Another time, he and the gang built a small coal-fired steam boiler out of an old dishpan and a large oilcan that blew up and set a fence on fire. Half a century later, his sister warmed to the memory. "Had I known what the future held for Henry in the way of mechanics," Margaret wrote, "I surely would have been more tolerant, patient, and understanding of his experiments."

"Fortunately, most of the time he got them back together again just fine."

Simply by glancing at a mechanism, Henry could comprehend the interdependence of its parts, pursuing a line of reasoning through gears, ratchets, wheels, pinions, and levers. Neighbors referred to him as a young man "with wheels in his head," and his father, speaking of Henry's younger brothers, remarked: "John and William are all right but Henry worries me. He doesn't seem to settle down and I don't know what will come of him."

Henry's mother, Mary, on the other hand, encouraged his mechanical interests. "She believed in his childish tinkering with tools, [and] her patience and understanding were appreciated by him," wrote Henry's sister Margaret Ford Ruddiman in her memoirs, published in *Michigan History* magazine. "There was a closeness between mother and son, which Henry missed after her passing."

Henry was only twelve years old when Mary died at age thirty-seven, following the birth of a stillborn baby. The house afterwards, he said, was like "a watch without its mainspring."

During the school year, Henry attended a red-brick one-room schoolhouse, the Scotch Settlement School, where he said he learned

Farming tools were useless for taking apart small mechanical objects, so Henry made his own tools: a screwdriver out of a shingle nail, tweezers from corset stays, and other devices from steel knitting needles. Margaret recalled that his pockets were full of boyish treasures—nuts, nails, pieces of string, a watch wheel, a spring, and other odds and ends.

Contrary to popular legend, Henry did not grow up poor. The farm was successful and he enjoyed a middle-class existence. He was expected to become a farmer like his father, a prospect that did not suit him. Destiny intervened in 1876, via a prophetic encounter with a self-propelled vehicle that irrevocably altered the course of his life.

PLOWING NEW GROUND

Having experienced the backbreaking toll of farm-work himself, Henry was determined to improve the lot of farmers. Here he sits on a 1907 experimental "automotive plow," the precursor to Fordson and later Ford tractors. Below: The 1935 Fordson tractor reconceived as a children's toy.

Henry and his father William were atop their horse-drawn wagon en route to Detroit when they spied a portable engine and steam boiler mounted on wheels. It moved slowly down the road, threshing grain. A chain connected the engine to the rear wheels. "I was off the wagon and talking to the engineer before my father knew what I was up to," Henry said. He shouted a fusillade of questions to the fellow shoveling coal into the behemoth, startling him with his audacity and keen mechanical insight.

"It was one of those events where something clicks," says Donn Werling, former historical director of the Henry Ford Estate, Fair Lane, at the University of Michigan—Dearborn, founder of the Henry Ford Heritage Association, and author of several books on Ford. "Here's this young man who has seen the burden of farming from the perspective of horse, oxen, and human toil, and along comes this steam-powered machine. It was an earth-shattering experience. With its noise and smell, the only similar image would be a large cannon. But, instead of exploding bombs, the machine exploded a way of life."

The year 1876 claimed many astounding events—General George Armstrong Custer's last stand at Little Big Horn, the formation of the National League in baseball, and the creation of an extraordinary invention, the telephone. But it was the Centennial Exposition in Philadelphia that captured Henry's imagination. William attended the show, which boasted the world's biggest steam engine: the two-story high, 1,600-horsepower Corliss. Millions of wide-eyed visitors also marveled at the giant Krupp cannons from Germany; the original band saw that would carve all those Victorian curlicues; and the torch from the Statue of Liberty, the rest of the lady not yet completed by her French sculptors.

William brought back to Dearborn an armload of printed materials, which Henry pored over. "He was completely captivated by the wonders his father described and the promise of a new mechanical age," says Michael Skinner, president of the Henry Ford Heritage Association. "He'd just seen with his own eyes his first self-propelled vehicle, and now he's told that machines exist that have the power of 1,600 horses! Given his mechanical bent, this new world of science and invention was enthralling."

In December 1879, Henry hung up his farmer's overalls and walked to Detroit to take an apprentice position at the Michigan Car Company, a railroad car manufacturer. He was fired after six days. "The shop foreman thought him too brazen," says Skinner. "A

WORK AND PLAY *Lured by the promise of the city, Henry headed to Detroit as a teenager, below. He courted and won the heart of Clara Bryant, pictured at right in 1888, the year they married. Left: A mustachioed Henry in 1892 with fellow employees of the Edison Illuminating Company. Overleaf: A replica of Henry's first workshop.*

number of older engineers were trying for hours to repair a machine. After they walked away in frustration, Henry went over, took one look at the thing, and fixed it in a matter of minutes. That didn't go over all too well."

Henry wasn't unemployed for long. William introduced him to the Flower brothers, who had a machine shop in Detroit, and Henry took an apprentice position paying $2.50 for a sixty-hour workweek. Since his room and board cost $3.50 a week, he had to take an evening job at the Robert Magill Jewelry Shop, repairing watches for $3 a week.

Thinking customers would be concerned if they saw a sixteen-year-old boy fixing their timepieces, Magill stuck Henry in the back room.

Shortly thereafter, in August 1880, Henry became an apprentice engineer at the Detroit Drydock Company, a large shipbuilding firm. He had quit the machine shop but kept his night job, working a grueling ninety-six hours a week. At Detroit Drydock, Henry saw his first internal combustion engine. The company's chief construction engineer, Frank Kirby, was experimenting with a gasoline power source for ships, albeit unsuccessfully. He liked Henry's inquisitive nature and took him under his wing. Kirby's mentoring had a deep impact on the young man, teaching him the scientific merits of constant trial and error. In the 1920s, Henry honored Kirby by directing that his name be carved alongside those of Galileo Galilei, Isaac Newton, and Thomas Edison on the portico of the Dearborn Engineering Laboratory.

Henry returned to Dearborn in the summer of 1882 to help William run the farm. He also joined a neighbor's threshing crew, operating a portable steam engine, the Westinghouse Agricultural Engine. Henry hauled the engine from farm to farm, hooked it up to a thresher (or other farm equipment), and fired it up. The piston turned a huge flywheel that powered the task at hand—cutting hay, sawing lumber, grinding feed, and so on. He was so adept at his work that Westinghouse hired him to service their steam engines, a job taking him from county to county.

Although these vital apprenticeships shaped Henry's life's work as an engineer, it was his decision to attend business school in December 1884 that prepared him to run a company. At Goldsmith, Bryant, & Stratton Business University in Detroit, Henry studied bookkeeping, business, and mechanical drawing, later crediting the school for his rudimentary understanding of business.

Henry's passion for work did not preclude an active social life. In 1885, he attended a New Year's Eve dance at the Martindale House in Greenfield Township, a short distance from the Ford family homestead. There he met eighteen-year-old Clara Bryant, "an attractive, earnest young woman with light brown hair and a very practical way about her," says Bryan. Given his father's relative success as a farmer, Henry was considered a catch. "She liked his serious-mindedness and his unique talents, and he liked her equally serious and appreciative demeanor," Bryan adds.

They participated in the courting rituals of the time: husking corn by moonlight, steamboat excursions, and plenty of dancing—an activity Henry took especial pleasure in. On April 11, 1888, Henry and Clara were married in the parlor of the Bryant home.

GREEN ACRES *Henry worked regularly as an engineer in Detroit but remained close to the land and his farm in Dearborn. The competing interests are reflected here: at right, Henry (back row, third from right) at Edison Illuminating Company, and at left, an Atlas drawing of his father's homestead in 1870.*

William gave the young couple a forty-acre farm he had purchased some years earlier. Henry cleared the land using a circular saw attached to a 12-horsepower Westinghouse engine, No. 345. Liking the activity, he even cleared his neighbors' properties of stumps and trees, earning a tidy sum of money that he augmented by servicing steam engines for Buckeye Harvester. "Some of the first of that lumber went into a cottage on my new farm and in it we began our married life," he said. Henry and Clara called the house the "Honeymoon Cottage."

It was a bucolic time. "Little groups gathered together to discuss the topics of the day," according to Henry's sister Margaret. "The ladies were interested in the latest styles and exchanged recipes, the men compared crops and discussed the new methods of farming." It was a period of reflection for Henry, a "time to think and plan," she observed. "He read a great deal about the new kinds of engines, particularly gasoline-powered ones."

Henry was consumed with building an engine that would ease the burden of farming and transportation. "For two years I kept experimenting with various sorts of boilers, and then I definitely abandoned the whole idea of running a road vehicle by steam," he said. The lumber or coal that had to be hauled along made the engine unwieldy. In the little workshop he constructed at home, he focused on making a double-cylinder engine that would propel a bicycle. Clara asked how it would work, prompting him to sketch it out on the back of a sheet of organ music.

In the midst of these efforts, Henry was offered a position as an engineer at the Detroit power plant of the Edison Illuminating Company, for $40 a month. "I took it because that was more money than the farm was bringing me, and I had decided to get away from farm life anyway," he said. The job afforded the opportunity to learn about electricity, crucial to Henry's long-planned gasoline engine.

Although dismayed at the thought of leaving the new house and moving to the city, Clara packed without complaint. "It was a great thing to have my wife even more confident than I was," Henry said. "She has always been that way." Clara was his "great believer," he often remarked. So, on September 25, 1891, with their furniture crammed in a hay wagon, Henry and Clara moved to Detroit, settling first at 570 Forest Avenue and moving a month later to a two-family house at 58 Bagley Avenue.

Detroit was burgeoning into an industrial center in the 1890s. The city was founded in 1701 by Antoine de la Mothe Cadillac, on the banks of what would later be called the Detroit River. In the nineteenth century, Detroit's access to the Great Lakes and its position as a rail hub allowed it to take advantage of the state's two primary raw materials, lumber and copper, which it exported throughout the region. Its large salt

A TIME OF DISCOVERY

The early 1900s was an extraordinary period of discovery and invention in all industries. Lightbulbs, color photography, telephones, and silent movies (the motion picture camera here is from 1915) made their debut. Science took a great

leap forward as Albert Einstein formulated his theory of relativity, Marie Curie discovered radium, and Sigmund Freud wrote his theories on human psychology. Astonishing feats of human endeavor, from the building of the Panama

Canal to Robert E. Peary's planting of the U.S. flag at the North Pole to the aerial accomplishments of the Wright brothers at Kitty Hawk, captured the public's admiration and awe.

CHAS. A. STRELINGER & CO.
MACHINERY,
TOOLS AND SUPPLIES.
HARDWARE. JUN 4 1898 P.M

Nos. 98 to 110 Bates St. Cor. Congress.

DETROIT, MICH. 189___

SOLD TO Henry Ford
c/o Edison Ill Co.

ORDER No. _____

1	Do 3/16 Nuts		12	
1	Bar Bess Rod		08	
1	Doz 1/4 nuts 10 Bess Rod 6		16	36

BUILDING FOR TOMORROW
In the brick shed behind his and Clara's home at 58 Bagley Avenue in Detroit, left, Henry constructed his first automobile, the Quadricycle, in 1896. The receipt from that year, above, is for parts used in making the vehicle. The 1902 portrait, below, is of Henry and his son, Edsel, born November 6, 1893. Henry often drove young Edsel and Clara in the Quadricycle from Detroit to his father William's farm.

deposits, yielding sodium carbonates, also helped it become a leader in the budding chemical industry. In short order, steel mills manufacturing stoves and railroad cars sprouted along the river, as did machine tool shops and metalworking firms. All this bustling activity fostered a skilled labor force that would be crucial to the advancement of the American automobile industry.

At the turn of the century, Europe was ahead of the United States in automobile development. A Belgian, Jean-Joseph-Étienne Lenoir, had invented an operable internal combustion engine in 1859, and in 1864, a Viennese, Siegfried Marcus, had built a primitive gas-powered road vehicle. Germany had contributed a four-cycle engine, built by Nikolaus Otto in 1876, and claimed Messrs. Daimler and Benz, makers of automobiles in the 1880s.

Henry's new employers allowed him to make use of a small workshop for his projects, and when not on duty, he could be found bent over his workbench. Indeed, he was so engrossed in building a gas engine that he often forgot to pick up his pay.

On Christmas Eve 1893, there were three Fords to celebrate the holidays—Henry, Clara, and Edsel Ford, born a few weeks earlier on November 6. Edsel was named for Henry's close friend from the Scotch Settlement School, Edsel Ruddiman, with whom he shared a desk and who, years later, married Henry's sister Margaret. While Clara busied herself with the holiday festivities, Henry lugged his first completed engine into the kitchen and mounted it to the sink. "It was a very simple one-cylinder machine, made up of a piece of pipe that Henry bored to permit the piston to move smoothly," says Robert Casey, curator of transportation at Henry Ford Museum & Greenfield Village.

"The flywheel was a handwheel off a lathe, and the carburetor, or at least what passed for one, was nothing more than a metal container allowing gas to drip. A piece of fiber with a wire through it served as the spark plug. Henry basically made the engine out of bits and pieces of things he had."

Clara was asked to help start up the contraption. Henry connected the crude spark plug to the house's electric current, then gave Clara the signal to start pouring gasoline into the carburetor while he turned a screw to let the gas trickle into the valve intake. The engine barked and shook violently, belching smoke and flames from the exhaust. But it worked! Now all he had to do was build a better engine and an automobile around it.

The rental house on Bagley Avenue had a brick shed behind it, where the landlord allowed the tenants to store coal and wood. In his half of the shed, separated by a brick partition, Henry set up a workshop to experiment further. The other tenant, an elderly man named Felix Julien, was so impressed that he moved out his coal and wood, tore down the partition, and let Henry have the whole shed. It was here, while Clara watched and Edsel dozed, that the first Ford automobile was built in the spring of 1896—the Quadricycle.

Henry was not the only engineer in the thick of such work. In March 1896, another Detroiter, Charles King, had built a 1,300-pound automobile. When it lumbered down the road, Henry followed it on his bicycle, transfixed. The Quadricycle, by contrast, weighed only 500 pounds. It had two cylinders, fitted into sections of a steam engine's exhaust pipe. Two belts, one attached to the flywheel and the other to a small wheel on its right face, gave the driver a choice of two forward speeds (10 miles per hour and 20 miles per hour). There was no reverse, no brakes and no steering wheel. A tiller guided a set of four bicycle wheels.

When the Quadricycle was ready to run, Henry discovered it was too wide to go through the door of the shed. So exhilarated by the prospect of driving his invention, he grabbed an axe and smashed the bricks out of the wall. At four in the morning on June 4, 1896, Henry Ford sat atop his first automobile and took it for a spin from Bagley Avenue to Grand River Avenue to Washington Boulevard, where it

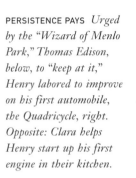

stalled from ignition trouble, drawing the taunts of transients outside the Cadillac Hotel. But Henry was jubilant—the Quadricycle was the crowning achievement of years of hard work. He had built an automobile.

The next month, Henry, Clara, Edsel, and Charles King drove the Quadricyle to the Ford farm to show William. Margaret recalled that their father wouldn't get into the automobile: "He saw no reason why he should risk his life . . . for a brief thrill. He liked his horses." Henry's sister, however, took her first ride, remarking that the experience was "better than bicycling."

Henry now devoted his attention to building a more advanced automobile. His confidence was boosted by another providential encounter. In August 1896, he attended an Edison Illuminating Company convention in New York City, where he was introduced to Thomas Edison, the inventor of the lightbulb and motion pictures. Informed that Henry had built a gasoline-powered motorcar, Edison was intrigued. Henry quickly made a few sketches of the Quadricycle on a menu. "You have it—a self-contained unit that carries its own fuel," Edison exclaimed. "That's the thing! Keep at it!"

LEISURE TIME *Henry and Clara relax at home, above. Not one to idle for long, Henry and two of his three grandsons, Henry II and Benson, right, "work" at the Ford farm. Below: Although he was among the richest men in America, Henry remained a man of the people.*

HENRY FORD: THE UNCOMMON COMMON MAN

The father of the Model T, the automobile assembly line, and commercial aviation was a crafty, workaholic businessman and an iron-fisted autocrat, who did things as he saw fit. He also was a social philanthropist, noted naturalist, and eminent folklorist. Henry Ford is so complex and so elusive that more than one hundred biographies have tried to delineate his character, shedding light on his facets while obscuring the whole.

What we do know is that Henry Ford the businessman and Henry Ford the man are not necessarily one and the same. He had very serious interests beyond automobiles, including global politics, industrial uses for

agricultural products, environmental conservation, and positive change in human behavior through work.

Henry bankrolled the sailing of a "Peace Ship" that set out to end World War I and publicly alleged that Jews had caused the war and controlled global banking. The latter action invited more outrage than adherents, and Henry ultimately renounced the printed comments in the *Dearborn Independent*.

He worked with the eminent scientist George Washington Carver to develop industrial uses for the soybean, as well as to promote the promise of soy milk as a highly nutritious alternative to cow's milk. A plant

that produced 150 gallons a day of Ford Soy Milk was built to supply the various Ford cafeterias and the Henry Ford Hospital. Henry remarked that the Model T "did away with the horse. Now, we're going to get rid of the cow."

Henry had one foot in the nineteenth century, the other in the twentieth century. Bound by a Puritan work ethic, he put more faith in honest labor than in things of the mind—scholars, intellectuals, and university degrees being of little practical use, he believed. Henry never attended high school, much less college, though he did spend a few months in a business preparatory school.

Henry collab
Michigan Audubon S
hundred birdhouse sa
imported six hundred
songbirds, including
thrushes, to be releas
grounds of his home,
be found walking in h
birdcalls.

His love of n
that he was one of the
responsible for the pa
Bird Treaty Act, whic
Congress for many ye
lined up influential fr

SOUND OF MUSIC *Henry Ford's Old Fashioned Dance Orchestra played the music Henry liked— Virginia reels, polkas, waltzes, and two-steps. The program, above, is from 1926.*

STEP IN TIME *Henry was committed to preserving the music he heard as a boy and the dances that accompanied it. Above: A 1926 book of records of old-time music "as revived by Mr. and Mrs. Henry Ford," high-stepping at right.*

KNOW THYSELF *Henry knew what he liked and didn't like. The former included old-fashioned music and dance; the latter, tobacco—the "Little White Slaver" he lambasted in the pamphlet, left. Above: Edsel Ford (at piano) chats with his father. Far left: Soloist Rose Brampton appeared at the Detroit Music Hall in 1945, broadcast on the Ford Sunday Evening Hour on ABC radio.*

Edison to urge passage of the bill, which would protect migratory birds. Thanks in part to Henry's efforts, the bill passed in 1913.

He had simple, rather folksy tastes, disliked ostentation and crowds, and would much rather stay at home with family and friends than mix with highbrow society. He enjoyed radio shows like *Amos 'n Andy* and comic strips, particularly *Little Orphan Annie*. He disliked liquor, gambling, and cigarettes and was a lifelong practical joker— he once put wooden croutons in the soup of Harvey Firestone, his friend and business associate.

Lean and quick-footed, Henry also made time whenever possible for "stepping out." Henry was "quite a good dancer," says Werling. "On the top floor of the powerhouse at Fair Lane, he had set aside an area for afternoon dancing, and would bring in a live orchestra and dance instructors to teach fellow workers the schottische, the varsovienne, different reels, and other dances." Henry enjoyed old-time fiddling, too—he sponsored fiddling contests in Detroit—and even learned to play "Turkey in the Straw" and other standards on a $75,000 Stradivarius violin.

He never parsed his opinions to suit populist trends, counseling against chewing tobacco, cigarettes (the "little white slaver," he called them in a pamphlet), rich foods, and liquor. "If booze ever comes back to the United States, I am through with manufacturing," Henry vowed in 1929, during the thick of Prohibition, a promise he did not keep. He believed in the full development of the human spirit, primarily through work. "The worst sin we can commit against the things of our common life is to misuse them," he said. ❖

EARLY BACKERS *Henry's early colleagues at Ford Motor Company included Alexander Malcolmson (seated on stool in center), a coal merchant, and James Couzens (standing), a quick-thinking businessman who helped Henry land several financial backers. The bearded man with the firmly clenched cigar is thought to be Ford backer John S. Gray, president of the German-American Bank and Couzens's uncle. Below: The Articles of Incorporation for Ford Motor Company.*

"Henry was exultant," says Terry Hoover, archivist of Henry Ford Museum & Greenfield Village. "To be middle-aged and not have achieved real success, and to be told to forge ahead—by Thomas Edison of all people—was life affirming." Buoyed by the inventor's support, Henry quit his job. He had been told by his boss at Edison Illuminating to choose between the company and the automobile. "There was really nothing in the way of a choice," Henry said.

So Henry Ford entered the automobile business. He would lead two small automaking enterprises before putting in motion plans for Ford Motor Company, as we know it today. On June 16, 1903, Henry and eleven associates dispatched incorporation papers to Michigan's state capitol in Lansing for the formation of Ford Motor Company. They had only $28,000 in cash, some tools, and a few blueprints. But they had a profusion of faith. Henry was thirty-nine years old.

The other stockholders were a coal dealer, Alexander Malcolmson; the coal dealer's business manager, James Couzens; a banker who trusted the coal dealer; two brothers who owned the machine shop that made the engines; a carpenter; two lawyers; a clerk; the owner of a notions store; and a man who made windmills and air rifles. Couzens had drummed up most of the investors. Apparently, a doctor also offered to invest money in the new venture, but Henry refused, fearing thirteen investors would bring bad luck.

Malcolmson, Henry's chief backer, put no money in the company, nor did Henry. The coal dealer invested his time and reputation, while Henry invested his patents, drawings, and experience. The hard-nosed Couzens was selected to oversee the business part of the company, freeing Henry to focus on design and engineering. Childe Harold Wills, a local engineer, was hired as his shop assistant.

Henry and his fellow stockholders had in mind a machine that could be made quickly and cheaply from contracted parts, removing the need for a large manufacturing complex. The company leased a small, converted wagon factory at 696 Mack Avenue, off a spur of the Michigan Central Railroad in Detroit. In an area illuminated by six lightbulbs, ten employees worked twelve-hour days, seven days a week, assembling the first Ford commercial automobiles, beginning with the Model A.

Henry and his engineers feverishly went through nineteen letters of the alphabet—from Model A to Model S— selling 20,000 cars between 1903 and 1908. While other automakers put their shoulders behind building automobiles for the rich, Henry sought to create a utilitarian car, "large enough for the family but small enough to run and care for," he said. "It will be so low in price that no man making a good salary will be unable to own one."

In early 1907, he set up a special workroom at the company's new plant on Piquette Avenue to work on his "universal car," as he called it. On October 1, 1908, the Model T—Henry's motorcar for the great multitude—was ready for full production.

It was exactly as he had promised. The Model T was the lightest and smallest car made in America, with a very powerful engine

in relation to its weight. It could turn within a twelve-foot circle, traverse rutted roads and rocky terrain, and pull itself out of loose sand. Owners could make emergency repairs with little more than a screwdriver, a few wrenches, and a pair of pliers—though some claimed chewing gum, clothespins, and twine also did the trick.

Bryan recalls that his father, "who wasn't particularly inclined toward mechanical things, learned to replace sparkplugs and lightbulbs, clean the timer, adjust the transmission, and dip a wooden stick into the gas tank to gauge how much gas was left" in his family's Model T. "Since there were very few service stations as such, quick, easy maintenance and repair was important," Bryan explains.

And, while it may have been homelier—a bit too high and square—than the more sumptuous cars of the rich, the Model T roused the common folk, who affectionately dubbed it the "Tin Lizzie" (Lizzie being popular slang for a good and dependable servant).

The Model T was as Henry predicted: the automobile that would put America on wheels. First-year production reached 10,660, breaking industry records. As the car dropped in price from an initial $825 to a low of $259, millions of American families bought their first automobile. The Model T also sold briskly in many European countries (a half million would be sold in Britain) and even in such faraway places as Mauritius, Siam (Thailand), Dutch East Indies, Ethiopia, Malaysia, Barbados, and Newfoundland—where it was the first car on the market.

The Model T was so versatile that it could be reconfigured by buyers to move cattle, haul freight, herd horses, fight fires, and even mow lawns. A farmer's wife in 1918 wrote Henry: "Your car lifted us out of the mud. It brought joy into our lives. We loved every rattle in its bones." And rattle it did: the powerful car with a maximum speed of 45 miles per hour got twenty-five miles to a gallon of gasoline, then twenty cents a gallon. The car was so beloved that in 1909, Henry announced Ford Motor Company would build only one car in the future—the Model T.

"The Model T made Ford Motor Company the most dazzling enterprise in American business," *Holiday* magazine proclaimed in 1957. It also made Henry Ford a multimillionaire. After moving from one rented home to another, ten in all, he and Clara built a stately red-brick mansion in 1907–08 at 66 Edison Avenue. They would not live there long. Henry also purchased two thousand acres in Dearborn, along the Rouge River he swam in and ice-skated on as a boy. In 1914, construction began on Fair Lane, the home where he and Clara would live the rest of their lives.

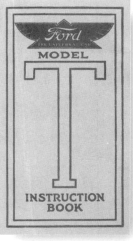

As cars rolled out of the Piquette Avenue factory, Henry realized more spacious production quarters were required, and he purchased sixty acres at Highland Park, an enclave within Detroit. He also recognized that he would have to scrap his manufacturing system, which was tedious and slow, taking twelve and a half hours to produce a single Model T.

Like other manufacturers, Ford built cars one at a time—the chassis stayed in one spot and didn't move until the car was finished. Stock runners literally ran around the factory floor fetching parts. The handmade automobiles required many hours of costly skilled labor that kept car prices high. A method of producing cars en masse, using both skilled labor and cheaper unskilled labor, was needed. *Harper's Weekly*, in January 1910, wrote: "The man who can successfully solve this knotty question and produce a car that will be entirely sufficient mechanically, and whose price will be within the reach of millions who cannot yet afford automobiles, will not only grow rich but will be considered a public benefactor." Henry Ford wanted to be that man.

After Ford built the new Highland Park plant in 1910, the impetus to develop mass production intensified. The public clamored to own a Model T, and the always business-minded Couzens wanted to capitalize on the demand. Henry latched on to a concept that was,

for manufacturing, rather revolutionary—instead of bringing the man to the work, work must be brought to the man.

He and Charles Sorensen, a hardworking Dane he had hired as his assistant in 1905, kept experimenting to find the solution. At first, cars were mounted on movable benches or "cradles" that were pushed from one workstation to the next, where parts were attached. Ford workers then tried moving parts along the production line on inclined slides. This speeded up production, but the cars were still largely handmade.

A breakthrough came in April 1913. A production engineer in the flywheel magneto assembly area tried a new way to put this component's parts together. The operation was divided into twenty-nine separate steps. Workers were instructed to place only one part in the assembly before pushing the flywheel down the line to the next employee. Previously, it had taken one employee about twenty minutes to assemble a flywheel magneto. When the job was divided among twenty-nine men, the time fell to thirteen minutes. Further advances trimmed it to five minutes. Gradually, this strategy was applied to the construction of the engine and other parts.

On October 7, 1913, the idea of moving the work to the man reached its zenith. On this historic day, the company rigged a rudimentary final assembly line at Highland Park, whereby a chassis

was pulled slowly across the factory floor by rope and windlass. Parts, components, and 140 assemblers were stationed at different intervals along the 150-foot line. As the winch literally dragged the chassis across the floor, workers attached parts to the car. When the first car was finished, production men were amazed at the time saved. Rather than twelve and a half hours to build a single car, they had performed the feat in five hours and fifty minutes.

"That line established the efficiency of the method," Henry said. The moving automobile assembly line was born and with it, a new era of industrial expansion.

Soon, the rope was replaced by a power-driven "endless" conveyor system that was flush with the floor and wide enough to accommodate the chassis, with room left over on both sides for workers to stand and complete their tasks. The first workers on the line fastened mudguard brackets to the chassis frame. The engine was at the tenth station. Some men performed only one task; others performed several. The fellow who put the bolt in didn't put on the nut, and the man who put the nut on didn't tighten it. Newer assembly lines were raised to waist level to reduce stooping. "Save ten steps a day for each of twelve thousand employees," Henry said, "and you will have saved fifty miles of wasted motion and misspent energy."

To further increase efficiency, Henry directed that Model T cars, as of 1914, be produced in only one color—black, since black-enamel paint dried faster than any other color. Hence, Henry's oft-quoted remark: "Any customer can have a car painted any color that

Here's a Ford Model T Touring Car

$690

Handsome—Foredoors—roomy—up-to-the-minute in desired details, strong, simple and backed with a record of five years' satisfaction—giving results in all parts of the world to more than 100,000 users. This beautiful motor car completely equipped for only $690 f. o. b. Detroit.

Ford Motor Company
Detroit, Mich., U.S.A.

MASS MARVEL *In 1914, when the image, left, was taken of a Model T chassis at Highland Park, workers built one Tin Lizzie every ninety-three minutes, causing the price of Fords to drop from $690 in 1911, above, to $360 in 1916. Overleaf: Installing seats in 1923.*

than all other automakers combined. By 1916, Model T production had risen to 585,388 and the price had plunged to $360. More than 700,000 Model Ts were churned out and sold the following year, and Ford's industrious dealer network was poised to sell every last one of them. "The perfection of the moving assembly line is Ford's greatest gift to history," says Werling. "It truly changed the world."

Rapid automobile production was not the only revolutionary change. Science and technology had made a quantum leap from the nineteenth century. Albert Einstein formulated his theory of relativity in 1905, Halley's Comet was observed in 1910, and the Geiger counter was invented in 1913. Anything seemed possible, including skyscrapers, like the fifty-story Metropolitan Life Insurance Building in New York City, built in 1909.

It was also a time for leisure. Gentlemen in homburg hats, stylish sack suits, silk scarf ties, and elastic braces and ladies in tight corsets, puff-sleeved blouses, voluminous skirts, and ornately feathered hats gathered at nickelodeons to see the new motion pictures or in public to hear the rousing patriotic marches of John Philip Sousa.

he wants so long as it is black." In later years, however, as competition from other manufacturers increased and improvements in paint eased the drying problem, the Model T was again available in colors other than black.

Constant revision improved the time it took to make a single car to ninety-three minutes in 1914. The results were immediate and extraordinary. In 1912, Ford had produced only 82,388 Model Ts, selling the touring car for $600. In 1914, it produced 308,162 cars, more

In this bourgeois society, Henry Ford was fast on his way to becoming a celebrity. "The first way for a man to set himself on the road toward glorious reputation is to win renown," Cicero instructed. Henry's rural background, wholesome habits, and love of nature had endeared him to many Americans, and his unabashed opinions were good copy for the journalists who shadowed his every move.

The next act in Henry Ford's revolution of industry, on January 5, 1914, secured his renown. On that day, Henry announced he would pay his workers the then incredible sum of $5 a day, more than double the previous rate. While Henry's primary objective was to reduce worker attrition—labor turnover from monotonous assembly line work ran high—newspapers all over the world reported the story as an extraordinary gesture of goodwill. Some called it plumb craziness.

Thousands showed up at the Ford employment office. Cotton pickers headed north from Alabama, Serbians rushed to apply for American passports, and Germans headed for the boat docks in Hamburg. But Ford was unable to hire them all, and small riots broke out when many were turned away at the plant gates.

'GOLD RUSH' IS STARTED BY FORD'S $5 OFFER

Thousands of Men Seek Employment in Detroit Factory.

Will Distribute $10,000,000 in Semi-Monthly Bonuses.

No Employe to Receive Less Than Five Dollars a Day.

As expected, employee turnover diminished. Moreover, by creating an eight-hour day, Ford could run three shifts instead of two, increasing productivity. The revolution was complete. Production on a grand scale performed by highly paid workers was dubbed "Fordism," a term that spread throughout the world. Ford's assembly process became standard in the manufacture of diverse products, from vacuum sweepers in Germany to radios in the United Kingdom.

But the assembly line was both a blessing and a curse. In 1914, the wife of a Ford worker captured the paradox in a letter to Henry. "The chain system you have is a slave driver, Mr. Ford," she wrote. "My husband has come home and thrown himself down and won't eat his supper—so done out! Can't it be remedied? . . . That $5 a day is a blessing—a bigger one than you know—but, oh, they earn it."

As Ford was making news with the hourly wage hike, Europe was heading toward war. On June 28, 1914, Archduke Francis Ferdinand, heir to the Austrian throne, and his wife were assassinated in Sarajevo. Germany declared war on Russia and invaded Belgium, Britain declared war on Germany, and Austria declared war on Serbia. President Woodrow Wilson advocated

THE GREAT WAR *During World War I, Ford equipped the U.S. armed forces with much war matériel, from the Eagle submarine chasers, left, that were built in 1918 at the recently opened Rouge plant to the Ford ambulance with storm curtains, right.*

a neutral position for the United States, but following the sinking of several unarmed American ships by German vessels, the United States declared war on April 6, 1917. "The world must be made safe for democracy," the president asserted.

Henry denounced the war in Europe. Before the United States had become involved in the war, Henry had funded a crusade to end the conflict. With fellow-minded sympathizers, Henry boarded the *Oscar II* (dubbed "the Peace Ship" by the media) in 1915 to cross the Atlantic and seek an immediate end of the war through mediation. As he explained:

"My opposition to war is not based upon pacifist or non-resistant principles. . . . Wars do not end wars any more than an extraordinarily large conflagration does away with the fire hazard. . . .

Fighting never settles the question. It only gets the participants around to a frame of mind where they will agree to discuss what they were fighting about."

When America finally joined the conflict, Henry put the entire company behind the effort. "I will place our factory at the disposal of the United States Government and will operate without one cent profit," Henry vowed, declaring he "would work harder than ever before." President Wilson immediately appointed him to the United States Shipping Board, charged with selecting designs for warships.

Henry kept his word. The company turned its attention from the production of domestic automobiles to a wide array of war matériel, sending the Allies more than 38,000 Model T cars, ambulances, and trucks and 7,000 Fordson tractors. "Tougher than an army mule," the Model T was used in World War I battles from the Somme to Amman. Journalists acclaimed it as the "Wonder Car of the Great War."

Partly because of Henry's position on the shipping board, Ford was selected to manufacture Eagle-class submarine chasers, which were built to hunt German U-boats. Sixty sub chasers were built on an assembly line at Ford's new manufacturing facility on the banks of the Rouge River. Ford also developed and produced steel "doughboy" helmets, caissons, shells, armor plate, two types of armored tanks, and four thousand Liberty airplane engines. It even worked on the development of guided missiles.

"Mr. Ford came in [to the engineering laboratory] with the idea of this robot bomber," according to the reminiscences of E. J. Farkas, a Ford engineer during the war. "He wanted it made as simple as it could, because when it reached its destination, it [would be] destroyed."

When the armistice came in November 1918, Ford returned its attention to making Model Ts, churning out a thousand a day by

late December. The company's ballyhooed role in the war added fuel to the Ford publicity machine. As troops returned, they recounted bully tales of the Tin Lizzie in action, calling Henry "Germany's greatest individual enemy."

President Wilson encouraged Henry to run for a Michigan seat in the U.S. Senate, believing he would tip the scales in favor of Wilson's proposed League of Nations. "You are the only man in Michigan who can be elected and help bring about the peace you so desire," the president wrote Henry, who replied, "If they want to elect me let them do so, but I won't make a penny's investment." Running on his name alone and without a campaign budget, Henry lost the 1918 general election by fewer than 4,500 votes out of more than 400,000 cast.

HENRY FORD
For UNITED STATES SENATOR

PREPARED AND SUBMITTED BY
NON-PARTISAN FORD-FOR-SENATOR CLUB

Henry again considered politics in the early 1920s, this time pondering a run for the presidency of the United States. A large volume of letters urged him to toss his hat in the ring, and placards declaring "We Want Henry" decorated many storefronts. Although he eventually rejected the idea, a letter from President Calvin Coolidge in 1924, thanking him for not running, indicates the prospect of a President Henry Ford wasn't too farfetched.

Even though many who knew him found him prickly and intractable, Henry had a heart for friendship, particularly with prominent men like Thomas Edison, naturalist John Burroughs, department store titan John Wanamaker, and tire magnate Harvey Firestone. Edison, of course, had played a crucial role by encouraging Henry's ambitions, and he and Henry developed a particularly strong bond. In later years they would own adjacent summer homes in Fort Myers, Florida.

The Fords often feted their friends at Fair Lane. The men would retire to the den, where carved oak busts of Edison, Burroughs, and Firestone were affixed to the heavy wood paneling. Edison dedicated the hydroelectric powerhouse at Fair Lane, and the Burroughs Grotto in the Fair Lane gardens was named in honor of the famous naturalist. And underscoring the importance of friendship to the Fords, the following memorable words of Ralph Waldo Emerson were carved into the fireplace mantel in the living room: "If I were sure of thee, sure of this capacity, sure to match my mood with thine, I should never again think of trifles."

The camping trips of Ford, Burroughs, Firestone, and Edison—the "vagabonds," they called themselves—into the Great Smoky Mountains in 1918 and the Adirondacks in 1919 were dramatized as roughneck adventures along the lines of Theodore Roosevelt's wild-game-hunting expeditions. One report chronicled the elderly Burroughs besting Henry in a wood-chopping contest.

Another postulated on Henry's alleged fondness for skinny-dipping. In reality, roughing it was a stretch: they'd brought along a caravan of vehicles and equipment, as well as cooks, chauffeurs, and even the photographers who would record the event.

The annual camping trips lasted until 1924 and sometimes included President Warren G. Harding. "[They] were good fun," Henry said, "except that they began to attract too much attention."

Generating even more interest was Henry's off-the-cuff remark, in 1916, that "history is more or less bunk." In June 1916, the *Chicago Tribune* printed an editorial alleging Henry would not continue to pay employees who, as National Guardsmen, had mobilized along the U.S.-Mexico border after Pancho Villa's attack on Columbus, New Mexico. The newspaper called Henry an "ignorant idealist" and an "anarchistic enemy of the nation." Henry demanded a retraction and when the *Tribune* declined, filed a libel lawsuit.

The much-publicized suit dragged on for years until coming to trial in May 1919. The case had the unfortunate effect of revealing Henry's unawareness of important dates, such as when the American Revolution was fought ("1812," Henry surmised). Cartoonists drew caricatures of him with a dunce cap on his head—hence his defensive follow-up that history was "bunk." Henry's point was that written histories presented a distorted view of life because they focused on the dates of political struggles and wars and not, as he told the New Orleans *Times-Picayune* newspaper in 1934, "the unconquerable pioneer spirit of man."

HISTORY MERE "BUNK"

Ford Simply Regards It All as Tradition

He Calls Professional Soldiers Murderers

Would Not Exclude Pershing or Grant

For League Without Delay or Another War

Mount Clemens, Mich., July 15—Testifying today in his $1,000,000 libel suit against the Chicago Tribune, Henry Ford admitted ignorance of history and said that more than ever he considered it "bunk" grow-

KEYS TO SUCCESS *A sumptuous print advertisement, opposite, targets women with images of affluent, leisurely pastimes. The Model T key rack at left features different numbered keys. When a key was lost, dealers took down the number of the car then gave the owner a new key of that number. Thus, many Model Ts operated using the same key! Far left: Henry's notorious "History is bunk" comment from a 1919 headline.*

In his oral reminiscences, Fred Black, a former business manager at the *Dearborn Independent*, said Henry believed history was "the way people lived and worked. He always said the history of America wasn't written in Washington, it was written in the country."

Werling concurs: "Henry had once said that 'there is more history in a plow than in the date of some long ago battle.'"

Although the newspaper ultimately was found guilty of libel and fined six cents, Henry's reputation suffered. Henry privately vowed to redeem himself by telling the "real story" of the American people. He had begun to collect the artifacts of early America, especially those that described rural life. Soon, he had a place to exhibit them—Henry Ford Museum & Greenfield Village, an institution that he built in Dearborn and dedicated to another poorly educated inventor—Thomas Edison. Many historic buildings were dismantled, transported to Dearborn, and rebuilt on the grounds, including the Wright Brothers' bicycle shop and Edison's famed Menlo Park, New Jersey, laboratory. Edison gibed at the time (1929) that the restoration was imperfect. "It's too clean," he said, much to Henry's amusement.

A new world order took shape in the wake of the Great War, with the United States a leading power. The United States was as rich as all Europe; indeed, 40 percent of the world's total wealth now lay in the hands of Americans. Trade and industry expanded, stock markets

boomed, and a new youth culture took hold. It was the Roaring Twenties, the era of unabashed consumerism and libidos liberated by bootlegged gin. Detroit flappers shimmied the Charleston to jazzman Bix Beiderbecke and his horn, and baseball fans swarmed to see the great Ty Cobb play for the local club, the Tigers.

Anything seemed possible in these whirlwind times, including safe, routine air travel. Although the war had speeded advances in aviation technology, the only airplanes in the early 1920s were those flown by wing-walking daredevils and airmail pilots. Henry, who had put America on wheels, now wanted to put America in the air. In 1925, he built the first of 196 Ford Tri-Motor airplanes, the first airplanes used by America's first commercial airlines.

The Tri-Motor is the story of aviation's coming of age. Nicknamed the "Tin Goose" and the "Model T of the Air," the Tri-Motor was the first all-metal, multi-engine transport in the United States, and standard equipment on all commercial airlines until the flight of the Boeing 247 in 1933.

Henry's interest in aviation began in 1910, when Edsel Ford, then sixteen years old, and some friends built an airplane modeled on the Louis Bleriot plane that had crossed the English Channel in 1909. Henry's curiosity deepened during Ford's wartime production of Liberty aircraft engines.

Then, in 1922, as a young man of twenty-eight, Edsel Ford subscribed to the stock of a new company, the Stout Metal Airplane Company, which named him a director. Edsel and Henry offered Stout land for an airfield, selecting 260 acres on Dearborn's Oakwood Boulevard as a viable site. Stout agreed. The airport was completed on January 15, 1925, and was hailed by aviation experts as one of the finest in the country. (Today, it's the site of the Dearborn Proving Grounds.)

Shortly thereafter, Henry discussed the future of aviation with William Stout. "This whole picture looks to me as if it was something that somebody has got to put a lot of money behind to make an industry out of it," he said. "I don't know why Ford Motor Company shouldn't do just that."

It was agreed that Henry and Edsel would buy the issued stock of Stout, keep William Stout on as an advisor, and form a brand new company, Ford Airlines. The airline would fly Ford mail and automotive

IN THE SKY *Passengers aboard a Ford Tri-Motor plane in 1929 look intently out their windows, left. Ford planes flew regionally, delivering mail and travelers, and even saw transcontinental service, via TWA.*

parts on a scheduled basis between Dearborn and Chicago, and would provide all financial knowledge gleaned from the effort to the burgeoning aviation industry. Edsel and Henry projected that investors, long convinced aviation was a precarious venture, would be stimulated by the Ford example.

In 1925, the one-plane Ford Airlines took off, with scheduled flights every other day. Later in the year, it added a second plane and daily service. Buffalo and Cleveland soon joined the schedule, and by the end of the second year, more than a half-million miles were flown and more than 3 million pounds of freight and mail were delivered.

In January 1926, Ford Airlines was awarded a government contract to carry U.S. mail to Chicago and Cleveland from Detroit. On February 15, bound for Cleveland, the first domestic airmail flight by private enterprise made history. Within another year, more than twenty airlines had sprouted nationwide and a growing network of air transport slowly spread across the country. Ford sold the Tri-Motor (so named for its three 1,260-horsepower Pratt & Whitney engines) to commercial airlines for about $40,000 each. Trans World Airlines, for example, flew twenty-five Fords in the 1930s.

The Smithsonian Institution in 1985 called Ford's entry into airplane manufacturing "one of the most important events in the selling of aviation to the general public." The Tin Goose saw service in every quarter of the globe in the 1920s and '30s—it carried freight in South America, smoke jumpers in Montana, and survey parties in Saudi Arabia. The plane was the first to fly over the South Pole and the first to be used for all-air transcontinental passenger service.

TWA, the originator of the transcontinental service in October 1930, re-enacted this historic flight in a restored Tri-Motor in 1963, operating the original schedule from Los Angeles to Newark, New Jersey, via eleven intermediate cities. With the Tri-Motor lumbering along at 110 miles per hour, the trip took thirty-six hours, including an overnight stay in Kansas City to give passengers a rest (same as in 1930, when airlines didn't fly after dark).

The last Tin Goose, No. 196, was assembled in January 1933. The company's losses from the business had risen to nearly $6 million in 1932, and Henry soon lost interest. "Ford car production was dropping fast at the time, so Henry had bigger fish to fry," says Timothy J. O'Callaghan, a Ford aviation historian.

Another culprit in the demise of the Tri-Motor was Black Monday, the crash of the stock market on October 28, 1929, a single day in which U.S. securities lost some

LUCKY HENRY

Charles Lindbergh was the first man to fly solo across the Atlantic Ocean, in the Spirit of St. Louis *in 1927. When he landed the small aircraft in Paris, he was an instant celebrity. Shortly after the historic journey, Lindbergh was asked by Henry to be taken aloft in the* Spirit of St. Louis—*Henry's first plane ride. It was the beginning of a long relationship. During World War II, Henry hired*

Lindbergh as an advisor on the building of the B-24 bomber at the Willow Run plant. The aviator also test-piloted several aircraft. In his reminiscences, Ford aviation engineer Emil Zoerlein wrote that "Lucky Lindy" even volunteered for an experiment to determine the highest elevation a pilot could ascend before losing his faculties. "Lindbergh went in, and we pulled him up at the rate of 3,000 feet a

minute up to 47,000 feet," said Zoerlein, who flew the plane with others by remote control. "He went like this and just blacked out. We dropped him to 35,000 feet and held him there for five minutes, [but] he wanted to go back up once more. He went up a second time to 49,000 feet, and blacked out again." Lindbergh's salary at the time was $666.66 a month.

$26 billion in value. The crash reverberated at Ford and two other Detroit-area automakers, General Motors and Chrysler, collectively known as the "Big Three." Car production dropped to half the prewar level since few could afford to buy a new car. Two-fifths of the working population in Detroit lost their jobs, and by the end of 1930, one in three Detroit families had no means of support.

Ford survived the tough times through a mix of cost-cutting initiatives, price reductions, and higher wages, which Henry correctly surmised would coalesce to sell more cars. He also earmarked more than $25 million for factory expansion and improvements, a move that startled economists. "You'd think at a time when a company is in such poor shape financially that it should not be looking to invest capital," says Bryan. "Yet Henry and Edsel literally poured money into expanding the Rouge," the manufacturing facility originally built by Ford beginning in 1917 and then used to make submarine chasers for the war effort. In later years, the Rouge plant would manufacture tractors, automobiles, and a range of other vehicles using modern "vertical integration" manufacturing techniques.

"Henry always went against the grain," Bryan adds. "He just refused to be depressed by the Depression. He knew financial recovery lay just ahead. And he was right."

But another provocation emerged during this bleak period, and it was a powder keg. Organized labor unions were proliferating to represent the rights of workers nationwide. On a bitterly cold day in March 1932, some three thousand unemployed Ford autoworkers, their families, and union organizers marched toward the Rouge plant to present a list of demands to Henry. They were interrupted by the Dearborn police, who hurled tear gas grenades to stop their progress. The marchers responded by tossing rocks and pieces of frozen mud at the police, who opened fire. Five marchers were killed and nineteen injured.

Three years later, during the pro-union administration of President Franklin Delano Roosevelt, the United Automobile Workers labor union was formed. General Motors and Chrysler, despite fierce resistance at first, eventually recognized the UAW to negotiate on their employees' collective behalf. Henry staunchly opposed union organization, convinced simply that one was not needed—he had always enjoyed solid relations with his employees and would continue to do so. Henry also distrusted the UAW, fearful it would erode the Ford work ethic and bring about reduced output from employees on the factory floor.

Henry bristled at the UAW's pamphleteering at Ford but could do little legally to stop it. So he resorted to more covert activities to crush the union before it took root. He had hired an ex-prizefighter with reported criminal ties, Harry Bennett, as head of security in 1916. Over the years, Bennett gained a reputation as someone who would do anything Henry asked.

Rising through the ranks, Bennett was appointed the head of Ford's service department, in charge of the company's labor policies. Instead, he used the department to gather evidence on union penetration of the workforce. He also had a network of employee operatives honeycombing the company. These spies warned him that the UAW, led by a group of union officials including Richard Frankensteen and Walter Reuther (a former Rouge worker and future UAW president), would organize a recruiting drive at the Rouge plant on May 26, 1937. Bennett was ready with a truckload of thugs to greet them.

As the union members handed out pamphlets to Ford workers walking along a street overpass, Ford security men attacked, repeatedly kicking Frankensteen and Reuther in the head and groin. Journalists and photographers recorded the bloodshed. The next day, photos of Reuther and Frankensteen dominated the national press, which portrayed the skirmish as the "Battle of the Overpass."

Edsel pleaded with his father to negotiate with the union, but Henry directed that Bennett handle the furor—a mistake. The National Labor Relations Board subsequently filed an unfair labor practice complaint against the company, which Ford denied, insisting its security force acted in self-defense. In December 1937, the company was found in violation of the federal Wagner Act and ordered to stop interfering with the right of Ford employees to organize. The case was appealed to higher courts and in February 1941 reached the U.S. Supreme Court, which declined to review it. Ford had lost the case.

Workers fired for their union activity were rehired and the company, having endured a walkout of 50,000 employees at the Rouge in April 1941, finally agreed to negotiations with the UAW. That May, a vote by workers made their intentions clear: only 2.7 percent voted in favor of no union.

IS EVERYBODY'S BUSINESS

UNITED WE STAND
Ford workers express solidarity, above, at the company's plant in Dagenham, England, in a dispute involving a fellow employee. Left: Union pins, one of which urges "Buy American." At right, a well-attended meeting of the United Auto Workers at Ford's Rouge plant, Gate 4, Miller Road Overpass in 1940.

THE UNITED AUTO WORKERS

Although Henry Ford considered the unionization of Ford Motor Company employees his "greatest disappointment" in business, Ford and the union—today's United Automobile, Aerospace, and Agricultural Implement Workers of America (UAW)—have worked together through the decades to ensure continually improving conditions for workers.

The UAW is one of the largest unions in the United States, formed as the United Automobile Workers in Detroit in 1935 following several years of self-organizing by

automobile workers. The UAW's early history is one of hard-fought, bloody battles on behalf of workers' rights, good wages, and worthy benefits.

The UAW was rejected by the U.S. auto industry as a bargaining body until a series of much-publicized sit-down strikes at General Motors plants in 1936 and 1937. One of the first was at GM's Flint, Michigan, plant on December 30, 1936—the famed Battle of Bulls Run, taking its name from the Civil War battle at a time when police were known as "bulls."

GM had obtained an injunction ordering the strikers out of the plant, but after it was discovered that the issuing judge owned a large amount of GM stock, the writ was rendered unenforceable. GM then decided to starve the strikers, precipitating a battle between police and women—who each day, for a month, had brought food to the strikers. Fourteen people were killed when police opened fire on the crowd. The Flint events precipitated other sit-down strikes at GM plants nationwide. The last of these, on January 13, 1937, involved more than 112,000 of GM's 150,000 production workers.

Finally, on February 11, 1937, GM capitulated to the UAW's demands, agreeing to a one-page contract with the union. After GM surrendered, the rest of the auto industry— eventually including a recalcitrant Ford Motor Company—followed suit. Since winning acceptance, the UAW has been a potent and forceful leader in collective bargaining with the auto companies, winning such benefits for workers as pensions, unemployment compensation of nearly 90 percent of paid income for one year, a cost-of-living wage increase, and a health security program. In the 1980s and '90s, Ford and the UAW built a strong relationship through policies and programs, such as hourly worker profit sharing and the UAW-Ford Visteon Family Service and Learning Centers.

In 1995, the union broadened to represent workers in the aerospace; trucking; agricultural; and technical, office, and professional industries. ❖

Embittered, Henry announced he would close down the plant before he would ever sign a contract with the union. "Let the union take over," he fumed. Informed the government would simply assume control of Ford if he shut it down, Henry grudgingly acquiesced and signed what was then the best contract the UAW had ever negotiated. It required that all employees join the union as a condition of employment, something the UAW had not bargained for.

Although Henry considered the union contract his biggest business defeat, it was a victory for American workers and a milestone in labor events. Says Bryan, "There was another reason why Henry finally signed that contract. Clara had told him if he closed down the plant, she'd leave him. She did not want this great company snatched from Edsel before he had an opportunity to lead it. Since they were married fifty-three years at the time, there was little else Henry could do."

By 1941, more than labor unrest confronted the company. Ford profits over the previous ten years totaled out to zero, and despite having the second most recognizable brand name in the world, just shy of Coca-

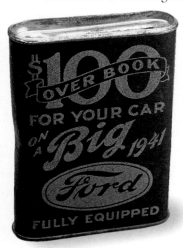

Cola, Ford was mired in third place among the Big Three auto manufacturers.

Even more serious problems were brewing for Ford of Europe. The Nazis had seized power in Germany and occupied Czechoslovakia in 1938. At the time, England's prime minister, Neville Chamberlain, declared that placating Adolf Hitler had achieved "peace in our time." The next year, however, Germany invaded Poland, starting World War II.

At Ford's factory in Cologne, which was off-limits to its own representatives from Dearborn after September 1940, vehicles were being manufactured for the German Army. The Dagenham plant in England, meanwhile, was producing 130 war-related vehicles a day for the Allies in 1940, despite being repeatedly bombed by the Germans. In effect, Ford plants were supplying both sides in the war effort.

At home, the company signed a contract with the U.S. government, which was not yet at war, to manufacture eighteen-cylinder Pratt & Whitney aircraft engines for defense purposes. Ford also built a new general purpose (G.P. or "jeep") military vehicle for the government in March 1941. Both would be developed at the Rouge Complex in a new $39 million factory.

Ford allowed the government to use its facilities to train U.S. Navy mechanics and was involved in developing a pursuit plane for the U.S. Army Air Force. Charles Lindbergh was hired as an aviation consultant, and a school was set up to train 1,100 aircraft technicians.

On December 7, 1941, the "day that shall live in infamy," Japanese bombers attacked Pearl Harbor, the major U.S. naval base in Hawaii. Nineteen U.S. ships, including eight battleships, were sunk or disabled; 180 planes were destroyed; and more than 2,300 soldiers, sailors, and civilians lost their lives. America declared war.

JAGUAR AND THE WORLD WAR II EFFORT

When war broke out in Europe in 1939, the United Kingdom decreed an end to automobile production. Jaguar, a Ford-owned brand today, turned its attention to making components for several British airplanes, including the Spitfire, below, and sidecars for

military use. Nearly 10,000 sidecars were manufactured by the Coventry, England–based automaker, which got its start in 1922 as the Swallow Sidecar Company. The war proved difficult for Jaguar and its workforce. Not surprisingly, Coventry was a target for raids by the German Luftwaffe. It was necessary to organize rosters of employees for what were called "fire-watching" duties—keeping one's eyes and ears attuned to the sight and sound of incoming German bombers. After the war ended, Jaguar SS (as it then was called) sold its sidecar division. The company also decided to drop the "SS" after its name, given its unfortunate wartime notoriety (the SS was the "elite guard" of the Third Reich). Its new name: Jaguar Cars.

We Can Do It!

WAR PRODUCTION CO-ORDINATING COMMITTEE

ROSE IN BLOOM *While their fathers, husbands, sons, and friends fought the Nazis in Europe and the Japanese in Asia, women served the war effort at home. Right: Kerchiefed women wielding power tools in the making of a B-24 bomber in 1944. Above: The popular depiction of "Rosie the Riveter" produced for the War Production Co-Ordinating Committee.*

WOMEN AT FORD: MAKING THEIR MOVES

The automobile industry was a male bastion until World War II, when women filled in quickly and capably for the male workers gone off to fight in Europe and the Pacific theater. In 1943, more than 30 percent of Ford workers in the machining and assembly departments were women. They built jeeps, B-24 aircraft, and tractors—operating drill presses, welding tools, heavy casting machinery, and, like Rose Will Monroe, riveting guns.

At work at Ford's Willow Run plant, Monroe was chosen by actor Walter Pidgeon

to appear in a promotional film for war bonds, becoming a real-life "Rosie the Riveter" as depicted in the "We Can Do It!" posters. She had been left with two young children after her husband was killed in a car accident and, like millions of other women nationwide, joined the workforce to fulfill a call to arms and to support her family.

When the war ended, Monroe and her female wartime colleagues were sent home so the returning soldiers could resume their prewar positions.

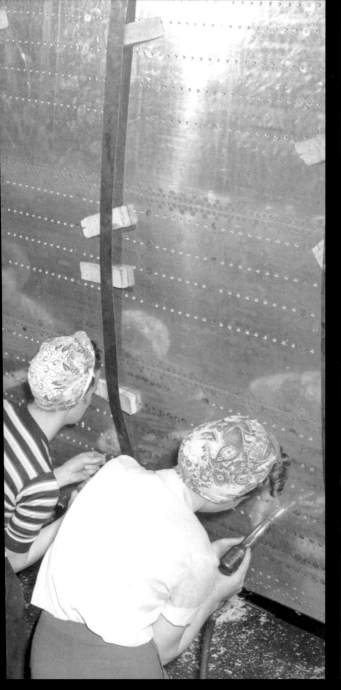

CLAIMING VICTORY *Women did more than just build aircraft during World War II; they also flew the planes. Left: Three test pilots emerge from a B-24, left, after a successful flight. Above: The Miss Bomber Plant trophy from 1943.*

Even before World War II, Ford was not completely male. One of Ford's first female employees was Georgia Boyer, who was chided politely in 1908 by James Couzens for stopping at a bulletin board during working hours to read a telegram announcing the results of a Ford stock car endurance race. Couzens was Ford's hard-nosed business manager and a founder of the company. Boyer operated the switchboard.

It wasn't until the 1970s that Ford opened the door wider to female job

applicants, a consequence largely of a 1972 law providing equal employment opportunities for women. While there were still no female vice presidents in 1972, there were at least ten female engineers, engaged in product development, safety research, and product planning. Mary Sohler, a twenty-year Ford employee, was one of them, a nationally regarded specialist in head-impact safety research. When asked once why young women proficient in science and math did not consider a career in engineering, Sohler

replied, "because they hear it's a tough occupation with a 'For Men Only' label. It's just not so."

Gradually, women began to change the face of Ford. Some who broke the gender barrier in the 1970s were Joanne Hardy, who worked in casting and core making at Ford's Michigan Casting Center; Barbara Robinson, an electrician at Ford's Stamping Plant in Chicago; Donna Carroll, a foreman at the Fairfax Transmission Plant in Cincinnati; and Ramona Bullock, a foreman at the General Parts Division in Ypsilanti, Michigan.

Bullock started with Ford in 1954 as a plastics assembler before being appointed a foreman in 1972. The eighteen men on her shift "call me 'Boss Woman' and 'Forelady,'" she said at the time, "but the teasing goes with the territory."

In 1976, the company announced that Marian Heiskell had become the first woman elected to its board of directors. Then there's Mimi Ornes Vandermolen— Ford's first female car designer. Over the years, Vandermolen developed an industry-wide reputation as a top designer of automobile interiors, working on the Mustang, Cougar, and many other 1970s-vintage vehicles. In the mid-1980s, she was selected to head up the design team for the interior of the 1986 Ford Taurus, the automobile considered responsible for the biggest turn-around in the company's history.

Vandermolen was born in Amsterdam, the Netherlands, and immigrated with her family to Toronto, Ontario, when she was six years old.

"I remember my backyard was filled with little cars," she told the *Detroit Free Press* in 1974. "The other little girls in my neighborhood thought I was weird."

Perhaps her greatest legacy is that she designed automobile interiors and exteriors with an eye toward women. Driver controls, for example, previously were configured to fit men, making it difficult for women to operate windows, gearshifts, and door handles, not to mention open a car hood. The idea of making cars women-friendly was novel until Vandermolen came along.

SAFE HOUSE *Veteran automotive safety pioneer and former vice president of environmental and safety engineering at Ford Helen O. Petrauskas, above, introduces the rollover airbag system at the 2000 North American International Auto Show in Detroit. Left: Dr. Roberta Nichols with one of the flexible fuel vehicles she helped to develop.*

Today, one is as likely to see women as men in all facets of endeavor at Ford. The "glass ceiling" is being challenged here and abroad. In 1995, Anne Stevens became the first female plant manager in Ford's Automotive Components Division, assuming her post at the company's Enfield, England, plant. And Dr. Roberta Nichols, a multitalented engineer who in the late 1960s held the women's world water speed record in boat racing, rose through the ranks at Ford to handle government and public relations for the company's Electric Vehicle Program before retiring in the 1990s.

Dr. Nichols, who has a Ph.D. in engineering from the University of Southern California, joined Ford in 1979, assuming a lead role in the company's propane, natural gas, and alcohol-fuel vehicle programs, including the design of the first flexible fuel vehicle. She is named on three U.S. patents for control systems for engine operation using two fuels of different volatility and volumetric energy content. In December 1989, Dr. Nichols became the first woman to be elected to the Society of Automotive Engineers' Fellow Grade of Membership, a prestigious honor.

Her fast-track career—she is listed in Who's Who of American Men and Women in Science—extends beyond the corporate and scientific worlds. The Los Angeles native is a former chair of the National Drag Boat Association and has been active in automotive racing since 1972. She is a throwback of sorts to Henry Ford himself, another engineer who thrilled at the prospect of zooming through space. ❖

TOP SECRET *During the war, Ford employees had to carry photographic identification badges, center top, color coded to permit or restrict plant access. Edsel's badge, center bottom, gave him unrestricted access to all facilities. The medallion beside it is his Ford Aircraft Division Badge. At right, Charles Sorensen (left) gives then–U.S. Senator Harry Truman a tour of Ford's Willow Run plant in 1942.*

The company—already heavily engaged in defense work at home—poured its energies into furnishing the tools of war. At a large tract of land he owned near Ypsilanti, Michigan, called Willow Run, Henry ordered the building of a mile-long L-shaped plant to produce B-24 Liberator bombers for the military. The four-engine B-24s were test-piloted by Lindbergh. "He was our first guinea pig," said Emil Zoerlein, a Ford aeronautical engineer during the war.

Edsel, head of production Charles Sorensen, and general manager Mead Bricker headed the Willow Run project. They worked tirelessly, as did Henry, said to have "rolled up both sleeves" for the war effort, even though Henry was seventy-eight years old.

By U.S. government decree, all civilian Ford automobile production in the United States ceased on February 10, 1942, and the company's immense manufacturing facilities in Michigan and branch assembly plants in many other states were brought under the control of the War Production Board. "The same assembly line that made Ford automobiles is now to be used for jeeps and staff cars for army officers," the press reported.

Ford's output of military products was stupendous. The $65 million Willow Run facility, staffed by nearly 50,000 workers at its peak, produced about 8,700 B-24 Liberator bombers for the war effort. In 1944, Ford alone contributed 48.5 percent of all the B-24s produced; in 1945, 70 percent of total output. The company also made M-4 tanks, parts, and engines; armored and reconnaissance cars; amphibious craft; swamp buggies; and a wealth of other war matériel. Overall, Ford led U.S. industry in producing high-power aircraft engines and large bombers. The company's ingenious manufacture of gliders played an especially important role. These silent aircraft were used in campaigns in Italy, New Guinea, Holland, and North Africa and often were at the forefront of an attack, flying at speeds in excess of 60 miles per hour.

Overseas, the Dagenham plant produced Ford military trucks and Bren-gun carriers for shipment to the conflict in North Africa. British Ford workers also built more than 30,000 super-charged V-12

PASSING THE TORCH *As the Allies claimed victory overseas, thanks to superb instruments of war like the M-10 tank at left, Ford lost one of its own. Edsel, below left, died in 1943 at the age of forty-nine. Below right: Edsel's oldest son, Henry Ford II, in his U.S. Navy uniform, poses with Henry and Clara. The twenty-eight-year-old became Ford's youngest president in 1945.*

engines for Mosquito and Lancaster bombers (more than were built by the British Rolls-Royce automobile company), helping England's Royal Air Force defend British skies against the German Luftwaffe. As for the rest of Ford in Europe, the Nazis exercised varying degrees of control over the company's plants in France, Belgium, Holland, Denmark, Finland, Hungary, and Romania as well as in Germany itself.

When the war ended in an Allied victory, the automobile industry was lauded for its pivotal role. "The Big Three and their suppliers produced more than 25 percent of the armaments used by America in the war effort," says Skinner. No wonder Detroit was called "the Arsenal of Democracy."

"The job of war production was a miracle," said Henry Ford II, the eldest son of Edsel. "It confounded our enemies and drew praise from our allies. In a very short time, we armed the largest fighting force ever mustered on this continent; we built, armed, and fueled combat ships and planes and tanks in quantities never before imagined; we put billions of dollars of weapons into the hands of our allies all over the world."

Henry Ford II had been released from service in the U.S. Navy during the war, upon the death of his father, Edsel, on May 26, 1943. Considered by many a moderating force in the company in addition to being a brilliant designer and visionary in his own right, Edsel was only forty-nine years old. Edsel's career had been more or less frustrated by his father. Although Henry named Edsel president of Ford in 1918, he never relinquished control. As Emerson wrote, "Wherever Macdonald sits, there is the head of the table."

At almost eighty years of age, Henry resumed the presidency of the company. Meanwhile, Henry II, upon his release from the military, was learning the ropes. By 1945, both Clara and Edsel's wife, Eleanor, insisted that Henry hand over the reins to Henry II. Eleanor threatened to sell her Ford stock unless he complied. "Eleanor alone owned about 45 percent of Ford family stock, so this was a weighty threat," says Skinner. On September 21, 1945, twenty-eight-year-old Henry Ford II became the new president of Ford Motor Company.

Henry in his early eighties was incapacitated by a series of strokes and no longer exuded his characteristic spry demeanor. On the evening of April 7, 1947, a storm caused some flooding at Fair Lane. "Henry went out to examine the damage, walking with his driver over the wet ground in his bedroom slippers—his 'clodhoppers,' he called them—to the powerhouse," says Bryan.

The hydroelectric facility was on the banks of the Rouge, which had overflowed, flooding the turbines and causing a blackout. Fair Lane was plunged into darkness when Henry returned to bed. Later that night, warmed by a wood fire, as candles flickered and the distinct odor of a kerosene lamp filled his senses, Henry Ford left the world.

His death was the top news story across the nation and much of the

world. Flags throughout Michigan flew at half-staff, and Henry's body lay in state at Greenfield Village, where a mile-long queue of some 30,000 to 100,000 mourners (depending on the source) paid their respects. His funeral at St. Paul's Cathedral in Detroit drew another 30,000 mourners.

The nation paid homage to perhaps its most productive native son. "There is none of us, rich or poor, whose life has not been bettered by his labor," said popular poet and Detroiter Edgar A. Guest in a radio tribute. "By the dreams he had, pursued, and achieved, the burdens of drudgery were taken from the shoulders of the humble and given to the steel and wheel."

Henry Ford was buried on the grounds of what would later become St. Martha's Episcopal Church. Three years later, his "great believer" Clara was laid to rest beside him. He had once said, "If I were to die and come back to another life, I would want the same wife."

Meanwhile, Henry II had taken control of the company as if he had been waiting his whole life for the opportunity. Ford was beleaguered by an inferior management system and other more serious problems, which Henry II and his top lieutenant, Ernest R. Breech, a former high-ranking executive at General Motors, tackled with fervor. The revitalized company met the postwar economic boom with a new Ford Division (led by Lewis Crusoe, another GM recruit) and a new car—the 1949 Ford, the first change in a Ford body since 1942 and the first change in a chassis since 1932.

America's sudden postwar prosperity made a brand-new car an attainable dream for millions. Many middle-class families had the financial wherewithal to buy a second car, and homes with two-car garages proliferated. Rock and roll hit the airwaves; TV overtook living rooms; and Elvis Presley, Marilyn Monroe, and James Dean—who drove a 1949 Mercury coupe in the 1955 movie *Rebel Without a Cause*—shocked the nation with their audacity. Amid it all, the dream car was born.

The 1950s liberated the automobile from its earthly bonds to soar into a futuristic vision of pop-up, push-button, retractable, tail-finned, multihued wonder, mirroring the optimism of a nation. Meanwhile, a mammoth government road-building program was under

SUBURBS AND THE "TWO-FORD FAMILY"

The end of World War II brought postwar prosperity to the United States. As employment soared and incomes rose, tract houses and highways sprang up coast to coast. Suddenly, "two cars for every garage" was no longer a financial *impossibility (although many garages would need enlargement). Ford Motor Company capitalized on the phenomenon, advertising that its affordable automobiles made two-car ownership within reach of the most modest family* *budgets. Ford raised the curtain on several colorful new models during the postwar period, including the 1955 Fairlane and Continental Mark II, the 1959 Galaxie, and the 1960 Comet and Falcon.*

FIFTIES GLAMOUR *The fanciful two-tone 1957 Mercury, left, reflected the buoyant optimism of the postwar era. Overleaf: The 1957 Ford Thunderbird, with its trademark porthole window, is a car design icon.*

way. The legendary American highway, Route 66, symbolized the romance of the open road. "The people buying cars in the 1950s had grown up during the Depression, fought in World War II, and had basically been through a lot," says Casey.

"Now come the good times they'd been waiting for since they were kids. They figured, rightly so, that they deserved the big two-tone car with the huge V-8 engine, tubeless tires, automatic transmission, and all that chrome—big cars that reflected big dreams. This was their reward."

Young people eyed the new Mercury Turnpike Cruiser, dubbing it the "original dreamcar," the Ford Sunliner (America's biggest selling convertible), and above all, the Thunderbird, Ford's first personal luxury automobile. The Thunderbird was introduced commercially in 1955, the same year James Dean died in an automobile crash, sealing his fame as an icon of cool. When unveiled at the Detroit Auto Show in 1954, the car had it all—the looks, the performance, and the promise—except for one important ingredient. It was nameless.

A contest, in which the winner would receive "a full suit of clothes," produced a long list of choices. A Ford car stylist won with "Thunderbird," the name drawn from the deserts of Arizona and New Mexico, where according to Indian legend the thunderbird was a divine

helper of man. Teenagers loved the "T-bird," whose appeal was immortalized during the 1960s in the Beach Boys' hit that celebrated the "fun, fun, fun" that could be had with it. More than 3,500 orders for the car were placed in the first ten-day selling period.

Ford had explored an uncharted market and come up a winner. In 1955, the company broke all previous sales records and Henry II was named *Time* magazine's "Marketing Man of the Year." The next year, President Dwight D. Eisenhower signed the Interstate Highway Act earmarking public funds to build a national grid of highways. Americans took to the road in record numbers, and a string of motels, drive-in movie palaces, and burger joints were built to accommodate them.

The economic boom echoed through the early 1960s, a time when "baby boomers" crowded the playgrounds and America's hopes turned skyward. The Soviet Union had beaten the United States into space with the first manned spacecraft, prompting youthful President John F. Kennedy to vow America would be the first to the moon. Jet aircraft flight became a symbol for Ford's designers and marketers, who captured the space-age spirit in three new cars, the 1959 Ford Galaxie, the company's new top-line series; the 1960 Mercury Comet, its first upscale compact car; and the 1962 Meteor.

More than rocket ship imagery inspired Ford. In 1965, the company's Philco subsidiary designed and equipped NASA's Mission Control Center in Houston, which would direct the Gemini and Apollo manned space flights. Ford had put people on wheels and in the air. Now it would play a part in putting them in space.

On Earth, the company's biggest success story of the 1960s was the Mustang. Ford division boss Lee Iacocca and product manager Donald Frey were the brains behind the flashy but practical car with its long hood and short rear deck. The Mustang was named for the famed fighter aircraft of World War II and not, as generally believed, for the horse that became its emblem. It was the right automobile at the right time for the baby boomers who were getting their first driver's licenses. The Mustang was small, light, sporty, and inexpensive, selling for a factory price of $2,368.

Ford and its marketing team went into high gear promoting the Mustang, arranging to have a sneak picture of the car taken on March 11, 1964, that was picked up by *Newsweek* and other magazines. More than one hundred Mustangs were loaned to reporters for test-drives in hopes of getting good reviews before the car was introduced to the buying public. The strategy hit the bull's-eye: journalists praised the car, and Iacocca and the Mustang made the cover of both *Time* and *Newsweek* the same week, a rare double feat.

THE 1964–65 WORLD'S FAIR

The great civil rights leader, Rev. Dr. Martin Luther King, Jr., and his daughter Yolanda enjoy a ride on the Ford Magic Skyway at the New York World's Fair, above. The fair, in Flushing Meadows, Queens, drew millions of people to visit the Unisphere; Michelangelo's magnificent sculpture, the Pieta *(on loan from the Vatican); and Ford's own creation—the 1964½ Mustang. Built on a marsh in the shadow of Shea Stadium, the home of the New York Mets, the World's Fair invited attendees to think about the past, the present, and the future through its many exhibits. Ford hired the original "imagineer," Walt Disney, to design the Ford Wonder Rotunda exhibit.*

The car that galloped away with America's heart had its first public showing as a 1964½ model on April 17, 1964, at the New York World's Fair. To promote the car, Ford worked with master showman Walt Disney to design and build the Wonder Rotunda a futuristic pavilion nearly three football fields long. Inside, a panorama of "yesterday, today, and tomorrow" greeted visitors, beginning with prehistoric images that ultimately blended into more modern achievements of humanity—all in Disneyland-style animation. The experience ended with a look at the cars of tomorrow.

Dealers were overwhelmed by customer demand for the Mustang, receiving more than 22,000 orders the first day it became available. Overall, 418,812 Mustangs were sold in a single year—besting the company's previous sales record of 417,000 Ford Falcons in 1960. More than one million Mustangs would be sold before the car had its second birthday.

The late 1960s were a more tumultuous time, marked by the assassinations of major public figures, the war in Vietnam, and rising civil unrest. Detroit, with its large African-American population, turned out to be particularly susceptible to racial tensions.

One hot summer night in July 1967, a police raid at an unlicensed bar triggered a civil disturbance. When the looting and

EASING TENSIONS *The 1960s and '70s were difficult times. After civil unrest took its toll on Detroit, a determined Henry II worked to bridge the divide between black and white. Right: Henry II presides at a meeting with Detroit mayor Coleman Young and UAW president Leonard Woodcock in 1974. Meanwhile, the first of two Mideast oil embargoes was sending gasoline prices sky-high and shock waves through the American auto industry. Below: A Lincoln assembly line. Opposite: Cars lined up at a gas station during the 1970s. Opposite, below: A FoMoCo parts sign from the 1960s.*

violence spread to other areas of the city, the National Guard was called in to restore order. It took days to quell the unrest. When it was over, forty-three people had died and the city had suffered significant damage—to its reputation as well as some of its neighborhoods and businesses. Henry II was stunned. "He was on the top floor of the headquarters building watching the city he loved literally burning in the distance," says Skinner.

The riot of 1967 was healed in part by the stunning come-from-behind victory of the Detroit Tigers in the 1968 World Series at Tiger Stadium. Ford's diverse workforce joined in unison to root for hometown slugger Willie Horton, an African American.

The civil unrest that characterized this period was evident also in growing public activism over the state of the environment. Polluted skies choked many cities, bringing cries for stricter

government controls on automobile hydrocarbon emissions. In 1964, California was the first state to mandate reduced amounts of nitrogen, carbon monoxide, and lead in car exhaust. The following year, the Motor Vehicle Air Pollution and Control Act of 1965 applied the California regulations to the entire country.

Although the automobile industry agreed air pollution was unhealthy and unacceptable, it insisted the technology to absorb pollutants was immature, complex, and costly. An unsympathetic public rendered these arguments moot, putting the onus on carmakers to find out how to reduce automobile emissions. More stringent antismog rules were issued, such as the Federal Clean Air Act of 1970, which imposed a reduction of almost 90 percent in vehicle emissions. The industry ultimately met these exacting mandates, which hiked the price of a car—from $50 more in 1977 to $530 more in 1980.

In a speech to Ford's worldwide managers in February 1973, Henry II predicted the environmental rules would become more restrictive as the public pressure increased. He also predicted another looming crisis—a major oil shortage. Later that year, an embargo by the Organization of Petroleum Exporting Companies (OPEC), which represented major oil exporters like Saudi Arabia, Libya, Iran, and Iraq, proved him right.

OPEC curtailed the production of oil from its members, creating a supply-demand imbalance that quadrupled the per-barrel price of oil sold to international oil companies. The oil industry had no recourse but to increase prices at the pump. Long lines and long waits at service stations became common around the country. Another major oil shortage followed in 1978, brought about by the overthrow of the Shah of Iran. Gas prices again spiked upward.

The U.S. automobile industry, accustomed to producing large gas-guzzling vehicles for a public that believed "bigger was better," was caught unawares. Forecasts after the first embargo indicated small cars would capture half the market share, and Ford quickly put its shoulders behind pint-sized cars like the Ford Pinto, a subcompact car introduced in 1971.

Ironically, in between the two oil crises, many Americans believed the worst was behind them since the price of gas had fallen, and they flocked back to larger vehicles. To unload their smaller cars, the auto manufacturers offered tempting rebates and discounts. Henry II even went to Washington to urge a 10 percent tax on gas to make smaller cars more enticing, to no avail.

Realizing that consumers apparently had curtailed their resolve to reduce the consumption of gasoline by buying more fuel-efficient automobiles, the U.S. government decided to make the car industry responsible for energy conservation. The Energy Policy and Conservation Act of 1975 instituted Corporate Average Fuel Economy (CAFE) guidelines requiring automakers to consistently improve their vehicles' miles-per-gallon metrics—to 18 mpg by 1978, 21.4 mpg by 1981, and 27.5 mpg by 1985.

Meeting these demands would not be easy for the U.S. auto industry. But for another group of carmakers from Japan—relative upstarts like Toyota, Honda, and Datsun—the regulations were less of an imposition. They already produced high-quality, fuel-efficient cars that suddenly found wide appeal in the United States, stunning the Big Three. "American carmakers didn't want to make smallish Falcons and Valiants; they wanted to make full-size Buicks and Fords," says Casey. "It was pure economics: It didn't cost much more to make a full-size Ford than it did to make a Falcon, but you could sell the Ford for a lot more money."

Made in Japan—once a scornful pronouncement of inferior workmanship—now meant solid, dependable merchandise. When the second oil crisis battered the public, the small-car craze returned and, this time, endured. But, instead of homegrown Fords and Chevrolets, the public wanted imports.

Complicating matters for U.S. carmakers was a favorable dollar-to-yen ratio, substantially lower labor costs in Japan, and soaring interest rates at home—21.5 percent prime in 1980. The stratospheric rates hurt makers of higher-priced cars mostly because of the higher financing costs required. By 1980, Japan had commandeered 21 percent of the U.S. car market.

The outlook for Ford was grim. The company's U.S. sales in 1980 were half the volume of 1978. Its market share fell from 23 percent in 1977 to 17.3 percent in 1980, a year in which it lost a staggering $1.5 billion. Suddenly, the press reported the unthinkable. On October 15, 1979, the cover of *Forbes* magazine asked: "Can Ford Keep Up?"

Ford would fight an uphill battle through much of the 1980s under a series of savvy CEOs, most of them former heads of Ford of Europe, whose experience buoyed the company financially during the turbulent period. Quality became Job 1 as Ford planned its counteroffensive, a long battle that would culminate in the introduction of another turnaround car, the 1986 Ford Taurus/Mercury Sable. There would be tough cost-cutting mandates and significant layoffs, but the company would persevere and prosper, thanks in large part to the sustaining strength of the company's widely dispersed dealer network.

By the late 1980s, Ford was a new company facing a changing market. The baby boomers who were captivated in their youth by T-birds and Mustangs now bought minivans like Ford's Aerostar, introduced in June 1984. Soccer moms were superwomen, running the office and running the home, and the minivan—the marriage of a station wagon and a van—was roomy enough to shepherd the kids to school and carpool fellow workers.

Mercury followed with the Villager minivan, and in 1993, Ford swapped the Aerostar for the highly successful front-wheel drive Windstar. More than thirty women—most of them engineers and most of them moms—were involved in creating the 1999 Windstar, which became the first minivan to earn the highest government rating for frontal crash safety.

Boomer dads searched for a vehicle that would satisfy their middle-aged yearning for adventure. The Ford Explorer, a sport utility vehicle launched in 1990 for the 1991

MAZDA RIDES WAVE INTO U.S. AND EUROPE

Today, Mazda is one of the many brands in the Ford galaxy, but in the 1970s the Japanese automaker was a major competitor. Japan's car companies seized upon novel production strategies to build vehicles more quickly, less expensively, and with lower gasoline consumption. The smaller cars invaded American shores and found a market desperate for economy in the recession-starved era. The first Mazda rolled off the assembly line in 1960. Ten years later, Mazda made its American debut, followed by the establishment of Mazda North America Inc. in 1981 and the beginning of vehicle production at its new U.S. facility in Flat Rock, Michigan, in 1987. Then as now, Mazda has stood for uncompromising quality, outstanding value, and breakthrough engineering. The company's unique rotary engine, aboard a Mazda 787B, won the Le Mans 24-Hour Endurance Race in 1991—the first victory for a Japanese automobile in this prestigious competition. Not bad for a company whose auto manufacturing origin in 1931 was a three-wheel truck for export to China.

As the new millennium dawned, only one automobile would be selected "Car of the Century." Hands down, that car was the Model T, Henry Ford's "universal" automobile. The Model T represented such a huge leap forward from previous automobiles, in terms of its engineering, durability, and, of course, its decelerating price.

Right: John Clinard, Ford Division Western Regional Manager of Public Affairs, with the fabled car and the notable award. Opposite: Chris Theodore, vice president of Ford North American Car, introduced the 2002 Thunderbird to members of the media at the North American International Auto Show in Detroit in 2001.

model year, appealed to this male hankering, though it wasn't confined to the likings of that demographic alone. "The Explorer was a high-end SUV, blending the rugged durability of a traditional SUV with stylish interiors, a comfortable drive, and softer lines," Casey says.

Marketers determined that highly active boomer progeny who enjoyed hiking and fly-fishing—and more extreme activities like mountain biking, rock climbing, paragliding, and parasailing—made up another market for the SUV; these marketers worked to position the Explorer as the boomer offspring vehicle of choice.

The world in the mid-1990s became the "global village" prophesied by Buckminster Fuller three decades earlier. The Iron Curtain had come crashing down, Third World countries morphed into emerging economies, and free trade blossomed. Many companies in the United States graduated into multinational corporations, hawking their goods and services from Argentina to Zaire. And the Internet connected diverse people in disparate lands and simultaneously created a new online global marketplace.

For Ford Motor Company, the planet had been its market ever since it ventured across the Detroit River in 1904 to produce and sell cars in Ontario. The company had planted flags in Europe, Australia, Latin America, and Asia well before other domestic companies even considered it. In the 1990s, Ford would extend its market, building or rebuilding operations in Vietnam, the Middle East, Russia, India, and the Philippines, to name but a few. The company launched Ford China, sold the new Ka car in Hong Kong and Moscow and the Ikon in India, and broke ground on joint venture assembly plants in Korea, India, and

Portugal. Yet, these foreign ventures barely scratch the surface of Ford's wide-ranging worldwide enterprises.

In this new era, Henry Ford's Model T appeared as antiquated as the horse must have seemed in Henry's day. But it was this car, after all, that ignited the revolution. As the twentieth century drew to a close, and journalists and car enthusiasts joined forces to pick the best of the last hundred years, only one car would forever carry the banner "Car of the Century." Hands down, the Model T was the most important automobile ever made.

Many other cultural icons from the Ford think tank also have earned their place in history. Two of these cars are bona fide "Living Legends"—the 2003 Thunderbird and the 2003 Mustang. In 2001, the T-bird and the Mustang Bullitt GT were the stars of a Ford-sponsored Living Legends tour across the continental United States. Everywhere the cars traveled, they stopped traffic and generated good vibrations. Oldtimers remembered their first T-bird tooling down the road or the Mustang that stole their hearts, and younger people celebrated cars that signified independence and freedom.

Here were some of the world's most treasured automobiles, reimagined for the twenty-first century, combining the best of the old and new. These vehicles are a part of history—in the making.

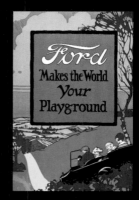

2

RISKS AND REWARDS

"The harder the conflict, the m[ore glorious]
the triumph. What we obtain to[o cheap we]
esteem too lightly; 'tis dearnes[s only that]
gives everything its value. . . . I l[ove the man]
that can smile in trouble, that [can gather]
strength from distress and grow[s brave by]
reflection. 'Tis the business of [little minds]
to shrink; but he whose heart i[s firm, and]
whose conscience approves his c[onduct, will]
pursue his principles unto [death.]"

—THOMAS PAINE

❖

Ford Motor Company has had its share of uphil[l climbs on the]
road to success. Here, a 1921 Model T is driven u[p the steps of]
Benson Polytechnic High School in Portland, O[regon. Inset:]
A Ford poster featuring Henry's enduring [slogan.]

For a company to endure one hundred years is notable in any industry, but to survive a century in the competitive automobile business borders the extraordinary. Hundreds of car companies have sputtered and stalled as Ford motored by them—Nash, Hudson, Packard, Stanley Steamer, Studebaker—the list goes on and on. But Henry Ford and his successors built a durable institution through dauntless decisions in automobile design, engineering, manufacturing, and marketing. In business, one reaps rewards by chancing risks others will not even consider. In Henry Ford's case, it was the ultimate gamble: He would risk his life.

The completion of the Quadricycle in the spring of 1896 brought renown to Henry in Detroit, and he set in motion plans to form an automobile company around his celebrated mechanical talents. With the backing and influence of Mayor William Maybury of Detroit, whose father came from the same town in Ireland as Henry's father, William, Henry Ford incorporated the Detroit Automobile Company in 1899. It had a short life, folding after one year and a loss of $86,000. Henry often quarreled with his backers, who disapproved of his plans to design a low-priced automobile, and resigned before a single car had been built.

Men of weaker substance might have moved on to other pursuits, but the failure only stiffened Henry's resolve and galvanized his energies. He decided to build a racecar that he himself would race. This was more than a middle-aged diversion. Henry's motive was pure business—the achievement of recognition through the personal demonstration of his product and its value. "I never thought anything of racing, but the public refused to consider the automobile in any light other than a fast toy," Henry remarked. "We had to race."

"It took tremendous courage, considering he had absolutely no experience racing a car at any speed," says Henry Ford Museum Curator of Transportation Bob Casey.

Henry built a swift vehicle with a confident name, *Sweepstakes*, helped by a team of engineers that included Oliver "Otto" Barthel and Ed "Spider" Huff. They entered *Sweepstakes* in a race sponsored by the Detroit Driving Club on October 10, 1901. Challenging Henry on the one-mile dirt oval in Grosse Pointe, Michigan, was the racing champion of the United States, Alexander Winton.

Winton was an established, successful car builder from Cleveland, so confident of victory that the club let his sales manager pick out the trophy, a cut-glass punch bowl that would look good in Winton's home. His racecar, the *Bullet*, was a proven winner with 70 horsepower, while *Sweepstakes* produced only 26 horsepower. Henry was the undisputed underdog, but the sentimental favorite of the hometown crowd. Eight thousand spectators crowded the grandstand.

At the start of the ten-lap race, Winton opened up a fifth of a mile lead and was well on his way to victory. But after five laps, Henry closed in. On the seventh lap, Winton's *Bullet* slowed and faltered, smoke streaming from the engine. Henry passed him in front of the cheering grandstand and won the race by a huge margin. Clara Ford wrote her brother, Milton, "One man threw his hat up in the air and when it came down he stamped on it, he was so excited."

ASTON MARTIN'S RACING ROOTS

Like Henry Ford, Lionel Martin raced cars in amateur competitions in the early years of the last century. A victory at Aston Hill prompted his car's name, and the firm was incorporated in 1913. After industrialist David Brown bought the firm in 1947, the company moved into the fast lane of international racing, taking the top three places in the 1958 Tourist Trophy Sports Car Race, left, and the checkered flag at the World Sports Car Championship in 1959. Ford acquired a 75 percent interest in 1987 and the rest seven years later. Since becoming part of Ford, Aston Martin is again receiving "bravos" for its world-class looks and speed. The sleek new Aston Martin DB-7 Vantage is capable of 180 miles per hour thanks to a 420-horsepower V-12 engine. The price also makes the heart jump—a whopping $160,000. At that price, it is Ford's most exclusive automobile.

Henry won the cut-glass punch bowl and a check for $1,000 (a pittance considering he spent five times that building the racecar). He also won priceless prestige: a car designed and built by Henry Ford had beaten a Winton, America's best automobile. Several spectators came forward after his great victory to offer financial support for another automobile company. Within weeks, the Henry Ford Company was incorporated.

"He'd persuaded people to invest their money in another automobile company by risking his neck to prove that his cars were on the cutting edge," says Casey.

But friction again developed between Henry and his backers. Henry wanted to build racecars, while his associates expected him to concentrate on automobile production. Sparks flew when the stockholders retained the services of another machinist, Henry M. Leland, to advise on Henry's engine design. When Leland disapproved, Henry resigned in March 1902, taking with him a $900 settlement and plans for another racecar. The Henry Ford Company was renamed Cadillac Automobile Company, after the founder of Detroit. General Motors acquired Cadillac in 1909, a historical irony.

Henry joined forces with Tom Cooper, a bicycle racing champion, to design and build two racecars, the red *Arrow* and the yellow *999*, the latter named after a New York Central train known for its record run between New York and Chicago. The cars' wheelbase and tread were larger than previous American racecars', and their four-cylinder engines galloped with 70 horsepower. "The roar of those cylinders was enough to half kill a man," Henry said.

Neither Henry nor Cooper wanted to race the speedsters, so they brought in another bicycle champion, Barney Oldfield, to race the cars for them. There was only one hitch—Oldfield had never driven a car before. "These cars were a far cry from *Sweepstakes*; they were brute force," says Casey.

On October 25, 1902, a rematch with Winton took place at Grosse Pointe. There were four other cars in the race. None came close— Oldfield won the five-mile event in a record time of five minutes, twenty-eight seconds. Racing remained in Henry's blood even after establishing the Ford Motor Company in 1903.

AUTOMOBILE RACES

At New Baltimore,
SATURDAY, JANUARY 9th, 1904.

Henry Ford of the Ford Motor Works of Detroit will attempt to lower
the World's Record.

There will also be ice boat racing for a valuable prize.

Come and see the fun.

CHECKERED FLAGS *Since its beginnings, Ford has been synonymous with auto racing. Above: A flyer for a 1904 race. Below: A Ford Model T in the state of Kansas, about halfway through a 1909 transcontinental race.*

100 YEARS OF FORD RACING

Ford Motor Company has been captivated by automobile racing right from the first, fueling an interest that began with the yearning of its founder for the thrill of victory. Henry Ford had built racecars and raced them himself, once holding the world land speed record for the mile, a feat accomplished with driving partner Spider Huff in the *Arrow* racecar in 1904.

Racing automobiles is not a lark for major automobile manufacturers. It is a proven method of evaluating car performance

limits, whether on the test track at the factory or at the world's great stock car and Formula 1 racing events.

In the early days of the automobile, races pitted cars in endurance contests, climbing rugged terrain and plowing through snow and mud across great distances. Henry's Model T won a much-publicized New York to Seattle endurance race in 1909, boosting Ford's reputation coast to coast. The publicity garnered by the victory led Henry to publish a booklet called *The Story of the*

Race that was distributed by the thousands to dealerships. Ironically, five months later the judges took the victory away from Henry upon learning that the driver had switched engines en route. The dispute did little to curtail the public's acceptance of the Model T as both durable and speedy.

"If my great-grandfather hadn't believed in the value of auto racing, the Ford Motor Company as we know it probably wouldn't exist today," said Edsel B. Ford II, a Ford director.

The company's introduction of a single-cast lightweight V-8 engine in the early 1930s made it the engine of choice among a generation of hot-rodders. Driving greats like Fred Flame and "Stubby" Stubblefield burned up the early stock car racing circuits from Elgin to Ascot to Monte Carlo, where a Ford V-8 won the 1936 and 1938 rallies.

Then, in 1949, a Lincoln driven by Jim Roper won the first-ever NASCAR Grand National race, held at Charlotte, North Carolina. Seven years later, Ford won its first NASCAR Manufacturers' Championship, in its first full season of factory-backed stock car racing. Below the border, Lincolns won the Carrera Panamericana, the famed Mexican Road Race, in 1952, 1953, and 1954.

Had Henry Ford been alive in the 1960s, when Ford sold as many as ninety different car models a year, he probably would have been most enthusiastic over the Total Performance cars, such as the Shelby Cobra. The company's focus on winning races from 1963 to 1971 brought many trophy cups, including 88 Indy car championships.

Ford also was active during the 1960s on the European racing circuit. Led by Sir Walter Hayes, who would become vice chairman of Ford of Europe, the company scored victory in the 1966 Le Mans race in a GT40 driven by Bruce McLaren. Ford had received its first win at the fifth running of the Daytona 500 in 1963 and its first Indianapolis 500 victory in 1965, a year in which Fords finished one through four. In 1967, Ford made its Formula 1 debut in the Dutch Grand Prix and would take first place in 155 Formula 1 races through 1983.

In 1970, Henry Ford II pulled Ford out of all forms of car racing because of the economic recession, the encroaching competition, and the need for deep budget cuts. In 1981, when Ford inaugurated a new unit, Special Vehicle Operations, as its administrative center for all racing activities, the quest for the checkered flag returned in earnest. Thanks largely to the unflagging efforts of Edsel B. Ford II, Ford was back at the track.

Ford would win many prestigious races in the next twenty years, including the first Winston Million in 1985, the 1992 NASCAR Manufacturers' Championship, the 1995 Indy 500, and the 1998 Winston Cup, in a Ford Taurus. In 2000, Ford won its fourteenth NASCAR Manufacturers' Championship. Also that year, Jaguar entered into Formula 1 racing, representing the British marque's first step into world championship competition.

Two years earlier, Ford had bought Cosworth Racing, its partner in Grand Prix race engine development for more than thirty years, positioning Ford well for future racing. ❖

BIRTHING PAINS *Henry's first car for Ford Motor Company was the original Model A, known as the Fordmobile and, in advertisements, right, as the "Boss of the Road." Trouble brewed for the nascent company when George Selden, below, charged Henry with infringing his patent on a gas-powered motorcar.*

In the winter of 1904, Henry and Spider Huff drove the *Arrow* on frozen Lake St. Clair, Michigan. As Henry gripped the steering mechanism, Huff stood on the running board feeding gas into the carburetor. They reached 91.37 miles per hour (39.4 seconds for one mile), which was a world land speed record at the time.

"The ice was seamed with fissures, which I knew were going to mean trouble," Henry said. "At every fissure the car leaped into the air. I was skidding, but somehow I stayed top-side up."

The mile record made news the world over, buoying the fledgling Ford Motor Company, then having a tough time staying afloat. Within the first thirty days of its incorporation on June 16, 1903, Ford was on the brink of collapse. Not one car had been sold. "The balance in the checkbook kept dropping," says Casey, "withering to a paltry $223.65."

Lack of demand was the problem. As Henry learned when the Quadricycle broke down in front of the Cadillac Hotel in 1896, many Americans regarded the automobile as a preposterous waste of time. Civil War veterans simply preferred their horses. Even in 1909, one year after the Model T made its debut, more than 25 million horses continued to provide primary transportation in America.

The public's curiosity about the horseless carriage gradually gave way to consideration and then demand. On July 15, 1903, a Chicago dentist, Dr. Ernst Pfennig, was the first person to buy a Ford, for $850 (although Dr. Pfennig's Model A was the eighth one shipped by Ford to customers). Thereafter, a steady stream of offers flowed in, and within a month nearly $20,000 in cars had been sold. At the end of nine and one-half months, business manager James Couzens's tally indicated 658 Model A automobiles had been purchased for a net profit of $98,851, a tidy 350 percent return on investment. New advertisements proclaimed the Model A the "Boss of the Road."

Trouble was brewing for the Boss, however. In 1903, a syndicate of automobile manufacturers sued Ford for patent infringement. The syndicate, the Association of Licensed Automobile Manufacturers (ALAM), had obtained a patent granted to the purported inventor of the gas-powered automobile, George Selden, a resourceful patent attorney who tinkered with internal combustion engines in his spare time.

Selden had developed a rudimentary gas-powered internal combustion engine on paper in 1878 and subsequently filed for a patent broadly covering all road vehicles powered by internal combustion engines. A series of technical delays helped Selden defer final issuance of his patent for sixteen years, during which time he filed more than one hundred amendments to his application encompassing technical improvements developed by others. In 1895, he was granted the patent, and notices were sent to U.S. carmakers that they must pay royalties to Selden.

THE HORSELESS AGE.

THE FORD

Boosted into Popular Favor by the Knocks of the Trust

You can't frighten a grown up man with a toy pistol; neither can you scare a man who wants the best car made from buying the Ford. The mechanical genius of Mr. Henry Ford enabled The Ford Motor Co. to produce a two cylinder car so perfect in construction and so low in price that it has sounded the death knell of the Trust. The cheapest two cylinder Tonneau car sold by the Trust is $1,500, so the Ford saves you $600.

Price with Tonneau, $900. *As a Runabout, $800.*

We agree to assume all responsibility in any action the Trust may take regarding alleged infringement of the Selden Patent to prevent you from buying the Ford—"The Car of Satisfaction."

Write for Illustrated Catalogue and name of our nearest agent.

FORD MOTOR CO., DETROIT, MICH.

Although many companies believed the patent was absurd, they found it cheaper to pay the royalty than fight it in court. In 1899, Selden sold his patent rights to the Electric Vehicle Company. Then, in March 1903, a group of more than two dozen manufacturers convinced Electric Vehicle to form a syndicate with them—ALAM—to decide which companies would be licensed under the patent. ALAM also would collect royalties of 1.25 percent on every gasoline automobile made.

At first, Henry concluded it would be easier to pay the royalty than fight it. But when he contacted ALAM about obtaining a license, he was rebuffed. The reason given was that Ford was an assembler and not a manufacturer, although Henry always believed it stemmed from his well-known difficulties at the two predecessor companies.

Far from being intimidated by this powerful organization and its $70 million war chest, Henry placed an emphatic notice in national newspapers guaranteeing his dealers, importers, agents, and customers protection "against any prosecution for alleged infringements of patents." Henry pledged the entire assets of Ford as a bond in this regard. As it turned out, only fifty customers asked for the bonds. Still, the risk for Ford was titanic.

The syndicate brought every pressure to bear upon the small, defiant company, using the press and advertisements to intimidate Ford customers and dealers.

Finally, in September 1909, after studying more than 14,000 pages and 5 million words of testimony, the court ruled that Selden's patent was, indeed, legal.

Henry immediately filed for an appeal. There was more at stake now for Ford—the Model T was setting sales records, exceeding 32,000 units in 1910. The entire industry watched Henry Ford fight for survival. On January 9, 1911, an appellate court ruled that Henry's engine did not fall within the scope of the Selden patent. The lower court ruling was reversed and victory was Ford's.

Had Henry abandoned the industry when the original lawsuit was filed in 1903, automobiles probably would have remained luxury items for another decade. The urbanization of America would have been delayed, and mass production and economic reform for workers would have been put off for several years. By fighting this grievance, Ford won national attention as a trust-busting David fighting a Goliath. "Nothing so well advertised the Ford car and the Ford Motor Company as did this suit," said Henry. "We were the underdog and had the public's sympathy."

Henry had promised the Model T would be so affordable that "everybody will have one. . . . The horse will be driven from the land." Horses remained, but people nonetheless adored the Model T, snapping them up at a rate of two thousand a month in 1910. Demand also sizzled outside U.S. borders. In 1903, Ford's first international venture was a shipment of a Model A, the sixth it manufactured, to a buyer in Canada.

Henry had only to look across the Detroit River to Windsor, Ontario, to visualize worldwide sales and manufacturing. Early sales in the provinces went through a distributor, Canada Cycle Company, but Henry soon comprehended that it didn't make economic sense to assemble cars in Detroit and then ship them worldwide, especially since the Canadians were exacting a 35 percent tariff on imported automobiles.

"Instead of wishing to keep [foreign markets] dependent upon us for what we manufacture, we should wish them to learn to manufacture themselves and build up a solidly founded civilization," Henry said.

On August 17, 1904, Henry invested $125,000 to form Ford Motor Company of Canada, Ltd., which received a provincial charter to conduct business in Walkerville, Ontario. A young wagon maker from Walkerville, Gordon McGregor, had come across the river in early 1904 and made Henry a proposal—he would turn his entire factory over to the making of Fords in return for the franchise on their manufacture and sale in Canada. Henry agreed. Ford Canada grew slowly, producing some 540 cars, mostly expensive Model Ks and inexpensive Model Ns, in its first three years.

International operations soon mushroomed. Ford opened its first overseas sales branch in Paris in 1908, and in 1910, sought a site for an assembly plant in England. It was found at Manchester, forty miles from the western coast but with direct water access to the sea through the Manchester Ship Canal. On March 6, 1911, Ford Motor Company Ltd. (England) was incorporated and a plant was built on a five and one-half acre site.

The following year, Henry, Clara, and Edsel traveled to England to meet with the Manchester plant's vigorous, erudite manager, Percival L. D. Perry. The four of them embarked on a tour of Ireland, visiting several cities and Cork, the county of William Ford's birth. In April 1917, Ford established its second European plant, in Cork, to produce low-cost Fordson tractors.

In swift succession, branches were established in 1913 in Buenos Aires, Argentina, and São Paulo, Brazil, and in 1919 in Copenhagen, Denmark. In 1920, a branch was opened in Cádiz, Spain. Two years later, branches were established in Asnières, France (near Paris); Hoboken, Belgium (near Antwerp); and Trieste, Italy. These cities were located close to the largest markets in their respective countries, and plans were soon put in motion to build assembly plants. By 1930, more than two dozen countries manufactured Ford vehicles. There were assembly plants in such far-flung places as Chile, New Zealand, Malaya, Australia, and South Africa.

From the very first models, automobiles have helped us define who we are. And advertising agencies over the last century have gone to great lengths to rouse people's emotional involvement with automobiles. The art deco grandeur of the 1920s print advertisement for the Lincoln, right, is one way such advertising makes its appeal to buyers. The passionate hues of the red ibis against a sea of gold, the misty silhouette of the passenger in the rear seat, just behind the uniformed chauffeur— "This could be you!" the ad suggests. ❖

LINCOLN

Semi-Collapsible Cabriolet

The Lincoln plan to create a new and higher standard in the automobile industry has succeeded beyond the hopes of its sponsors, the Ford Motor Company. It was expected that the public would appreciate what could be done when such vast resources were behind the work, but results have exceeded expectations. The process of refinement goes steadily forward but it will never be expressed in terms of yearly or periodic models. Only changes of unquestioned value will ever prevail; only progress along sound and proven lines may be expected.

L I N C O L N M O T O R C O M P A N Y
Division of Ford Motor Company

1904

1925

1935

1946

1952

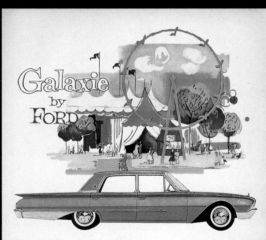

1960

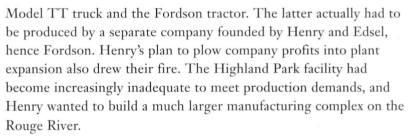

At home in the 1910s and '20s, the erect, dignified Model T had become a national institution. A huge billboard of an illuminated Model T with actual turning wheels crowned the Detroit Opera House in 1916. It was the most exuberant electric sign the world had ever seen, advising passersby to "Watch the Fords Go By."

The much-loved car was the subject of numerous publicity stunts. A "Ford Clinic" in New York, with mechanics in doctor's garb and an operating room with seats for spectators, demonstrated how to "operate" on an ill or injured Model T. The "surgeons" attended ailments from "sprained axles" to "rheumatic valves." Ford's clever advertising staff rigged up a one-hundred-foot assembly line at the 1915 International Exposition in San Francisco. Visitors were awed each time a Model T came together from piles of parts.

In 1914, Henry had a risky marketing idea—a $50 refund for each customer who bought a car in the next twelve months, providing 300,000 cars were sold during the period. When sales reached 308,213, the company cut more than $1.5 million in checks, sending one to President Woodrow Wilson, who had just bought a Model T.

Henry's fellow stockholders were indignant over the $50 rebate. They also begrudged his plans in 1917 to manufacture the

Model TT truck and the Fordson tractor. The latter actually had to be produced by a separate company founded by Henry and Edsel, hence Fordson. Henry's plan to plow company profits into plant expansion also drew their fire. The Highland Park facility had become increasingly inadequate to meet production demands, and Henry wanted to build a much larger manufacturing complex on the Rouge River.

As Henry saw it, the Rouge would encompass everything required to build a car—blast furnaces, coke ovens, a massive foundry, coal and ore bins, railroad yards, and large dock facilities—all in one place. The idea was not at all farfetched. The two thousand acres Henry owned on the Rouge River lay halfway between major sources of iron ore to the north and soft coal to the south. The site offered passage through the Great Lakes and access to North America through a junction of major railroads. Ore could be shipped down the Great Lakes on Ford ships, where foundries, steel mills, and an array of plants and assembly lines would perform the process of turning ore into automobiles.

To capitalize the project, Henry cancelled the dividend paid to stockholders from company profits. "A reasonable profit is right, but not too much," he explained. His backers took a dim view. Two leading stockholders, co-founders Horace and John Dodge, whose chassis components were used in many early Fords, filed a lawsuit

Ford Industries. Dearborn. Mich.

INDUSTRIAL MIGHT *Upon its completion in 1925, the self-contained Rouge Complex encompassed diverse industries—steel mills, paper mills, a glass factory, and a power plant that could generate enough electricity to power the city of Boston. It was the chief reception depot for coal, iron ore, rubber, and lumber. Left: The Rouge during its construction in 1917. Above. An artist's depiction of the finished plant.*

against Henry in 1916 to provide "reasonable dividends." At the time, Henry owned 58.5 percent of Ford stock.

"The Dodge brothers had ambitions to make their own cars, which required capital," Casey explains. "So when Henry cut the dividend, he was cutting short their ambitions."

Henry lost the case in 1919 and was forced to pay a delayed dividend of some $19 million to his fellow stockholders. The Dodge brothers later achieved their dream of making their own cars. The Dodge Motor Company was acquired by Chrysler in 1928.

The lawsuit was the last straw for Henry, and he made up his mind to buy out his stockholders and gain sole control of the company. Alexander Malcolmson and several other original partners had sold their stock in 1905 to pursue other interests, and James Couzens had resigned in 1915, in part over Henry's public position against the brewing war in Europe. Henry's Peace Ship crusade was the climax in a series of increasingly bitter relations between the two men, and Couzens felt he could no longer work *for* Henry, though he said he could still work *with*

him. Couzens, moreover, had budding interest in a career in politics and would later become the mayor of Detroit and a U.S. senator.

Only six stockholders remained now, and Henry concocted a strategy to separate them from their Ford holdings. At a stockholders meeting, he named Edsel Ford, who was just turning twenty-five, company president as of January 1, 1919, and announced he would step aside to start an automobile company that would manufacture a car less expensive than the Model T. Alarmed stockholders immediately offered to sell Henry their shares. Now all he had to do was scrape together $106 million to buy the 41.5 percent of company stock he didn't already own.

Some money came out of Henry's own pocket. Henry borrowed the rest, $60 million, in July 1919, from a New York financial syndicate, figuring he'd pay off the loan through earnings. However, economic prospects darkened in the early 1920s, and Ford Motor Company revenues fell. Wall Street salivated at the possibility of another huge Ford loan.

Henry had another strategy in mind. In 1920, he liquidated the entire Ford inventory and required his dealers to take whatever vehicles Ford had in stock—paying cash for the cars on delivery—or lose their franchise. The pressure was extreme, and the dealers had to borrow from local banks to remit Ford. Here is where Henry's close ties with Ford's dealer network paid off in spades. They were the company's point of customer contact, the face of Ford to the world. They showcased Ford cars, talked them up as the greatest vehicles on the road and received complaints with attentive ears. Although Henry had

THE CAR COMPANIES THAT CAME AND WENT

QUALITY
IN EVERY DETAIL

CORD

The automobile in the United States is a story of fortunes won and lost, careers made and squandered, and companies born and prematurely dead. The cemetery of car companies that breathed their last includes Cord, Packard, Studebaker, Stanley Steamer, and Peerless—and more forgotten vehicles such as the

Waverley, the Carterear, and the crazily named Locomobile, which made its debut in 1899. Many car companies were created to capture the wallets of the upper classes, their products pleasing to the eye in a way that the utilitarian Model T was not. Most sputtered and soon perished—the stiff competition for the small

number of individuals with enough money to buy them was the culprit. So why did Ford accelerate as other car companies fell behind? "The impression was that . . . only wealthy people were in the market for cars," Henry said. With the low-priced Model T, he proved them wrong.

changed the assembly process so he could build vehicles for the masses, it was the dealers who provided mass availability—making cars and trucks available in even the smallest communities. Thanks to strong demand for the Model T, Henry's strategy worked. Car lots emptied fast and Ford's cherished dealers quickly repaid the loans. Henry's bold plan was nothing short of financial wizardry.

Both banks of the Rouge now bustled with activity as Henry's planned expansion project took shape. The river was straightened and dredged in some places from four feet deep to twenty-seven feet deep. Although parts for the Model T first came off the Rouge assembly line in the fall of 1919, it would take another six years before the massive complex was ready to complete within its gates the whole process of converting ore into steel and steel into cars.

Today, we call this strategy "vertical integration," but when Henry, head of production Charles Sorensen, and Edsel Ford

envisioned the project, their conception was "flow." The moving assembly line had demonstrated that the flow of parts in the factory was of vital importance. It was now recognized that without the flow of raw materials to the point of manufacture, the flow of parts might be impeded or stopped, curtailing the production of automobiles.

Upon its completion in 1925, the self-contained Rouge Complex encompassed diverse industries—steel mills, paper mills, a glass factory, and a power plant that could generate enough electricity to power the city of Boston. It was the chief reception depot for coal, iron ore, rubber, and lumber. Ford established a lumber operation in northern Michigan to provide wood for car components and a rubber plantation in Brazil for tire production. Not everything was produced at the Rouge, however. Many smaller plants, located on rural riverbanks and powered by hydroelectricity, produced parts and components for Ford automobiles. Henry called these manufacturing outposts his "Village Industries."

Edsel and the Arts Commission of the Detroit Institute of Arts commissioned the renowned Mexican muralist Diego Rivera in 1931 to capture the spirit of the Rouge Complex in the famed *Detroit Industry* murals for the museum. Although he was only the titular president of Ford, Edsel presided over Ford's business, branch, and marketing operations and over all foreign developments. Much more so than Henry, Edsel had a clear picture of the world around them. He had driven across America with Charles Edison (the inventor's son and Edsel's best man at his wedding to Eleanor Clay) and other close friends in a Model T as a teenager, seeing life in cities large and small, prosperous and squalid.

He also had an eye for style and beauty. In the 1930s, Edsel and another Ford automobile designer, E. T. Gregorie, collaborated

UPPER CRUST *Ford bought Lincoln Motor Company in 1922, and through the artistic vision of Edsel and another Ford car designer, E. T. Gregorie, re-branded the Lincoln nameplate, below, on a radiator shell plaque, to more clearly associate it with classic style. The Lincoln factory, left, produced the kind of car Ford lacked—a high-class vehicle for the affluent consumer. The car had great appeal—police departments liked it for its speed and British consumers were impressed by the novel cigarette lighter.*

on some of the most strikingly beautiful cars ever to roll off an assembly line, manufactured by a new Ford acquisition, the Lincoln Motor Company.

Lincoln was owned by Henry Leland, the same Henry Leland called in as an advisor to the Henry Ford Company in 1902, which had compelled Henry to hand in his resignation. In 1917, Leland, his son Wilfred, and a group of investors organized Lincoln Motor Company to produce Liberty engines for Allied aircraft in World War I (as had Ford). After the war, Lincoln shifted its attention to building a big, high-end car. But with the market in an economic downturn in 1920, the pricey automobile failed to attract a following. Heavily overextended, the company was forced into receivership in 1921.

Learning of Leland's plight, Henry made the only bid at the receiver's sale, and on February 4, 1922, Ford purchased Lincoln Motor Company and all its assets and debt for $8 million. Leland and his son were bought out shortly thereafter, and Edsel took firm command of the unit. His and Gregorie's artistic touches soon elevated the Lincoln nameplate to one of the most prestigious in the automobile industry, a car synonymous with luxury and style. The

Lincoln provided access to a market that the Model T did not— nouveau riche Americans eager to display their sudden prosperity.

Although in 1926 the Model T was again available in colors besides black, the public had grown fickle. Fatter wallets made them more willing to pay for the "extras" offered by the competition, such as flashy paint schemes and nickel trim. "Ford didn't keep up in styling or mechanics," says Henry Ford Heritage Association President Mike Skinner. "The only thing that kept the Model T going was its price."

Chevrolets and Dodges kicked up 30 horsepower, while the Model T was saddled with 22.5 horsepower. Their interiors were lavishly appointed, while Ford's were simple. Their cars had electric starters, hydraulic brakes, and sliding gear transmissions that shifted reliably, with a clutch and accelerator pedal. Henry stuck to manual cranking ignitions until 1919—and mechanical brakes and his now-antiquated planetary gear system with its pedals on the floor through the 1920s. "Today you could sit in a 1922 Chevrolet and drive it without instruction," says Casey. "You couldn't do that with a 1922 Model T."

Had Henry retired and let Edsel run the company, Ford likely would have retained its market share. However, Edsel's

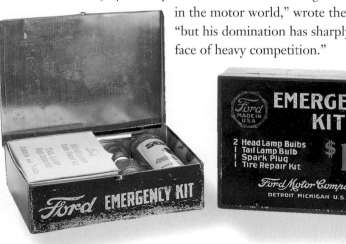

MODEL BEHAVIOR *Fifteen million Model Ts were manufactured between 1908 and 1927, when the ceremonial last one was driven off the line, right. Soon, Ford was assembling 40,000 Model As a day, opposite. Below: "Emergency Kits" from the Model T era.*

advanced industrial concepts and cultivated tastes clashed sharply with his father's flinty individualism and homespun preferences. Edsel had appealed many times to update the styling and performance of the Model T, but Henry insisted he had already created the perfect car that, with proper care and maintenance, would last an owner a lifetime. Henry had misjudged the market, and many customers abandoned him.

The consequences were dire. Ford's market share in the second half of 1926 fell to one-third of all automobiles sold, compared with two-thirds in 1924. "Henry Ford continues to be the greatest single influence in the motor world," wrote the *New York Times*, "but his domination has sharply declined in the face of heavy competition."

Henry finally accepted the fact that the Model T had run its course. The end of the line was marked with a ceremony on May 26, 1927, upon completion of the milestone 15 millionth unit, a car that Henry and Edsel drove off the assembly line together. He subsequently closed Ford plants all over the world to retool for a new car. He and his engineers now worked patiently behind closed doors to perfect a new car to replace the Model T.

For six months, the public waited patiently to see what Henry would bring out next. Ford suffered: workers were laid off, suppliers sweated it out, and only the strongest dealers survived—by selling used cars. The standstill gave an edge to the competition, causing a further loss in market share that would be difficult to regain.

Henry and his engineers sought to create a chassis more advanced than the Model T, as well as a new four-cylinder engine, a new sliding transmission, and a novel electrical system. Edsel was given the job of styling the car. By now, the Lincoln was among the finest-looking cars in America, and he would adapt its finely sculpted lines to the new Ford. On December 22, 1927, the new vehicle—christened the Model A to signify a new beginning—wheeled off the Rouge assembly line and into dealers' showrooms. Ten million people stood in line for two days just to get a glimpse of the new automobile from Ford.

"A" FOR EFFORT *The Model T was a tough act to follow. Yet Henry's "lady," right, exceeded public expectations with its smooth lines—similar to those on the Lincoln—and lighter, quieter four-cylinder engine. The build-up in the press also created an instant sensation when the car was unveiled, and Ford dealers were ready to show them, left, to meet demand. Below: A 1931 Model A brochure. Overleaf: New York City teems with people and cars in 1935.*

HENRY'S MADE A LADY OUT OF LIZZIE
Written in 1928 by Walter O'Keefe

Have you seen her, Ain't she great?
I'm sure you understand what I mean,
Everybody, everywhere is falling for her now,
I'm talking about the new Ford,
And boy, it's sure a wow!
Lay off people, Lay off folks,
None of your sarcastic jokes,
Henry's made a lady out of Lizzie.

No more bruises, no more aches,
Now she's got those four wheel brakes;
Henry's made a lady out of Lizzie.

She's even got a rumble seat,
And lots of style and class;
The horn just seems to holler out
"Toot, toot they shall not pass."
The Lincoln cars just yell out loud,
That they are mighty, mighty proud.
Henry's made a lady out of Lizzie.

It was the biggest introduction in the history of the automobile and an event considered among the most momentous of 1927, a year that saw Lindbergh's solo flight across the Atlantic, the execution of Sacco and Vanzetti, and the Jack Dempsey–Gene Tunney heavyweight championship fight in Chicago. Thousands of cash deposits to buy the low-priced, fashionable car were taken on the spot, even when it was announced that it would be weeks before production would commence.

Henry capitulated to another trend in the industry, forming Universal Credit Company in 1928 so his dealers could sell cars on credit, something else Edsel had recommended for years to no avail. Altogether, Ford sold more than 5 million Model As through 1931, finally signifying to Henry that speed, comfort, and—most of all—styling had become just as important in an automobile as engineering. As the song goes, "Henry's Made a Lady Out of Lizzie."

Despite its stellar start, the Model A was unable to sustain Ford through the economic turmoil of the Depression. In 1931, Ford sales slipped to half that of 1930, roughly 620,000 automobiles sold for $460 million, and the company went into red ink for the first time.

Only eight of Ford's thirty-five U.S.-based assembly plants were active by 1933, the others turned temporarily into parts depots or sales offices. Ford dealers kept alive by resorting again to used-car sales.

Although the Depression took a toll on Ford and its dealer base, Henry was optimistic the country would pull through. In a national telephone hook-up with dealers, Henry told them to "pitch in and do all the business [you] can to help the President pull the country out of the hole." Henry understood full well the value of his dealers, who even in dire times would spend their own money to advertise his cars. They largely remained loyal to him, even when he was forced to cut their commissions during the difficult economic period or when he blasted off about the evils of tobacco and alcohol and FDR's New Deal, distancing many prospective customers. When a few dealers did bolt for the competition in the 1930s, Henry retaliated by raising commissions for those who stuck by him.

To encourage demand, Henry slashed automobile prices, raised wages, and spent capital on expansion of the Rouge. "A business that makes too much profit disappears almost as quickly as one that operates at a loss," he explained. Price before cost was his maxim—if you offered the right price, the cost would take care of itself.

These were tough years for Henry Ford personally. His close friend Thomas Edison passed away in 1931, and Henry's reactionary views on unions distanced many in the working class.

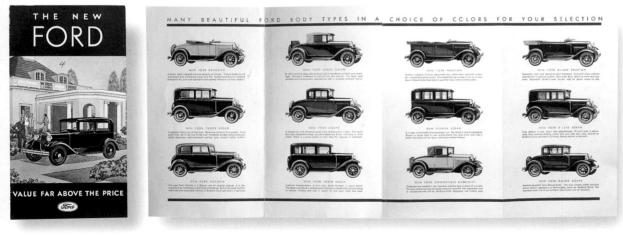

THE NEW FORD
VALUE FAR ABOVE THE PRICE

MANY BEAUTIFUL FORD BODY TYPES IN A CHOICE OF COLORS FOR YOUR SELECTION

His seeming insensitivity to the impact of the Depression hurt his public standing further. When Henry said in 1931 that "these are good times but only a few know it," the poor and downtrodden wondered just whom he was talking about. Many people also were put off by his vitriolic comments concerning President Franklin Delano Roosevelt and his New Deal for America. Henry jibed that the eagle emblem of the National Recovery Administration, a cornerstone of the New Deal, was "Roosevelt's Buzzard."

Henry's anti-Semitic publications also took a toll. A series of articles in the *Dearborn Independent*, a weekly newspaper he purchased in 1918, opined that the Jewish people had caused many of the problems confronting the world, including World War I. Some of these articles were reprinted in a series of books entitled *The International Jew*. These preposterous claims eventually caused the demise of the newspaper. When the *Independent* reported that Jews were attempting to gain control of wheat farming in the United States, Henry was charged with libel in a lawsuit filed by Aaron Sapiro, a powerful attorney involved in organizing Midwestern farm cooperatives.

When the case came to trial in 1927, the defense took the position that the editor of the *Independent* had not made Henry privy to any articles prior to printing. The case was declared a mistrial on a legal technicality, giving Henry an opportunity to settle with Sapiro out of court. Henry then printed an apology in the *Dearborn Independent*, writing that he had no knowledge of what had been published in the newspaper and promising to see to it that no more anti-Semitic material would be circulated in his name.

In 1938, the German consul in Detroit presented Henry with an award on the occasion of his seventy-fifth birthday. Later that year, Henry issued a statement saying that he considered the award a gift from the German people and that his acceptance did not signify any sort of support for the Nazi government. In 1942, Henry wrote to the founder and chairman of the Anti-Defamation League of B'nai B'rith, denouncing anti-Semitism and all sectarian hatred.

In succeeding years, both Edsel and Henry Ford II would endeavor to strengthen ties to the Jewish community. Upon assuming the presidency of Ford, Henry II fired the man who had edited the anti-Semitic articles in the *Dearborn Independent*. In 1972, he paid a visit to the nation of Israel, spending some time at the Wailing Wall. The following year he sent Ford trucks to Israel for use in the Yom Kippur war. Henry II also single-handedly fractured the prohibitions preventing Jews from joining the exclusive Detroit Club, of which he was a member.

While Ford coped with negative publicity and competitive pressures in America, its varied European operations in the late 1920s had become unruly and unproductive. Henry had split his European interests after the war into twelve separate companies, a strategy that now proved costly and ineffective. "The European companies had become splinter groups trying to run their own organizations," Skinner explains.

Henry summoned Percival L. D. Perry, the original manager of the Manchester plant, to help craft a new organization for Europe. Sir Percival (knighted for his service during World War I) had resigned from Ford in 1919 and retired to the Channel Islands. In October 1928, Henry and Sir Percival announced a new strategy for Ford in Europe— "the 1928 Plan."

The centerpiece of the strategy was the centralization of Ford's European activities in England under Sir Percival's oversight and the formation of a new company, Ford Motor Company, Limited, to serve this purpose. The giant automobile manufacturing plant that Ford had built in 1924 to replace the old plant in Manchester was located in Dagenham. Situated on the north side of the Thames River twelve miles from London, Dagenham offered excellent railroad and port connections, as well as a large pool of labor and parts suppliers.

The plan called for Dearborn to design and engineer automobiles and parts and for Dagenham to produce and distribute them for assembly by other Ford plants in Europe. Ford Limited also was directed to acquire the stock of the various Ford companies on the continent. In 1932, the first of the cars to be made for the European market made its debut—the Model Y. The small automobile was a hit, capturing 54 percent of the British market in 1934 for all vehicle types.

Although the 1928 Plan looked sound on paper, it caused turmoil on the European continent. Plants objected—from nationalistic considerations—to buying cars and parts from England. Realizing the plan had sprung a leak, in 1934 Henry allowed the Continental companies to buy parts and automobiles from either Dagenham or Dearborn, an action antagonistic to Sir Percival.

Outside Europe, Ford's far-flung empire fared less divisively. The company's plant in Geelong, Australia, built more than 4,000 Model Ts, 2,400 Model TT trucks, 665 Fordson tractors, and 3 Lincolns in its first six months of production in 1925. Geelong was chosen as the headquarters for Ford of Australia because of excellent road and rail facilities. The city also offered sufficient land resources at a reasonable cost for future development, an adequate supply of labor, and close proximity to the wealthy Western District of Australia.

In 1928, Ford of Australia unveiled the Model A to the same fanfare the car received in the United States. More than 100,000 people lined up to see the car in Melbourne, and in Sydney a similar turnout caused huge traffic jams. Even more sensational was the introduction of the Model Y, a smaller lightweight car, in 1933.

Ford's Mexico City plant, built in 1925, employed native Mexicans to manufacture Model T cars and Model TT trucks, "using machinery and equipment similar to that used in Dearborn," *Ford Times* reported. The 48,000-square-foot facility carried a large service stock and employed a standard assembly line and body-painting department, producing twenty-five cars and trucks a day.

Elsewhere in Latin America, Ford ventures proliferated. In 1924, the company opened its first branch west of the Andes in Santiago, Chile, and the following year, at the Grand Exposition of Brazil, it unveiled an assembly line for publicity purposes, as it had in San Francisco in 1915. Three plants were in operation in Brazil by the late 1920s. Meanwhile, new branches were established in San Juan, Puerto Rico, and Caracas, Venezuela. By 1927, Ford boasted eleven companies and plants operating in Latin America, selling through some 1,700 dealers, more than any other auto manufacturer.

POWER FOR LESS *Ford's 1932 breakthrough V-8 automobile, right, was built at the company's Rouge manufacturing plant. Charles Sorensen wrote that the car "was a production man's dream come true." Opposite: At New York World's Fair in 1939, visitors waited in line to drive the latest Fords, Lincolns, and Mercurys around the cork and rubber "Road of Tomorrow" exhibit.*

In the United States, the lean years of the Depression required a change in marketing. Ford advertised its new V-8 automobile as providing the same power as its rivals but at a more economical price. This theme was conveyed through Ford's "thrifty Scotsman," a Scottish gentleman in kilts accompanied by his faithful Scottish terrier dog. Ford dealers capitalized on the new advertising strategy, bolstering it with additional print ads paid for with their own funds. Many dealers also exploited the V-8's reputation as the only car in the low-price field with a V-8 engine. The pavement pounding paid off—Ford's V-8 outsold Chevrolet's in 1935 by a substantial margin.

Ford's advertising ingenuity also was evident at the Ford Rotunda, the company's eleven-acre exhibit at the 1934 Chicago World's Fair. Designed by Albert Kahn in the shape of a cluster of gears, the Rotunda was made of steel and covered with weatherproof papier-mâché. Inside the novel structure were exhibits on the latest industrial, manufacturing, and transportation methods, as well as the new Fords. More than 25 million fairgoers visited the Rotunda, prompting Henry

to have it reconstructed in Dearborn in 1936 as a visitors' center. Tragically, it was lost to fire in November 1962.

As the decade wore on, the public wanted more product options from the Big Three. Ford, however, lagged in this regard, selling only two models through 1937 (Ford and Lincoln), while GM offered six and Chrysler four. The company took notice and in 1938 unveiled a new line of automobiles—the medium-priced Mercury.

The Mercury filled the market void between the low-priced Ford and the high-priced Lincoln. The first Mercury, the 1939 Mercury 8, had a distinctive streamlined body style, a V-8 engine with ten more horsepower than a Ford, and hydraulic brakes. It competed against a potpourri of brands, including Buick, Oldsmobile, Pontiac, Dodge, Graham, Hudson, Nash, and DeSoto. Cars now came in colors and body styles to suit every whim and were priced to suit every pocketbook.

Ford had fallen to third place among the Big Three in the 1940s. Other serious interests, including the historical museum in Dearborn and soybean research, diverted Henry's attention, and he increasingly delegated management responsibility of the motor company to Sorensen, Edsel, and Harry Bennett.

In 1943, the hard-driving Sorensen resigned as Ford's head of production, after thirty-nine years of service. The departure of "Cast-iron Charlie," a nickname derived from Sorensen's love for casting but also a sly allusion to his brusque demeanor, left a hole in Ford's management. He had partnered with Henry to create the automotive assembly line, had overseen the building of Ford plants around the world, and had transitioned the company to wartime production in two world wars.

RISE OF LAND ROVER AFTER THE WAR

From three wheels to four describes the evolution of Land Rover. Founded as Starley & Sutton in 1877 to produce tricycles, the company today, owned by Ford, is a world-class maker of specialty SUVs. The company's most profound transformation occurred after World War II, when the two owners of the British

firm Rover—brothers Maurice and Spencer Wilks—decided to make a light four-wheel-drive utility vehicle. The British government was urging manufacturers to create products for export. U.S. Army Willys jeeps were popular after the war—though their parts were hard to come by—so the

Wilkses attached existing Rover parts to a jeep-like chassis and transmission. Orders soon poured in from all over the world. They intended the vehicle primarily for agricultural use—working the land—hence the name, Land Rover. At left is Winston Churchill alongside a Land Rover Series I.

ROTUNDA

The Ford Rotunda, a spectacular monument to free enterprise, was first erected at the 1934 Century of Progress Exposition in Chicago. The Rotunda, designed in the shape of a cluster of gears by noted architect Albert Kahn, was so popular that Henry later had the building re-erected in Dearborn, right. ❖ From 1936 until its destruction by fire in 1962, the Rotunda hosted more than 18 million visitors. Guests marveled at its beautiful nighttime lighting and at the striking geodesic dome designed by R. Buckminster Fuller in 1953 (previously the Rotunda center court was open to the skies). ❖ Opposite: The Rotunda during its various incarnations and examples of the exhibits inside it in 1957. ❖

DEARBORN ROTUNDA

GEARSHIFT KNOBS

ROTUNDA CHINA

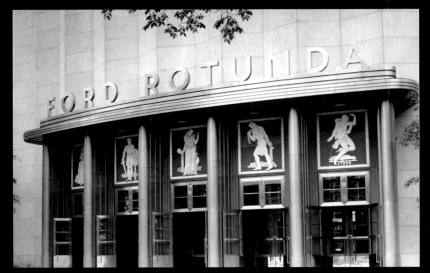

ROTUNDA ENTRANCE IN 1937

ROTUNDA EXTERIOR IN 1939

1957 STYLING EXHIBIT

1957 ALASKA EXHIBIT

THIS GAVEL AND BLOCK WERE MADE FROM WOOD FROM THE YACHT "ONIKA" BELONGING TO MR. EDSEL FORD

With Sorensen gone, Bennett, the one-time Ford bodyguard who had a battalion of employee spies and thugs at his command, set out to solidify his power base. *Time* magazine in 1944 said there was no one except Henry and his twenty-seven-year-old grandson, Henry Ford II, "to challenge Bennett's absolute power."

Bennett was fearless, alleged to have decked several employees who disagreed with his decisions. He was licensed to carry a firearm and is said to have once shot a cigar out of the mouth of a visitor who broke Henry's no smoking policy. Some reports maintain he kept cages of lions and tigers hidden in a tunnel underneath his home.

Henry felt strong allegiance to Bennett, who had settled the Sapiro case for him and been injured during the 1932 altercation between unemployed Ford autoworkers and Dearborn police near the Rouge complex. Beginning in 1927, Bennett claimed, Henry often picked up Bennett for the drive to work, and nearly every evening he called him on the phone before he went to bed. In his book, *We Never Called Him Henry*, Bennett wrote: "I became [Henry's] most intimate companion, closer to him even than his only son."

By the 1940s, Henry was convinced Edsel lacked the fortitude to replace him and lead the company. Bennett had a lot to do with this assessment. "Henry thought Bennett a sharp guy because he seemed to agree with everything he said," says Henry Ford Museum archivist Terry Hoover. "When Edsel wanted to change the style of a car and Henry disagreed, Bennett always threw his support behind Henry. He didn't have the company's interests at heart, only his own."

With Edsel's passing and Henry's health deteriorating, rumors circulated in early 1945 that Bennett had in his possession a codicil to Henry's last will and testament stating that, upon Henry's death, control of Ford would pass to a small group of people that included Bennett and others under his influence. Henry II, a Ford executive vice president at the time, sent John Bugas, a former FBI agent heading up Ford's government relations department, to obtain a copy of the alleged codicil.

When approached by Bugas, Bennett purportedly produced the document and, always flamboyant, set it afire. No copy of the codicil has ever been found, prompting speculation that Bennett simply made it up to assure Henry II—Henry's heir apparent—that Bennett was behind him 100 percent. If that was the objective, it failed. Upon assuming the presidency of Ford in September 1945, Henry II fired Bennett and hundreds of other employees in his command. The mass firings sent a clear message: Henry II was now in charge.

Henry II's first job at Ford was as a grease monkey, taking cars apart and putting them back together in the experimental garage. He had attended Yale University for four years. In the spring of 1941, he

had secured an ensign's commission in the U.S. Navy and was promoted to lieutenant prior to his release upon Edsel's death.

Neat, orderly, and punctual, Henry II expected Ford to share the same characteristics. But, as he surveyed the company upon assuming control, he soon realized it was in tatters, losing $9 million to $10 million a month. Feeling a bit "green," he sought counsel from his uncle, Ernest Kanzler, a former director of the War Production Board who had helped secure his release from the navy. Kanzler was a member of the board of directors at Bendix Aviation, then part of General Motors, and had come in contact with the president of Bendix, Ernest R. "Ernie" Breech.

Breech was a candidate for the top spot at GM, but when it was apparent that he would be passed over, Kanzler suggested that Henry II make him an offer. Breech joined Ford as an executive vice president in July 1946, bringing another top GM executive, Lewis Crusoe, a thirty-two-year veteran of the industry, with him.

Breech and Crusoe, a Ford vice president, worked with Henry II to direct a team of ten bright new executives, all of them former U.S. Army Air Force officers. They had gained fame during the war by creating from scratch a management information system that provided data on airplanes, personnel, and munitions required by top generals for decision making. Their new mission: resurrect Ford Motor Company.

The new recruits visited one Ford department after another, asking so many questions that employees nicknamed them the "Quiz Kids," later amending it to the "Whiz Kids." What they discovered from this fact-finding mission astonished them.

Ford was bedeviled by a complete lack of cost accounting, estimating its expenses by measuring or weighing the stacks of invoices that arrived in the accounting department. The company had no balance sheet, crude property records, scant bookkeeping, and, most disturbingly, dead people on the payroll. The only reliable numbers the team could find were bank slips, and that's because the bank produced them.

Ford desperately needed financial controls. Three Whiz Kids, Ed Lundy, Arjay Miller, and Robert McNamara, were directed to prepare the company's first Financial Review. The effort indicated that Ford would have enough cash to avoid borrowing only if proper actions were taken. Fortunately, there was pent-up demand for cars in postwar America, helping Breech forecast vehicle production costs fairly closely

SHOWSTOPPERS *The waxed-up paint jobs of used cars, shot in 1951, reflect the bright lights at the Jefferson Lincoln-Mercury used car lot in Detroit.*

since they depended largely on the price of steel, then fixed by the government.

"That still left dozens of assumptions to be made, like efficiency of labor, cost of raw materials, sale of assets, and accounts payable and receivable," Miller told the company's publication, *Ford World*, in 1996.

Breech and Crusoe were determined to remake Ford in the image of other large corporations such as Standard Oil and General Motors, which had decentralized structures. Henry II had read Peter Drucker's *Concept of the Corporation*, a book evaluating GM's decentralization, and is said to have been so influenced by it that he put a chart depicting GM's organizational structure on his office wall. The book's chief tenet: No institution could exist under one-man rule.

Ford stepped away from the autocratic management structure of its founder. The company installed individual accounting systems for individual operations, so that the steel mill, for example, would have its own set of books and benchmarks. If steel cost more from its own mill than the open-market cost of steel, Ford would buy from outside steel manufacturers.

The same practice was instituted in all other operations. Each division became a "profit center," a term that passed into the corporate lexicon. They included the newly combined Lincoln-Mercury Division, headed by General Manager Benson Ford, a younger brother of Henry

II. Ford required that each profit center produce an estimate of costs and balances every quarter.

Unprofitable operations were put on the block, including many of Henry Ford's pet projects—the soybean venture, sixteen Village Industries, and the Brazilian rubber plant. The company plowed the capital into new plants and Ford's first automated machines and computers.

The Financial Review became the company's monthly report card, monitoring how the new financial controls were performing. "Where it once suffered from figure famine," wrote *Fortune* magazine in 1947, "Ford now has figures running out of its ears."

In 1946, Ford reported a $2,000 profit. The reorganization gelled, and Ford was back on its feet, earning more than $64 million in 1947. A profit of $94 million was reaped in 1948, and in 1950, following the totally redesigned 1949 Ford, profits skyrocketed to more than $258 million. Ford at last edged out Chrysler for second place among the Big Three. Modern management had replaced chaos and confusion.

Dealers rallied behind Henry II to assist with the company's comeback, introducing the automobile-starved public to Ford's newest machines. Dealers also conveyed with candor the postwar problems affecting supply, again proving their merit as the public's main point of contact with the company. Many suppliers were threatened by strikes and

TOTAL U.S. CAR REGISTRATIONS
IN MEDIUM AND HIGH PRICE PASSENGER CAR FI
Showing Lincoln-Mercury's Share

stoppages that affected their production, which dealers explained calmly and rationally to buyers irate over late car deliveries.

The reorganization extended to Ford's overseas operations in seventy-eight countries. By now, the Dagenham factory was considered the best in Europe, and Ford was the top-selling car manufacturer in Britain, buoyed by demand for the Ford Anglia, Prefect, and Consul automobiles. Latin America had emerged as among the most important wholly owned subsidiaries in the Ford pantheon. The Mexico City plant manufactured some 12,000 cars annually, and Brazil had the capacity to make 18,000 vehicles a year. Australia also boomed.

A decision that had been brewing was now made final: Ford Motor Company in Dearborn would obtain the majority of voting stock in all its foreign subsidiaries and, where feasible, full ownership. Only with 100 percent stock ownership, Henry II reasoned, could these semi-autonomous branches be operated with the same stringent regard for profitability that guided Ford at home.

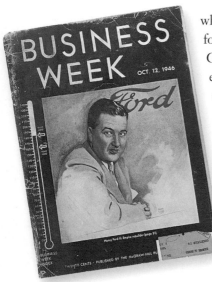

In 1949, Ford International, Inc., which would oversee this dominion, was formally activated in New York City. Graeme H. Howard, a former GM executive with long experience in foreign affairs, was named to lead it. The new division reported a year hence that its sales in 1950 were more than $713 million, generating a net profit of $48 million. Both domestically and abroad, Ford was again a reckoning force.

The rebuilt Ford Motor Company in 1955 was ranked fifth in size among U.S. corporations although it was still a private company owned by the Ford family and one outsider, the Ford Foundation. Henry Ford had established the foundation in 1936 for the public welfare, as well as to assure smooth transfer of company control to his heirs. In November 1955, the foundation announced it would diversify its vast wealth by splitting the Ford shares it owned and offering this huge block for sale to the public.

Beginning in January 1956, for $64.50 per share, average Americans from every walk of life could buy a piece of the historic company that had given them the Model T, aided two war efforts, and ushered in the commercial aviation industry. The demand for the stock was astounding. More than 350,000 investors plunked down their money, ranging from a 103-year-old woman in North Carolina who had admired Henry Ford to a 7-year-old boy in Maine whose uncle lent him the cash.

To encourage automobile sales, a new subsidiary, Ford Motor Credit Company, was formed in 1959, offering financing, leasing, credit life insurance, and other services to Ford car owners. GM had operated such a credit company since 1919, and Ford dealers had expressed their concerns over a perceived competitive disadvantage. Ford Credit today provides financing to more than 10 million consumers across forty countries.

The 1950s were not without disappointment. A decision to create a new division to manufacture and market a new car via a new

Watch the Fords go by!

You may buy a Ford yourself thru

UNIVERSAL CREDIT COMPANY

presenting the Only Authorized

Ford Finance Plan

"WE BETTER GET A NEW FORD THRU UCC"

UCC Finance Plans AVAILABLE THROUGH FORD DEALERS EVERYWHERE

CREDIT CLOUT *To help consumers finance a car, Ford Motor Credit Company was formed in 1959. Ford first extended credit to customers in 1928, when Henry launched Universal Credit Company as the "only authorized Ford Finance Plan," advertised in the brochure and tabletop display at left and above. UCC was sold during the banking crisis of 1933. Below: Henry II and Robert McNamara, former "Whiz Kid," Ford president in 1960. Overleaf: Members of the press, wearing promotional lab coats emblazoned with an Edsel emblem, check out the new Edsel.*

dealership network backfired. Henry II had announced in 1955 that Ford would introduce a new line of cars that would embody daring styling and state-of-the-art engineering. After months of speculation, he confirmed the new line would be called the "Edsel" to honor his father's design contributions. Unfortunately, the Edsel was a legendary flop.

The car was meant to be a medium-priced addition to the Ford family of vehicles, falling between the Mercury and the Lincoln. It turned out instead to be a big car with a large engine, spacious interior, and voluminous cargo space. As promised, the design was daring and unique, with a prominent vertical "horse collar" grille, wide horizontal taillights, and a pushbutton gearshift on the steering wheel. But it was the wrong car for the wrong market at the wrong time. A minirecession in the late-1950s steered consumers away from big gas-guzzling vehicles that screamed "excess."

The horse collar nearly strangled the company. The Edsel cost Ford $250 million to bring to market and lost roughly $350 million during the three years it was in production. Ford sold fewer than 111,000 Edsels between 1957 and 1960. In 1958, the company killed the separate Edsel division and formed the new M-E-L division, which assumed responsibility for the Mercury, Edsel, and Lincoln automobiles. Two years later, Ford discontinued the Edsel line altogether. Ironically, the cars are a prized collector's item today.

As the Edsel faded from the spotlight, Ford's Mercury division brightened under the guidance of Benson Ford, another of Edsel's sons. Benson assumed control of the Mercury division in 1948 and relinquished it in 1956 to head up the company's relations with its dealer base. His former position put him in good stead with Lincoln-Mercury dealers, as did his good-humored nature. Benson was a consummate charmer, able to make anyone, from a high-level Ford executive to the lowest-selling salesman at a tiny dealership, feel he had him as a friend in Dearborn. As Henry II ran the company with an iron fist, Benson was out in the field glad-handing the troops.

Although Ford would usher in a series of presidents in the 1960s and '70s, Henry II, as chairman, retained firm control of the company. Robert McNamara became president in 1960, only to resign a few months later to become U.S. secretary of defense. John Dykstra replaced McNamara as president in 1960, followed by the quiet, competent Arjay Miller, elected in May 1963. Semon "Bunkie" Knudsen, another former GM executive, was named president in 1968.

Lee Iacocca, credited for riding herd on the Mustang introduction, emerged as a leading candidate to replace Knudsen in September 1969. But Henry II installed a triumvirate of top executives instead, consisting of Iacocca, Robert J. Hampson, and Robert Stevenson. Although Iacocca nominally was Ford president, he and Henry II rarely saw eye to eye.

In 1977, Ford's board of directors approved recommendations by the consulting firm McKinsey & Company to restructure senior management, creating a new Office of the Chief Executive. The OCE would consist of Henry II as chairman and chief executive officer, Philip Caldwell (a former Ford of Europe president) as vice chairman, and Iacocca as president and chief operating officer. Henry II indicated that when he was unavailable to make decisions, Caldwell should make them.

In June 1978, Phil Caldwell became deputy chief executive officer. Reportedly unhappy at the prospect of reporting to Caldwell and unable to convince Ford's board that he should lead the company, Iacocca resigned in October 1978. Caldwell immediately became both company president and deputy chief executive officer.

Leading up to the resignation, Iacocca and Henry II had clashed constantly. The increasing tension spilled over into the executive suites at Ford, dividing the ranks. Years later, each man vented his bitterness. In his autobiography, *Iacocca* (with William Novak), Iacocca said Henry II was a "dictator . . . who never had to work for anything in his life." He added that he believed that his ouster had been planned years before:

"In 1975, Henry Ford started his month-by-month premeditated plan to destroy me. Until then, he had pretty well left me alone. But in that year he started having chest pains, and [began] to realize his mortality. He turned animal. I imagine his first impulse was: 'I don't want that Italian interloper taking over.' . . . But he didn't have the guts to just go ahead and do his own dirty work. [Instead], he played Machiavelli, determined to humiliate me into quitting."

Iacocca blamed Henry II for Ford's troubles during the 1970s, castigating his slow response to the Mideast oil crisis and his overspending at a time when belts needed tightening. But what really ruffled his feathers was Henry II's appointment of Caldwell as his second in command in 1977. Fourteen months later, Iacocca dropped another rung in the Ford hierarchy, when William Clay Ford, Henry II's youngest brother, joined the Office of the Chief Executive.

Shortly thereafter, the two men met in Henry II's office, whereupon it was decided that Iacocca would "resign" on October 15, 1978, his fifty-fourth birthday. To this day, Iacocca maintains that Henry II never gave him a reason for his discharge.

Not unemployed for long, Iacocca was snapped up by Chrysler Corp. to lead a comeback at the ailing automobile company. He staved off bankruptcy at the number-three automaker, arranging a $1.3 billion government loan that Chrysler eventually repaid—with interest. His autobiography became a national best seller and a source of great displeasure to Henry II.

In a wide-ranging interview with historian David Lewis in the 1980s, published in the *Detroit News* in 1994, Henry II explained why he had fired Iacocca:

"There are lots of reasons I let him go. One of them is he's not really a good chief executive—not from a broad viewpoint.

Secondly, he's too conceited, too self-centered to be able to see the broad picture. To me, he's socially—not in the sense of friendships but socially in the broader sense—very insecure. . . . Iacocca had another very bad failing. He had a coterie of his own people. . . . I don't know if it was for empire-building purposes. . . . There was [sic] a lot of shenanigans, as well. I mean there was just a lot of dirty work. I got the proof, but what the hell. I don't want to get into it. . . . He was just not my cup of tea."

While these machinations kept the finance press busy in America, Ford's overseas operations blossomed calmly. Ford's Latin American subsidiaries posted record sales in 1968, up 49 percent to more than 128,000 units sold. Ford led the industry in combined car and truck sales in Mexico, Peru, and Venezeula, and its trucks were the industry leaders in Argentina, Brazil, Peru, and Venezuela.

In Australia, William O. Bourke, an expatriate American with a flair for fast cars, presided over the development of a four-door Gran Turismo sedan, the first-ever Down Under. Behind Bourke's decision was his desire for a Ford to win the annual five-hundred-mile Australian production car race. In March 1967, the Falcon GT was unveiled, carrying a 225-horsepower engine and "four on the floor" (four-speed) transmission. The car took the checkered flag and attracted a solid following through the 1970s.

In Europe, the Ford Escort and Capri cars, introduced in Germany and England in the late 1960s, spurred record sales. The sporty, compact Capri, in particular, achieved high public acceptance throughout the continent, and like the Mustang in the U.S., virtually created a new market segment.

Further restructuring of Ford's European operations in 1967 led to the development of Ford of Europe, a wholly owned subsidiary comprising Ford's national companies in Britain, Germany, France, and ten other countries in Europe and Africa. Previously, each of the national companies was a separate entity with a separate product range, engineering organization, and manufacturing operation. While this structure seemed sensible at the time, given the language, cultural, and currency differences separating the nations, it had the unfortunate effect of restraining communications among the different companies.

Creating a single Ford of Europe would solve the problem by coordinating the development, manufacture, and sale of cars in Europe and Africa. The timing was fortuitous, since foreign markets were in high-growth mode. Ford of Europe also became fertile breeding ground for future Ford Motor Company CEOs, including Caldwell, Don Petersen, Harold "Red" Poling, Alex Trotman, and Jac Nasser.

Perhaps the biggest overseas development during this period was the decision to build a massive new Ford plant in Almusafes, Spain (near Valencia), to manufacture the new front-wheel Ford Fiesta, a minicar designed by a team of American, British, Australian, German, and Italian engineers. The car's major components would come from a variety of countries, would be assembled at Almusafes and two other

INTERNATIONAL APPEAL *The 1979 Volvo 245, right, garnered a global customer base in the late 1970s. Below: A 1976 Ford Fiesta Ghia.*

plants—Dagenham and Saarlouis, Germany—and would be distributed to markets in Europe, Canada, and the United States.

At $870 million, the Fiesta budget was the costliest in the company's history. But for the kingdom of Spain, suffering economic malaise, the new plant was a much-needed shot in the arm.

On October 25, 1976, Henry II, with King Juan Carlos in attendance, dedicated the Almusafes plant. As Henry II walked through Valencia that day, thankful Spaniards of all ages shouted "Viva Henry Ford."

The Fiesta broke the one-year sales record established by the 1964 Mustang, selling more than 441,000 units in 1977 worldwide. Ford became Spain's largest automotive exporting company, earning the country more money than tourism in the 1980s.

Upon Henry II's retirement in March 1980 as chairman, Phil Caldwell succeeded him (he'd become CEO the previous October and president in 1978). The passing of the baton represented the first time in the history of the company that a non-Ford family member had complete operational control. In the thirty-four years that Henry II had guided the company, Ford's income had catapulted from $11.2 million to $1.2 billion. In 1946, Ford sold about 900,000 cars, trucks, and tractors; in 1979, it sold nearly 6 million.

The years of hard work and long travel finally caught up to this vital man at age seventy. On September 29, 1987, Henry Ford II died in his bed at the Henry Ford Hospital after a brief illness. He had always said the company came first in his life. Like his grandfather, he was mourned by the business world and common folk alike. His legacy was to have preserved an American institution, one that happened to bear his surname. "For Henry II, reviving Ford was a matter of pride," says historian Ford Bryan.

It is said that history repeats. Like Henry II when he took control of Ford four decades earlier, Caldwell in 1980 had a company

Pinto had performed as safely as other small American and foreign cars at the time.

Ford also struggled with an undigested mass of government regulations involving safety, emissions, and fuel economy. Meanwhile, the company was retooling virtually every one of its factories and all its cars and trucks, applying new processes and new materials to reduce the weight of vehicles to make them more fuel efficient.

in deep trouble on his hands. Ford's problems were a many-headed Hydra—competition from Japan, big cars out of synch with the mood of the market, no small front-wheel-drive car (in 1980), and deepening public perceptions of inferior quality.

Consumer confidence had deteriorated following a series of lawsuits involving the Ford Pinto automobile. The litigation alleged the Pinto's fuel tank was vulnerable to explosion upon a rear collision. Although some cases ended in Ford's favor, and more than 1.5 million Pintos were recalled to correct the purported defects, Pinto sales suffered. The car had been the top-selling subcompact in America, with more than 3 million sold from its introduction in 1970 through its discontinuation in 1981. Federal data later revealed the

These pressures only added cost to the bottom line at a time when top-line revenues were threatened by Japanese imports.

Ford's share of the American car market continued to dwindle, falling from 20.7 percent in 1979 to 16.6 percent in 1981, lowest in its history. Owner loyalty also deteriorated—to 35 percent in 1981—the lowest level since this measurement was adopted in the early 1960s. Public ridicule greeted Ford products, and jokes were told that Ford was an acronym for "fix or repair daily." Between 1980 and 1982, the company lost $3.3 billion—a staggering 43 percent of its net worth.

The economy didn't help—the country was mired in the longest and deepest economic depression since the 1930s. Car sales

are the first to suffer in a recession, hence the saying "When the economy sneezes, Detroit catches a cold."

Like Ernie Breech and the Whiz Kids, Caldwell and his executive vice presidents— "Red" Poling, Bill Bourke, Don Petersen, and Louis Ross—left no stone unturned. "Ford's new managers are actually a return to the kind of serious men who ran the company years ago, before it was overrun by flamboyant marketing men," the *Wall Street Journal* wrote in May 1980.

To the redheaded Poling fell the difficult task of cost management. The former chairman of Ford of Europe cut a huge swath in production costs. In short order, he pulled one million units from production, laid off some 60,000 Ford employees (reducing payroll expenses from $6.2 billion to $5.2 billion), and closed five plants (saving another $500 million).

Despite these budgetary reductions, Ford spent $14 billion between 1980 and 1984 on plant improvements, new products, processes, machinery, and equipment and another $9 billion on research and development. It also earmarked $5.4 billion for its overseas facilities.

"While we were engaged in this extraordinary financial balancing act, we never sacrificed Ford's future by failing to invest in our businesses around the world," Caldwell commented.

The hardest cuts were in personnel. Poling made an unprecedented effort to communicate with UAW officials before the downsizing. He explained that quality had to improve and only those plants that understood this objective would remain open. Poling also confided that the difference between Ford and its Japanese competitors was not the quality of workers but Ford's inferior management philosophy, which did not emphasize continuous improvements in product quality.

This rare admission eased tensions. It also fostered a historic agreement between Ford and the UAW in 1982, whereby union workers consented to wage and other concessions in return for a moratorium on plant closings and, in the event of future layoffs, income guarantees for workers with seniority.

Caldwell articulated the mission before all Ford workers— "Quality is Job 1." Continuous improvement in quality was the cornerstone of Japanese manufacturing, preached by management gurus such as W. Edwards Deming. "Quality is Job 1" now permeated the culture at Ford facilities all over the world. Instrumental in the Q-1 campaign, as it came to be called, was the UAW and employee involvement in the initiative. "Quality is Job 1" was more than a popular advertising message: it signified a new collaborative working relationship between the UAW and the company.

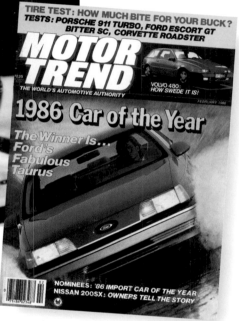

In the first quarter of 1983, Ford was profitable both at home and overseas for the first time in the past sixteen quarters; by the end of the year, Ford was the car sales leader in all of Europe for the first time in its history. To celebrate the company's remarkable comeback, Red Poling presented both Phil Caldwell and Ford's new president, Don Petersen, with a bottle of black ink.

The rewards earned by an emphasis on continuous quality were shared with the workers who made it happen. Ford's groundbreaking 1982 agreement with the UAW included another industry trendsetter—an incentive profit sharing provision. In 1983, each Ford worker in North America received a check for $400. As the company continued its recovery, the checks kept coming: $2,000 in 1984, $1,200 in 1985, $2,100 in 1986, and $3,700 in 1987. Over the years, Ford has paid billions of dollars to its employees in profit sharing bonuses.

The many business decisions that combined to change the quality of Ford cars culminated in the creation of the 1986 Ford Taurus and Mercury Sable, two cars designed on the same platform. Not since the 1949 Ford had there been such a pronounced change in a Ford automobile. Don Petersen, named chairman and CEO upon Caldwell's retirement in February 1985, approved a $3.5 billion budget for the Taurus/Sable—a company record. The Fiesta budget, by comparison, was $870 million.

Not just the budget was daring—the cars would feature a radical aerodynamic design that reduced drag to increase fuel efficiency (a 10 percent reduction in wind resistance causes a 2.5 percent improvement in gasoline mileage). Ford had experimented with an aerodynamic design in the 1983 Thunderbird and would improve upon this work with the Taurus/Sable.

The question was, would buyers accept the new look or reject it, as they had the Edsel and its horse collar grille? Vice chairman William Clay Ford, youngest brother of Henry Ford II, headed the company's design committee and had final say on the new design. Said to have inherited his father's artistic touch, William unhesitatingly offered his firm approval. Given his stockholdings in the company, he had a lot to lose.

Fortunately, Ford had undertaken long-term planning of a kind never before seen in the automobile industry. Team Taurus contracted outside experts in ergonomics, insurance, and car repair to offer their specialized advice and criticism, and they implemented many suggestions. Ford engineers literally tore apart hundreds of cars sold by competitors, a process called "reverse engineering," to

learn others' best practices firsthand. Marketing worked side by side with design and engineering and conducted public research, gauging opinions on everything from aerodynamics to how the cars would be accepted overseas.

The Taurus and Sable had an elegant debut rivaling a Hollywood film premiere. Advertisements beseeched, "Have You Driven a Ford Lately?" The reception was overwhelming. The Taurus won *Motor Trend* magazine's "Car of the Year" and the Sable took the runner-up. Ford brought both cars in under budget ($2.9 billion), realizing an impressive 11 percent return on investment. The company's pretax earnings in 1986 were better than GM's for the first time since 1924, and the next year, Ford's stock price climbed an astonishing 76 percent from its 1986 high.

The irony is that the Taurus and Sable weren't the top-selling cars for Ford in 1986—that honor belonged to the Ford Escort, the number-one car in America.

A new image of the Ford Motor Company took shape in the public consciousness, and a new confidence in the company's products and services beckoned. Ford's relentless efforts to improve

quality, its tough cost-cutting mandates, and its strong partnership with its dealer base had resurrected a company that many thought had breathed its last. As the *Wall Street Journal* summed up in October 1986: "Ford has everything in motion."

In the mid-1980s, Ford continued to evolve, embarking on an ambitious agenda to acquire large financial services companies. Its objective was twofold: to offset the cyclical nature of the automobile business and to provide Ford's customer base with a broad range of financial services products.

In 1984, the company acquired First Nationwide Financial Corporation, which operated one of the largest savings and loan networks in the United States. Two years later, Ford acquired U.S. Leasing, the nation's oldest equipment leasing specialist. Both subsidiaries became part of Ford's Financial Services Group. FSG also oversaw Ford Motor Credit Company, the second largest finance company in the world, and the financing operations of Ford's overseas automotive affiliates. From 1991 to 1998, Edsel B. Ford II was the president of Ford Credit. Under his oversight, the company emerged as the industry's largest automotive leasing firm.

FORD EXAMINES USE OF FORCED AND SLAVE LABOR UNDER NAZI REGIME

In a sad footnote to history, rumors had circulated for years after World War II that Ford-Werke, the company's German subsidiary, had been run using slave and forced labor. In response to questions raised by the media and a class action lawsuit in 1998, Ford commissioned a study of the activities of its German subsidiary during World War II. The report, released in 2001, summarized more than 98,000 pages of documents and other materials gathered from more than thirty international archival repositories. Under control of the Nazi regime, Ford's prized manufacturing plant in Germany was required to use labor provided by the German government, as were other companies under the Third Reich. In Ford-Werke's case, many of the laborers were Eastern European civilian workers forced to work by the Nazis. "By being open and honest about the past, even when we find the subject reprehensible, we hope to contribute toward a better understanding of this period of history," the company stated at the time. In conjunction with the study's release, Ford announced that it would contribute $4 million toward human rights studies and humanitarian relief.

CAPITAL CONSIDERATIONS
As part of its diversification into financial services, Ford acquired the Associates Corp. in 1989. The company, then the third largest finance firm in America, was spun off to shareholders in 1998. Below: Executives of the Associates in 1996, (from left) Joe McQuillan, Ken Whipple, Keith Hughes, William Johnston, and Harold Marshall.

Ford Credit today remains the world's largest automotive finance company.

In 1989, FSG acquired the Associates Corp., the third largest finance company in the U.S., for $3.35 billion. The Associates owned diverse enterprises, offering home equity loans, mortgage banking, and even corporate relocation services.

Ford entered another new business in the 1980s, acquiring a large share in the leading car rental company, Hertz Corporation, in 1987, buying it outright in 1994. Ford also provided $300 million in financing to invest in Budget Rent a Car in 1988.

In 1997, Ford created Visteon Automotive Systems for the design, development, and delivery of fully integrated automotive systems, replacing the company's automotive products division. Other new Ford subsidiaries were incorporated to deliver premium automobile service and repair. Ford acquired Kwik-Fit, an

automotive repair unit with more than 2,400 outlets throughout Europe; Quality Care, Ford's vehicle service shops in the United States; Master Service, its repair chains in Mexico; and B-Quik, a similar series of shops in Thailand. Ford studies had unearthed a powerful connection between vehicle maintenance and car sales: seventy percent of customers who had their automobiles serviced by dealerships returned to buy their next vehicle from that dealer.

Ford also developed another important subsidiary that fit its strategy of improving the customer experience—Top Driver, the country's leading provider of driver education and training. These were business ramifications that extended well beyond the service bay.

In the mid-1990s, Ford began reviewing these decisions. First Nationwide was deemed outside FSG's core competency and was divested in 1994. The Associates and Visteon were spun off to shareholders in 1998 and 2000, respectively.

Other subsidiaries also were reexamined. Rouge Steel Company, a subsidiary formed in 1981, was sold in 1989, and the Great Lakes ore ships that Ford had operated were dismantled. Ford Aerospace, the company's communications satellite business, was divested the following year. The steel and ship businesses no longer fit lean manufacturing objectives, marking a goodbye to the great vertical integration strategies of Henry Ford. Outside tiers of suppliers now contributed the lion's share of parts used in Ford vehicles, linked to Ford and each other beginning in 2000 through Covisint, an Internet-based supply chain system owned by Ford, GM, and DaimlerChrysler.

The company's dealer network also blossomed during this period, in large part because of the efforts of Edsel Ford II, son of Henry II. Edsel was a known and trusted face among dealers, and with his easygoing and affable demeanor, he helped bridge the gap that often erupts between a manufacturer and its independent sales force. As the Internet beckoned as an additional sales channel, Edsel reassured dealers that the company was not going direct to consumers—it was merely tapping the power of the information superhighway for the benefit of Ford's dealer body.

To penetrate many emerging markets, Ford entered into joint ventures in the 1980s and '90s with a veritable Who's Who of international automotive companies. They included Autorama (with Mazda, to distribute Ford products in Japan), AutoLatina (with Volkswagen, to provide automotive products and credit operations in Brazil and Argentina), and AutoEuropa (also with Volkswagen, to produce multipurpose vehicles at a new plant in Portugal). Other alliances were announced with carmakers in Korea, Argentina, China, India, and Thailand, to name a few. Some have ended; others continue.

Red Poling had become chief operating officer in 1985, and succeeded Petersen as chairman and CEO in 1990. As Ford opened doors the world over, Alex Trotman, who succeeded Poling as chairman and CEO in 1993, hinged together an ambitious plan in 1995 to cut costs, boost productivity, and grow the bottom line. Called Ford 2000, the strategy sought to reshape Ford by combining the separate North American and European units into a single operation.

Eventually, other Ford units around the world—such as Ford of Australia, Ford South America, and Ford Asia Pacific—would be blended into this organization, unifying Ford's purchasing, engineering, and manufacturing. Global product teams would create cars that would be sold around the world, thereby reducing waste and duplication of effort. A more efficient, leaner company would result. As other changes in industry and the economy took root in the latter half of the decade, Ford 2000 was modified to provide more autonomy to branch managers. But the goal of a more nimble international company embracing teamwork, new technology, and a worldwide outlook—one far less bureaucratic and insular—remained the same.

The most notable evolution of Ford in modern times is its acquisition of some of the most important automobile names in the world—Volvo Cars, Jaguar, Aston Martin, Mazda, and Land Rover. For Ford, a company defined by a single brand through much of its early history and only three brands well into the 1980s, these acquisitions marked a confident, new direction.

EXCITING LINEUP

As Ford headed into the twenty-first century, it introduced an exciting group of new cars, led by the Ford GT40 concept, which was to go into production the year of the company's one-hundredth birthday. This extraordinary mid-engined sports car is a modern interpretation of the speedster that won the prestigious Le Mans auto race in 1966, 1967, 1968, and 1969. ❖ This Living Legend from Ford's racing heritage joins other hot cars such as the Mercury Marauder. Like the GT40 concept, the Marauder has an impressive past, based on the 1975 Grand Marquis. Add the Thunderbird Sports Roadster and Ford's new Expedition SUV, boasting ultra-low emission, and another century of well-defined and memorable vehicles is clearly on tap. ❖

2003 GT40 CONCEPT INTERIOR

2002 ASTON MARTIN DB7 VANTAGE COUPE

2003 VOLVO XC90

2003 LINCOLN NAVIGATOR

2002 JAGUAR X-TYPE

2003 RANGE ROVER

2002 KA STYLE

the 1964 Jaguar 3.8 S-type, bottom, to unveiling the 200-mph "supercar," the Aston Martin V12 Vanquish, right, Ford has embraced a multibrand global strategy.

This multibrand global strategy was devised to generate multiple benefits. By creating diverse cars across multiple platforms, the thinking was that Ford could reap synergies in design, engineering, and manufacturing, helping it squeeze purchasing and production costs and amortize new technology and research expenses. Moreover, by building a much larger company, Ford would have the financial wherewithal to spend the billions of dollars required to design and manufacture new car models spanning much wider demographics.

Ford today is a collection of automobile brands that consumers admire and trust. The first company to join the Ford family in recent times was Aston Martin Lagonda, the venerable British sports car manufacturer, perhaps best known for the car Agent 007 drove in the James Bond movies. Aston Martin, whose origins date to 1913, is a small specialty company making high-priced superior sports cars. Ford acquired a controlling interest in Aston Martin in September 1987, taking full control seven years later. Aston Martin remains Ford's most exclusive brand. It also is the company's "laboratory on wheels," testing leading-edge technologies that one day could be used in larger series production.

Next to join was Jaguar PLC, another blue-blooded British company with a gilded marque, known for some of the world's most luxurious sedans. Ford acquired Jaguar for $2.5 billion in 1990, edging GM in a much-publicized bidding war. Jaguar's origins stretch back to 1922 and the formation of the Swallow Sidecar Company, which moved into automobile production shortly thereafter (the Jaguar brand sprang upon the scene in 1935). Jaguar sedans, with the familiar hood ornament in frontal pursuit, enjoy a high recognition factor among well-heeled American consumers, who perceive the Jaguar marque as standing for the highest in luxury—a classic, elegant look few other lines can match. Ford is leveraging the distinct

LEVERAGING LEGACIES
*Ford's blockbuster brands
at the end of the twentieth
century included two other
great companies—Mazda,
of which Ford Motor
Company controls a
majority interest; and
Volvo Cars, which it*
*bought outright in 1999.
Both brands convey
distinctive consumer
strengths and have unique
histories. Left: A 1990
Volvo S-70. Below: A
1964 Mazda K360, their
three-wheeled truck.*

emotional core message conveyed by the Jaguar brand—power, sportiveness, and natural sophistication.

Mazda Motor Corporation joined the Ford family in 1992. Ford owns 33 percent of Mazda today, a "majority" interest under Japanese law. The company had owned a 25 percent equity position in the Japanese car manufacturer since 1979. Ford and Mazda have collaborated on many projects over the years, such as the Festiva minicar and the Probe sports coupe. The 1989 Probe culminated a decade of work to build the first "global car"—designed and manufactured by Ford, engineered by Mazda, and aimed at the sports car market in Asia, Europe, and North America.

Mazda started life as a tiny cork manufacturing company in Hiroshima in 1920. First making three-wheeled trucks for the Chinese market, Mazda began manufacturing passenger cars in 1960. In 1999, Ford acquired a majority interest in the Norwegian company that was known for the zero-emission electric city car, TH!NK.

At the end of the twentieth century, Ford added Land Rover and Volvo to its lineup of leading brands. Ford bought Volvo Cars in 1999 for $6.45 billion. Considered one of the world's great brands, Volvos are esteemed for their focus on safety, quality, durability, and environmental responsibility—attributes increasingly important to

Ford and its customers. Founded in 1927, Volvo built a strong following in Europe, where its laser-like focus on customer satisfaction is enviable. Women make up a large percentage of buyers—51 percent, compared to 31 percent for Jaguar and 26 percent for Lincoln—bolstering this demographic in Ford's lineup.

Land Rover, acquired by Ford in 2000, boasts a lineage even older than Ford Motor Company. The company's history stretches back to 1877 and the founding in Coventry, England, of Starley & Sutton, a manufacturer of Rover tricycles. Later, the company introduced a revolutionary two-wheeled "safety" cycle that became the model for the modern bicycle.

The first Land Rovers emerged in war-torn Europe in the 1940s as light four-wheel-drive utility vehicles targeting the agricultural and military markets. A higher-cost spin-off, the Range Rover, made its debut in 1970, followed by the Freelander, Europe's best-selling SUV. These "purpose-built" cars are considered the best 4x4s on the market, as imperturbable plying deserts or inching through rivers as they are coasting uptown to the opera.

Each of these distinctive brands benefits from Ford's technological know-how, marketing expertise, and capital strength. Ford, on the other hand, gains greater market breadth, wider demographic appeal, and the emotional goodwill these familiar brands leverage in the marketplace. The new family members combined to produce more than 1.65 million additional units sold under the Ford banner in 2000, a year in which Ford Motor Company as a whole sold nearly 7.5 million vehicles, a company record.

In the last year of the twentieth century, another Ford namesake—William Clay Ford, Jr.—assumed the chairmanship, and

Jacques Nasser, a former president of Ford of Australia and a former chairman of Ford of Europe, became CEO and president. The former Ford chairman and CEO Alex Trotman, who had presided over Ford's multibrand strategy, retired on January 1, 1999.

Born in Lebanon and reared in Australia, Jac Nasser hired a cadre of skilled executives to pare costs and improve productivity. He gave Ford's global managers more say about local brands, efforts that were praised, at first, by automotive analysts. They also lauded his unflagging efforts to promote diversity within the workforce, leadership training of Ford executives, and greater involvement of employees in community endeavors.

But Nasser experienced a difficult relationship with Ford's dealership base and employees. When he attempted to implement company-owned dealerships, independent dealers complained bitterly. He distanced many executives and managers when he abandoned promotions from within the company and went outside Ford to hire key executives. And his forced ranking of the company's 18,000 top managers, which guided bonuses and salary raises and threatened dismissal of the lowest tier, hurt morale and spawned several workplace discrimination lawsuits.

There were other problems—daunting business losses in Latin America, falling profit margins from European operations, severe production overcapacity and manufacturing quality issues, several recalls, and a dire need to streamline operations further to reduce corporate expenses. The *Detroit News* and others criticized Nasser for losing focus on the business basics—the making and selling of vehicles—and exercising too much interest in e-commerce, recycling, and Ford's quick service operations.

Finally, the dual power-sharing structure itself broke down. With Nasser and Bill Ford at times appearing to pursue different agendas—"They were at odds over how to run the company," *Fortune* magazine reported in October 2001—a change at the top was inevitable. On October 30, 2001, Ford's board of directors ousted the fifty-three-year-old Nasser as CEO and named Bill Ford to replace him, consolidating day-to-day operating responsibility in the hands of a Ford for the first time in twenty-two years. The board also

INTERNATIONAL CACHET
Former Ford president and CEO Jac Nasser, below, brought years of overseas experience to the company at the turn of the millennium. Nasser was a former chairman of Ford of Europe—the breeding ground for so many Ford leaders. Nasser worked hard, but he faced many formidable problems, including mounting business losses and the Firestone tire recall debacle.

promoted Nick Scheele, group vice president of Ford's North American Group, to chief operating officer.

Son of former vice chairman William Clay Ford, Bill Ford vowed to get the company back on course and back to basics. He brings a thoroughly modern sensibility and vision to the company launched by his great-grandfather a century before. His career with Ford began in 1979 as a product planning analyst and over the years has encompassed diverse positions and responsibilities, from head of commercial vehicle marketing for Europe to chairman of Ford Switzerland to chairman of Ford's influential finance committee.

At the dawn of the new millennium, Ford Motor Company encountered serious problems, both business and emotional. In 1999, an explosion at the Rouge resulted in six fatalities, an incalculable loss. Rushing to the scene of the disaster, Bill Ford told a writer for *Fortune*,

"This has to be the worst day of my life." Late into the night, he visited the hospitals at which the injured and dying received care, consoling the families and, the magazine reported, "making it perfectly clear he did not intend to be a buttoned-down, twentieth-century executive."

As Bill Ford assumed the role of chief executive officer, the company was undergoing intense public and government scrutiny of Ford's top-selling Explorer sport utility vehicle, introduced for 1991. Several Explorers with Firestone Wilderness AT tires had rolled over after the tires came apart, resulting in driver and occupant fatalities and injuries. In 2000 and 2001, the company voluntarily recalled and replaced all Firestone Wilderness AT tires on the Explorer—close to 20 million tires in all. Although federal authorities maintained that there was no evidence the Explorer's design was at fault in the rollovers, Ford Motor Company spent millions of dollars to settle more than one hundred Firestone-related lawsuits, in addition to the massive replacement effort.

"The Firestone tire recall reinforced everything we believe about the critical importance of being responsive and responsible in everything we do as a corporation," Bill Ford said. "I deeply regret the anguish this tragic situation has caused, and the anxiety felt by our customers. I am proud of the way our team stepped up to this difficult challenge. There is nothing more important to us than the safety and trust of our customers."

The expensive incident also marked the end of a nearly century-old business relationship, at least temporarily. Henry Ford and Harvey Firestone had been close friends and business associates since 1906, when Firestone won a contract to supply tires for the Model N. The Ford and Firestone families also are intertwined: Bill Ford's mother, Martha, is Harvey Firestone's granddaughter.

Bill Ford is intent on remaking Ford into the world's best corporate citizen. Intelligent and charismatic, he is an unapologetic

environmentalist, long involved in environmental issues. As a teenager in the 1970s, he volunteered on many clean water and recycling projects. As a corporate scion, Bill led the Big Three in withdrawing from the automotive industry group that had taken the position that global warming was not a pressing problem. Once Ford pulled out—quietly and without fanfare—General Motors and Chrysler soon followed. Small wonder that Bill has been asked by the Greenpeace organization to speak about his pro-environmental opinions.

"He is that rare corporate executive who says boldly that his company will do best for its shareholders if it takes care of its employees, its community and the environment—all of which, he says, will enable Ford to attract better talent, develop loyal customers, enhance its brand, sell more cars and services and, over time, boost its share price," *Fortune* said of him in 2000.

Bill Ford believes Ford can distinguish itself among competitors by leveraging improved technologies to create vehicles that are more environmentally responsive. He is vitally involved in the company's approach to greenhouse gases, fuel economy, and conservation efforts, and he has pledged Ford's financial clout to build a better world. Like Henry Ford, Bill Ford insists that the company must be a leader on social issues, from education to the environment. "There's no incompatibility between doing the right thing and making money," he told *Business Week* magazine in 1998.

The centerpiece of Ford's environmental stewardship is the Rouge Complex in Dearborn, Michigan, where Ford has undertaken the largest industrial redevelopment project in the world, remaking the Ford-owned half of the 1,100-acre facility into a flagship of sustainable manufacturing.

Imagine flexible manufacturing techniques, open space areas with trees and shrubs, living greenery on roofs, climbing plants cooling buildings, natural water-runoff management, supplemental solar energy, and reconditioning of contaminated soil through the use of mediating vegetation. These stalwart plans and more are on tap for the Rouge Complex. As Bill Ford said, "We need to make it easy for people to say, 'I'm an environmentalist and an auto enthusiast.'"

The forty-six-year-old chairman and CEO is as passionate about building great cars as he is about enjoining the company to make the world a better place. Like his great-grandfather, Bill Ford is not averse to risks that advance human progress and achieve greater rewards for the company whose lineage and legacy he shares.

It's in the blood.

1914

1956

1949

1964

1928

1960

1950

1964

1939

1961

1954

1964 1/2

1941

1961

1955

1968

1948

1962

1955

1969

1970

1971

1986

1990

1991

HEART AND SOUL

TWENTY-FIVE VEHICLES THAT HAVE GENERATED EXCITEMENT AND INSPIRED PASSION

❖

Over the past one hundred years, the eight brands in the Ford Motor Company have produced some of the most memorable vehicles to ever hit the road. In the following pages, twenty-five of these vehicles, selected by members of the auto industry and automotive media, are presented in their full soul-stirring glory.

1914 FORD MODEL T

Henry Ford introduced the Model T in 1908 and it quickly became the best-selling car in the country. Ford kept looking for ways to manufacture the cars faster and at lower cost. In 1914, he found the ultimate answer—the moving assembly line. By the early 1920s, half the cars sold in America were Model Ts.

ENGINE *The Model T had a one-piece cylinder block and a removable cylinder head, which were modern features when the car was introduced in late 1908.*

WINDSHIELD SAFETY *The 1914 Model T was the first to switch from forward-folding windshields—which could fold or unfold while the car was in motion—to the less hazardous rearward-folding ones.*

HEADLIGHTS *Headlamps burned acetylene gas. Electric lights didn't appear on Model Ts until 1915.*

GREAT DIVIDE *Americans leaped across scientific and geographic boundaries in the second decade of the twentieth century. The noted African American scientist George Washington Carver began his breakthrough experiments, fostering wide agricultural and industrial uses for the lowly peanut. The forty-mile-long Panama Canal, opened in 1914 to connect the Atlantic and Pacific Oceans, is considered one of the most extraordinary engineering feats of all time. The same year, the United States' first traffic light went up in Cleveland, Ohio. By 1931, when the stoplight at left was operating, the country was populated with them.*

ENGINE	in-line 4, 177 cu. in., 20 h.p.
WHEELBASE	100 in.
WEIGHT	1,200 lbs.
ORIGINAL PRICE	$550.00

COLORS *The year 1914 marked the first time Model Ts were available only in black, which was the fastest color to dry. Other colors would not become available again until 1926, one year before production formally ended.*

MODIFICATIONS *Model T owners got pretty creative when it came to modifying the "Tin Lizzie." At top is a Model T "mobile home." Above: A Model T modified to be driven on snow.*

CURVED DOOR EDGES *The doors of the 1914 Model T had curved bottom edges—an improvement over the sharp corners on earlier models. The driver-side "door" did not actually open; it was just a simulated door.*

OPERATION *A Model T would confuse a modern driver. The pedal on the right worked the brake. The one in the middle put the car in reverse. The pedal on the left shifted the transmission between high and low.*

1928 FORD MODEL A

The new Model A was eagerly awaited by loyal Ford customers. They were not disappointed. The car was well made and technologically modern, and it performed well and looked good. The Model A allowed Ford to recapture sales leadership from Chevrolet.

SAFETY *Model As featured safety glass windshields, an unheard-of feature for a low-priced car.*

DESIGN *Model A styling was inspired by the Lincoln. The curve of the front fenders and the design of the radiator shell especially recalled the look of more expensive cars.*

THINKING BIG *In 1928, kids were blowing big bubbles while men were realizing big dreams. Fleer's released the first bubble gum; U.S. aviator Richard E. Byrd began his technologically sophisticated exploration of the South Pole; and the original "Imagineer" himself, Walt Disney, introduced the world to Mickey Mouse, star of his first movie, Steamboat Willie.*

COLORS *The new Fords came in a variety of attractive colors with equally attractive names like Arabian Sand, Niagara Blue, and Dawn Grey.*

SPECIFICATIONS
1928 Ford Model A coupe

ENGINE	in-line 4, 200 cu. in., 40 h.p.
WHEELBASE	103.5 in.
WEIGHT	2,225 lbs.
ORIGINAL PRICE	$550.00

WELCOME UPDATES *The Model A had a more powerful engine and a sliding gear transmission— an improvement over the obsolete planetary transmission that Henry Ford favored for the Model T.*

Ford

MODEL "A"
**Instruction
Book**

Ford Motor Company

INSTRUCTION BOOK *Like other manufacturers in the late 1920s, Ford provided owners with detailed instructions for tasks like lubricating the chassis and adjusting the brakes.*

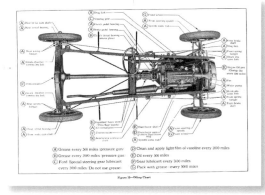

COMFORT *After test-driving a prototype, Henry Ford ordered that hydraulic shock absorbers be installed to improve the ride.*

1939 MERCURY EIGHT

In 1939, Ford Motor Company introduced a new car intended to fill the large gap between the most expensive Ford and the least expensive Lincoln. It was the brainchild of Jack Davis, Ford's top sales executive, and Edsel Ford. They named the new car Mercury, after the fleet-footed messenger of the gods from Roman mythology.

ENGINE *Mercury's 95-horsepower version of the Ford V-8 made the new car an excellent performer.*

NOT IN KANSAS ANYMORE
In 1939, the world became a smaller place. PanAm began regular transatlantic passenger flights, whisking twenty-two travelers from New York to Portugal. A new broadcasting medium, the television, made its debut, bringing news and entertainment into people's living rooms. That same year, the world became a bit more vibrant as well. MGM released The Wizard of Oz, *highlighting the wonders of Technicolor by juxtaposing black-and-white film with the bright colors of Oz.*

BODY *Mercurys were 16 inches longer and 250 pounds heavier than similar Ford models.*

SPECIFICATIONS
1939 Mercury Eight four-door sedan

ENGINE	V-8, 239 cu. in., 95 h.p.
WHEELBASE	116 in.
WEIGHT	3,168 lbs.
ORIGINAL PRICE	$930.00

CLAY MODEL *In the late 1930s, Ford stylists began using clay models to work out their designs. Here is the 1939 Mercury under development.*

SMOOTH RIDE *The Mercury Eight, considered a lavish upgrade for a Ford owner, boasted ample seats with a new soft construction, soundproofing, and a center-poise design that made for a smoother ride.*

DESIGN *Mercury styling bore a strong "family resemblance" to the Ford and Lincoln Zephyr, shown at right.*

1941 LINCOLN CONTINENTAL

The Continental grew out of a customized Lincoln Zephyr that E. T. Gregorie and Edsel Ford designed for Edsel's use. Both designers were inspired by the "continental" cars they saw in Europe. Ford's wealthy friends were so impressed by the car that Edsel decided to put it into production.

ENGINE *The Continental and its sister, the Lincoln Zephyr, had the only V-12 engine in the American auto industry.*

STILL AROUND
Some icons with staying power came out in 1941. The precursor to Cheerios, Cheeri Oats hit breakfast tables. "Wunderkind" film director Orson Welles released his seminal work, Citizen Kane, *a thinly veiled account of the life of* newspaper tycoon William Randolph Hearst. Another monumental effort that obviously hasn't gone away also made its debut in 1941—Mount Rushmore.

SPARE TIRE *Edsel insisted that the spare tire be mounted outside, "continental style." Such mountings have been known forever after as "continental kits."*

SPECIFICATIONS
1941 Lincoln Continental cabriolet

ENGINE	V-12, 292 cu. in., 120 h.p.
WHEELBASE	125 in.
WEIGHT	3,860 lbs.
ORIGINAL PRICE	$2,778.00

RIDING IN STYLE *The convertible top on the 1941 Lincoln Continental was operated electrically, replacing the vacuum-operated top.*

DESIGN *Both Edsel and Gregorie loved boats, so it is no accident that the Continental's front end resembles a yacht carving its way through the water.*

DOOR HANDLES *Clean lines were enhanced by nearly invisible pushbutton door handles.*

BODY *The Continental was also available as a coupe. All the 1941 Lincoln Continentals came standard with wheel trim rings.*

1948 FORD F-SERIES

The Ford trucks that appeared in 1948 were completely new postwar designs. They ranged in size from the one-half-ton capacity F-1 to the three-ton capacity F-8. Ford has used some variation of that numbering system ever since. The new designs stayed in production through 1952 and put Chevrolet on notice that competition in the truck market was going to be fierce.

POSTWAR PANORAMA
In 1948, the Polaroid "Land Camera" hit stores, becoming the first camera that developed its own prints. That same year, the U.S. became a member of the United Nations Security Council, the "castle of the great powers," sharing top billing with the Soviet Union. The frigid relationship between the U.S. and the Soviet Union following the end of World War II marked a new kind of war, a Cold War of espionage and counterespionage. Musical styles also turned down the thermostat, influenced by trumpeter Miles Davis and his "Birth of Cool."

TRUCK BED *The 6$\frac{1}{2}$-foot-long bed of the Ford F-1 could hold 45 cubic feet of cargo.*

SPECIFICATIONS
1948 Ford F-1 pickup

ENGINE	V-8, 239 cu. in., 100 h.p.
WHEELBASE	114 in.
WEIGHT	3,061 lbs.
ORIGINAL PRICE	$1,232.00

"MILLION DOLLAR CAB" *Ford ads claimed that $1 million had been spent on designing and tooling the new roomier, more comfortable cabs.*

ENGINE *Standard engine on the pickups was the 95-horsepower six-cylinder that first appeared on the 1947 passenger cars. Of course, the famous V-8 was available as an option.*

DESIGN *Broad fenders and a horizontal grille gave the new truck a huskier, more substantial look, matching the durability promised in the "ten-year life expectancy" promotion.*

BORN TO BE WILD *This 2002 Ford–Harley-Davidson F-150 truck is one product of the cooperation between Ford and Harley-Davidson. Each company celebrated a centennial in 2003.*

1949 FORD

The 1949 model was as big a break with Ford tradition as the Model A had been. The smooth, modern, slab-sided body was mounted on an all-new chassis. Even the venerable V-8 engine was updated to reduce oil consumption and improve cooling.

ANGST AND ANTICS *Postwar audiences were rocked by the tragic story of Willy Loman in Arthur Miller's* Death of a Salesman. *Silly Putty had just the opposite effect on the masses of people who played with the puzzling substance. Meanwhile, the wild popularity of danceable swing started to give way to the dissonance of be-bop jazz.*

COMFORT *For the first time, a Ford had independent front suspension, giving a much smoother ride.*

BODY *The body was also available in two- and four-door sedans, two-door club and business coupes, and a station wagon.*

SPECIFICATIONS
1949 Ford convertible

ENGINE	V-8, 239 cu. in., 100 h.p.
WHEELBASE	114 in.
WEIGHT	3,274 lbs.
ORIGINAL PRICE	$1,949.00

UPGRADES *The new Ford not only looked better, it also was more practical. The trunk held nearly twice as much luggage as the 1948 Ford trunk.*

DESIGN *The art deco–inspired hood ornament was distinct to the 1949 Ford. It gave the car an added sense of luxury usually associated with Lincolns.*

DESIGN *The "spinner" grille reminds one of an airplane propeller. Aircraft motifs would appear on many cars in the 1950s.*

THE "WOODIE" *The only station wagon available in 1949 was this striking wood-bodied two-door. In that year 31,412 were sold.*

1950 MERCURY

The 1949–1951 Mercurys were favorites with young car enthusiasts. The sleek, rakish styling appealed to customizers, while the improved V-8 engine that developed 110 horsepower was easily hopped up to make the car even faster. James Dean drove one in the classic 1955 movie Rebel Without a Cause.

HISTORY *The one millionth Mercury, a four-door sedan, was built in August of 1950.*

CARTOONS AND CONVENIENCE Peanuts *character Charlie Brown and his gang of friends showed up in seven newspapers, keeping adults as well as children entertained. Other 1950 debuts made more of a difference to adults: The automatic dishwasher became available and the Diners Club Card became the first credit card. Its inventor, Frank McNamara, enjoys a meal before flashing the plastic.*

RACING *A Mercury convertible was the pace car for the 1950 Indianapolis 500. Benson Ford, general manager of Mercury and grandson of Henry Ford, drove the car.*

SPECIFICATIONS
1950 Mercury two-door club coupe

ENGINE	V-8, 255 cu. in., 110 h.p.
WHEELBASE	118 in.
WEIGHT	1,980 lbs.
ORIGINAL PRICE	$3,430.00

ADVANCE *In June of 1950, Mercury introduced the Monterey, a high-style coupe with one of the industry's first vinyl roofs.*

CUSTOM CAR CRAZE *The smooth lines of the Mercury were an ideal platform for the endless creativity of custom car builders.*

DESIGN *For the first time, Mercurys did not bear a strong resemblance to Fords. Instead, Mercury borrowed from the styling of the upscale Lincoln.*

NEW FEATURES *The 1949 Mercury was the first post–World War II Merc not based on a prewar design. The body and chassis were all new.*

1954 JAGUAR D-TYPE

The D-Type Jaguar was one of the great racing sports cars of the 1950s, finishing second in the Le Mans twenty-four-hour race in 1954 and winning in 1955, 1956, and 1957. Jaguar built a total of seventy-one D-Types, very high production for an all-out racing car.

THE ROYAL COURT *As Godzilla, "King of the Monsters," was storming Japanese movie theaters, fashion queen Coco Chanel reopened her famed Paris* *fashion house. That same year, Lord of the Flies, written by William Golding, shown here a decade after the book's release, hit bookstores.*

FIN *The distinctive fin was added to improve straight-line stability at high speeds.*

BRAKES *Jaguar was one of the first builders to adopt four-wheel disc brakes, when even Mercedes-Benz and Ferrari were remaining loyal to drum brakes.*

BODY *The D-Type was among the first racing cars to utilize a monocoque chassis that did away with separate body and frame. This design, borrowed from aircraft practice, has become virtually standard for competition vehicles.*

PURPOSE-BUILT *The D-Type was designed to excel on the long straightaways of Le Mans.*

SPECIFICATIONS
1954 Jaguar D-Type

ENGINE	in-line 6, 231 cu. in., 300 h.p.
WHEELBASE	90.5 in.
WEIGHT	1,860 lbs.
ORIGINAL PRICE	$10,000.00

INTERIOR *A tiny passenger seat met the letter (if not the spirit) of the rule requiring racing sports cars to be two-seaters.*

DESIGN *Jaguar made use of wind tunnels to refine the design of the D-Type's sensuous body. In 1955, the "nose" of the car was made longer.*

393 RW

1954 OPTIONS *Jaguar also made this XK140 Roadster that year.*

LOW TO GO *Engineers fitted the D-Type with dry sump lubrication, a feature—still found in race cars today—that allowed the hood to be lower to the ground and helped oil supply during acceleration.*

1955 FORD TAUNUS

In the 1950s, Taunus carried the Ford banner in the German sedan market. Named for the Taunus mountain range in Germany, the cars came in three versions: the 12M with a 1.2-liter engine, the 15M with a 1.5-liter engine, and the 17M with a 1.7-liter engine. For most of the decade, the Taunus resembled a scaled-down version of the 1949–51 American Fords.

SAD LOSSES, HOPEFUL GAINS

In 1955, teenagers all over the world mourned the loss of James Dean, the anti-hero of Rebel Without a Cause, *and parents breathed a sigh of relief as Dr. Jonas Salk's polio vaccine was released for use. That same year, West Germany became the fifteenth member of NATO.*

CONSTRUCTION *The 17M not only had a larger engine, it also had a wheelbase 4.5 inches longer than the 12M and 15M.*

LUXURY *The styling of the 17M resembled a 1956 U.S.-built Ford.*

SPECIFICATIONS
1955–1957 Ford Taunus 15M

ENGINE	in-line 4, 91 cu. in., 55 h.p.
WHEELBASE	98 in.
WEIGHT	1,904 lbs.
ORIGINAL PRICE	$1,473.00

INTERIOR *The deep-dish "safety" steering wheel appeared in both foreign and domestic Fords in the mid-1950s.*

FOGLIGHT *A distinctive element of the 12M and 15M front end was the central foglight that resembled a round ornament.*

BR 549•656

HISTORY *The original 1952 Taunus 12M.*

1955 FORD THUNDERBIRD

During the 1950s, Ford was determined to fight Chevrolet on every front. The debut of the Corvette in 1953 prompted Ford to develop a two-seater of its own. The Thunderbird was marketed as a "personal" car, not as a pure sports car, and outsold the Chevrolet by a wide margin.

DESIGN *Thunderbird hoods were hinged at the front, in the style of famous European sports cars like the Mercedes-Benz 300SL.*

CHALLENGING CONVENTIONS
In 1955, Rosa Parks refused to play by others' rules, standing up for the civil rights of African Americans by balking at sitting in the back of a segregated bus. Marilyn Monroe was at the height of her popularity and famously posed over a subway vent to promote her film The Seven Year Itch. *That same year, the first mall in the United States, the Southdale Regional Shopping Center in Minneapolis, irrevocably altered the nature of shopping.*

COMMON SENSE *Most of Thunderbird's parts were interchangeable with those of other 1955 Fords.*

DESIGN *The only Thunderbird body style was a convertible. The folding top was supplemented by a removable hardtop that came as standard equipment.*

SPECIFICATIONS
1955 Ford Thunderbird

ENGINE	V-8, 292 cu. in., 198 h.p.
WHEELBASE	102 in.
WEIGHT	2,980 lbs.
ORIGINAL PRICE	$2,944.00

STYLE AND COMFORT *The Thunderbird was equipped with roll-up windows while Chevrolet's Corvette still had transparent side curtains that snapped into place.*

DESIGN *The Thunderbird's round taillights and prominent dual exhausts gave the car a jet-powered look.*

A NEW BREED *The new Thunderbird, which was unveiled in 2001, harked back to the original—even sporting the porthole window on the hardtop. The porthole window was inspired by the 1956 model.*

LOW PRIORITY *At the time the Thunderbird was released, its ultra-low silhouette was the lowest ever offered on a Ford vehicle.*

1956 CONTINENTAL MARK II

The Mark II displayed clean, elegant lines that contrasted sharply with the flamboyant styling of other 1950s cars. With only three thousand made between 1955 and 1957, each Mark II was shipped to the dealer in a custom tailored, fleece-lined cover. At nearly $10,000 it was the most expensive American car one could buy.

SPARE TIRE *The spare tire was mounted under a hump in the trunk lid that recalled the original Continental's outside-mounted spare.*

BEAT BY BEAT *The postwar economic prosperity that characterized much of the 1950s had a profound impact on science, entertainment, and the arts. New drive-in theaters accommodated the booming suburban car culture, researchers photographed the DNA molecule for the first time, and Beat poet Allen Ginsberg, seen here on television after the release of his signature poem "Howl," pushed society in directions it heretofore had not considered.*

DESIGN *The heating and ventilating controls emulated the throttle levers of a modern airliner.*

ELVIS AND HIS '56 *Elvis Presley was not the only famous owner of a Mark II. Nelson Rockefeller, Frank Sinatra, and the Shah of Iran also drove this exclusive car.*

OPTIONS *The only option available on the Mark II was air conditioning. Power assists were standard on the brakes, seat, windows, and steering.*

DETAIL *Each Mark II received eight coats of paint with hand sanding after every two coats. The final coat was also rubbed and polished by hand.*

THE GRILLE *Although virtually every American car in the 1950s had a large chrome grille, most were not nearly as elegant as the Continental's.*

1960 AUSTRALIAN FORD FALCON

The 1960 Falcon was the first Ford to be truly manufactured in Australia. All previous Fords were simply assembled from parts made in the United States or Great Britain. Falcons started out as copies of American cars but were gradually modified for Australian conditions. Today's Falcon is Australian-designed and Australian-built.

LIGHTS. CAMERA. ACTION
The same year that T. H. Maiman was demonstrating the power of the laser he invented, Federico Fellini was poking fun at Italian society in La Dolce Vita. *Meanwhile, the townsfolk of Parkes, Australia, were awaiting the installation of "the dish," the radio telescope's base having been completed. The Australian radio telescope would aid NASA in its first trip to the Moon.*

STYLING *The Falcon's smooth good looks gave the car a sales advantage over its chief competition, the General Motors–built Holden.*

CONSTRUCTION *Falcon's unitary construction did away with separate body and frame and was lighter than rival Holden.*

MARKETING *Despite the fact that it was designed in the United States, Ford advertised the Falcon as "Australian—with a world of difference."*

SPECIFICATIONS
1960 Australian Ford Falcon standard sedan

ENGINE	in-line 6, 144 cu. in., 90 h.p.
WHEELBASE	109.5 in.
WEIGHT	2,463 lbs.
ORIGINAL PRICE	A$2,274.00

STEERING *The Australian Falcon was an exact copy of the American-built Falcon except for one thing—the Aussie car had right-hand drive.*

ENGINE *Falcon's 144-cubic-inch, six-cylinder engine was rugged and got good gas mileage for that time— 20 to 25 miles per gallon.*

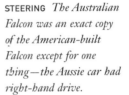

CURRENT FALCON *Although it has gone through several restylings, the Falcon is still one of Australia's most popular six-cylinder cars.*

1961 LINCOLN CONTINENTAL

Proving once again that less is more, the new Continental had clean, classic lines and was 15 inches shorter and 230 pounds lighter than the 1960 Lincoln. Before being shipped, every Continental was given a twelve-mile road test that checked 189 separate items.

DESIGN *The 1961 Continental was one of the few automobiles ever awarded a medal for excellence by the Industrial Design Institute.*

BIG HITS *Roger Maris beat the home-run record set by Babe Ruth the same year a new dance craze, the pelvis-challenging Twist, hit. Dancing to the Chubby Checker single "The Twist," teenagers, their younger siblings, and even their embarrassing parents brought new meaning to the term "cutting the rug." Young Baby Boomers also found hours of pleasure from a new and enduring toy—Lego, introduced to America in 1961.*

STYLING WITH STAMINA *The sleek, clean, knife-edged styling introduced in 1961 would remain part of the Lincoln look for two decades.*

PRESIDENTIAL HISTORY

After four years of planning by the Secret Service, this stretch version of the 1961 Lincoln was delivered to President Kennedy complete with retractable footstands. The president was riding in this car when he was assassinated.

SPECIFICATIONS
1961 Lincoln Continental sedan

ENGINE	V-8, 430 cu. in., 300 h.p.
WHEELBASE	123 in.
WEIGHT	4,927 lbs.
ORIGINAL PRICE	$6,067.00

CONTINENTAL AD *This ad illustrated that the new Lincoln was at home with modern "International Style" architecture.*

DOORS *For the first time since 1951, Lincolns had center-opening doors.*

BODY *The 1961 Lincoln Continental was also available as a convertible.*

1961 JAGUAR E-TYPE

The first public appearance of the new E-Type Jaguar was at the Geneva (Switzerland) auto show in March 1960. The car rocked the automotive world. Rarely had a production car ever combined such sensational looks, outstanding performance, and relatively affordable price.

DESIGN *The new car featured a monocoque main body structure that was inspired by the racing D-Type.*

STRETCHING THE IMAGINATION
As Soviet cosmonaut Yuri Gagarin made the first-ever manned space flight, a young troupe of British actors, led by Dudley Moore and Peter Cook, took to the stage with their comedy and musical review, Beyond the Fringe. *That same year,* *French cartoon characters Asterix and Obelix made their appearance in the first of over thirty albums about the duo,* Asterix the Gaul. *Four decades later, their thirty-first volume of comics was publicized at the International Book Fair in Frankfurt in 2000.*

INTERIOR *The E-Type's cockpit was elegant yet functional, with simple round gauges and efficient-looking toggle switches.*

JAGUAR AD *The Jaguar E-Type was introduced in coupe and roadster models. The coupe (top) and the roadster were equally striking and both sold well.*

This is the new Jaguar X-K-E!

ENGINE *The 3.8-liter engine was fed by three carburetors and pushed the car to a top speed of nearly 150 miles per hour.*

HEADLIGHTS *Covered headlights preserved the car's smooth lines and reduced aerodynamic drag.*

END OF AN ERA *The 1974 E-Type Series III V12 was the last in the E-Type line.*

1962 FORD CORTINA

Cortina was named for a ski resort in northern Italy. Both customers and stockholders regarded it as one of Ford's better ideas: For years it contributed nearly half the profit Ford of Britain made on its car lines. The most famous version was the high-performance Lotus-Cortina, which garnered many race and rally wins.

ELEVATING SUCCESS
In 1962, Lawrence of Arabia's *success was as sweeping as its epic drama. The Brazilian music style Bossa Nova achieved a note of prestige to add to its international popularity when the genre's most heralded musicians, including Antonio Carlos Jobim, played Carnegie Hall in New York City. The Americans sent their own man, John Glenn, into space that same year.*

TAILLIGHTS *Cortina's distinctive taillights resembled the symbol used by the peace and nuclear disarmament movements. They became known as "ban the bomb" lights.*

ENGINE *Cortina's 1.2- and 1.5-liter engines were strong and easy to modify, making them popular with builders of small racing cars.*

RACING ROOTS *By the end of 1964, Cortina GTs and Lotus-Cortinas had accumulated some two hundred race and rally wins.*

SPECIFICATIONS
1962 Ford Cortina

ENGINE	in-line 4, 73 cu. in., 53 h.p.
WHEELBASE	98 in.
WEIGHT	1,775 lbs.
ORIGINAL PRICE	$1,820.00

HOOD *Even on the racing versions, the Cortina's small hood scoop was for looks only.*

HISTORY *The last Cortina rolled off the assembly line in England in 1982.*

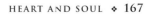

1964 ASTON MARTIN DB5

Tractor and gear manufacturer David Brown bought the venerable but moribund Aston Martin company in 1947 and transformed it into one of the world's great makers of high-performance luxury sports cars. And luxurious the DB5 was: from the elegant contours of the body to the styling and comfort of the interior to the fast, powerful engine, affluent customers found all that they could desire in the DB5 line.

ENGINE *The Aston's smooth double-overhead cam six-cylinder engine was made of aluminum, just like the car's body.*

TURN, TURN, TURN *The Beatles were turning out tunes, Catherine Deneuve was turning heads, and Jean-Paul Sartre was turning down awards in 1964. It was the year that the Beatles exploded onto the scene, performing two weeks in Paris, touring Australia, and appearing on* The Ed Sullivan Show *in America. Deneuve catapulted to stardom in the French musical* The Umbrellas of Cherbourg, *and Sartre won—but rejected—the Nobel Prize in Literature.*

DESIGN *The shape of the grille was modified over the years but retained a distinctive outline that said "Aston Martin."*

BOND CAR *No doubt the most famous Aston of all time was the DB5. A special version of the car appeared in the James Bond movie* Goldfinger.

ENGINE	in-line 6, 244 cu. in., 282 h.p.
WHEELBASE	98 in.
WEIGHT	3,233 lbs.
ORIGINAL PRICE	$12,775.00

BODY *The DB5's Italian-made aluminum body utilized the "superleggera" principle: the panels were supported by a lightweight latticework of small steel tubes welded together.*

2002 VANQUISH *With the V12 Vanquish, James Bond was again driving an Aston Martin. The Vanquish is the fourth Bond car made by the British automaker.*

INTERIOR *Aston Martin claimed that three-and-a-half cowhides were required to provide leather upholstery for the DB5.*

TOP SPEED *Since the DB5 had the ability to reach a speed of 141 miles per hour, this was the view most people had of the car.*

1964 VOLVO 1800S

Volvo introduced its sports car in 1961 as the 1800S. Road & Track *magazine said that it "... gave us the impression it would run forever at near maximum speed." Sales were helped by the fact that the car appeared regularly on the British television series* The Saint.

HISTORY *The 1964 models were the first actually assembled in Sweden. From 1961 to 1963, the cars were built by Jensen in Great Britain.*

WAVE OF THE FUTURE *New television sets allowed watchers to see the world in living color. People were seeing a lot of bobs, the chic 'do updated by legendary coiffeur Vidal Sassoon. Sassoon gave the cut a futuristic edge. A new leisure activity rolled into the future of youngsters—skateboarding.*

SAFETY *Like all Volvos, the 1800S featured three-point seat belts long before they were required by government regulators.*

TV STAR *Roger Moore, as the Saint, opens the door of his Volvo for his leading lady. The Volvo pictured here is the 1965 model.*

SPECIFICATIONS
1964 Volvo 1800S

ENGINE	in-line 4, 108.5 cu. in., 108 h.p.
WHEELBASE	95.5 in.
WEIGHT	2,320 lbs.
ORIGINAL PRICE	$3,920.00

MADE FOR SPEED *The 108-horsepower engine of the 1800S was small by American standards but it could push the lightweight car to over 110 miles per hour.*

AGE BEFORE BEAUTY *At this time, Volvo's advertising slogan was "The car that lasts eleven years in Sweden." In 1964 the car was named "Most Beautiful Sports Car" at the Concours d'Elegance at Baden-Baden, West Germany.*

BODY STYLING *The unique styling of the 1800S was like nothing else on the highway. In 1971, Volvo introduced a striking station wagon version of the car.*

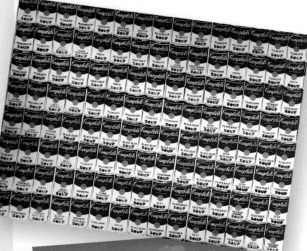

1964½ FORD MUSTANG

The Mustang took America by storm when it was released in 1964. By the end of that first year, more than 500,000 cars had been sold—a record for Ford. The Mustang was available with a long list of options. Buyers could make it a six-cylinder economy car, a mini-luxury car, or a high-performance sports car. But in any incarnation, the Mustang offered good looks and good value for the money.

ENGINE *Mustang offered six engine options, from the 101-horsepower six-cylinder to the 271-horsepower "hi-po" V-8.*

THE TIMES A'CHANGING
The culture changed dramatically in the 1960s. Andy Warhol revolutionized the world of art with his pop images of Campbell's Soup cans. Civil rights leader Rev. Dr. Martin Luther King, Jr. led a different revolution, non-violent protests on behalf of racial equality, which won him the Nobel Peace Prize. And the Beatles revolutionized music, dance, and fashion styles when they appeared on Ed Sullivan's Sunday night variety program on CBS. That's not Ringo, by the way; it's Sullivan clowning in a Beatles wig.

DESIGN *The Mustang's proportions drew on decades of automobile history. From Duesenbergs to Jaguars, long hoods and short decks promised powerful engines and driving fun.*

SPECIFICATIONS
1964 ½ Ford Mustang coupe

ENGINE	V-8, 260 cu. in., 164 h.p.
WHEELBASE	108 in.
WEIGHT	2,449 lbs.
ORIGINAL PRICE	$2,308.00

DESIGN *Clean lines and rakish proportions made the Mustang the only car ever to win a Tiffany Award for Excellence in American Design.*

2003 MACH 1 *Ford built 6,500 special edition Mach 1s as part of their Living Legends series. The 2003 version of the popular Mustang delivers over 300 horsepower from its 4.6-liter V-8 engine.*

SEATS *Bucket seats and a floor-mounted shifter symbolized sportiness. They were soon adopted by many other carmakers.*

1968 FORD ESCORT

Escort was introduced in 1968 as Ford's new weapon in the fierce European small-car market. It was offered as a sedan and as an "estate" (station wagon) as well as a sporty GT model. Escort also did its bit in motor sport, becoming Ford's most successful entry in rallies and doing well in "saloon" (sedan) races.

STEERING *The 1968 Escort was the first Ford with rack-and-pinion steering.*

ENGINE *The engine in the Escort GT had a piece of equipment rarely seen on an economy car—an expensive race-bred Weber carburetor.*

FULL OF STARS *Written by British science fiction writer Arthur C. Clarke and filmed in England, 2001: A Space Odyssey, made its European debut in 1968. French skiing legend Jean-Claude Killy, shown flanked by the runners-up in the giant slalom, took the "triple crown" in that year's Olympic alpine skiing events. Students at Colet Court School in London saw the first expressions of Tim Rice and Andrew Lloyd Webber's Joseph and the Amazing Technicolor Dreamcoat—at that time a mini-play commissioned by the school's headmaster.*

STYLING *Escort's front-end styling would be borrowed for the new Capri in 1969.*

ENGINE *Dealer brochures for the new Escort went into great detail about the efficiency of the engine's cross-flow cylinder head.*

RACY PAST *The Escort was both fast and rugged, making it a favorite of rally drivers.*

SPECIFICATIONS
1968 Ford Escort De Luxe

ENGINE	in-line 4, 79 cu. in., 63 h.p.
WHEELBASE	94.5 in.
WEIGHT	1,640 lbs.
ORIGINAL PRICE	£761.00

SUPER LOOKS *Escort's clean styling accomplished the difficult task of making a small car look good.*

2002 EUROPEAN FORD ESCORT
At the beginning of 2002, Ford announced that it would phase out the Escort by the end of the year.

1969 MERCURY MARAUDER

Mercury introduced the name Marauder in mid-1963. It was applied to a two-door hardtop with a distinctive sloping fastback roofline. The name was revived in 1969 for another hardtop with equally distinctive styling that blended sportiness and luxury.

MARQUIS BROUGHAM AND MARQUIS 4-DOOR HARDTOPS

DESIGN *Marauders shared their elegant, clean front styling with the top-of-the-line Mercury Marquis.*

BIG TRIPS *On a small farm in upstate New York, young people by the tens of thousands gathered to turn on, tune in, drop out, and protest the war in Vietnam. The Woodstock rock festival was a smorgasbord of free love, illegal substances, mud, and rock,*

from Jimi Hendrix's electric rendition of "The Star Spangled Banner" to Country Joe's rousing sing-a-long, "What Are We Fighting For?" Neil Armstrong had walked on the moon, a gigantic yellow bird was a TV star, and everything seemed possible, even the end of the war.

HEADLIGHTS *Hidden headlights were a popular styling feature in the late 1960s and early 1970s.*

ENGINE *The base Marauder had a 390-cubic-inch, 265-horsepower engine. The lower-production, higher-powered Marauder X-100 boasted the 429-cubic-inch, 360-horsepower powerplant.*

DESIGN *Marauders were easily identified by their wide, flowing C-pillars. Because of the inset rear windows, this style was sometimes called a "tunnel-back."*

2003 MARAUDER *Ford brought the Marauder back in showrooms for the 2003-model year, calling it a "rebel with a cause." Still a muscle car, the new Marauder boasted modern standards of safety, performance, and efficiency.*

WHEELS *Aluminum wheels and fender skirts were standard on the Marauder X-100.*

1970 RANGE ROVER

After World War II, Land Rover became known as one of the world's best off-road vehicles. In 1970, Rover introduced a new, even more capable but much more civilized vehicle—the Range Rover. With V-8 power and a clever suspension design, it virtually defined a new market—the luxury sport utility vehicle.

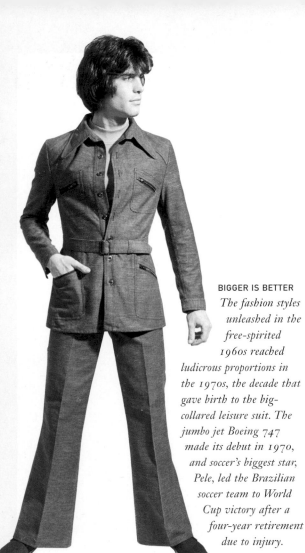

BIGGER IS BETTER *The fashion styles unleashed in the free-spirited 1960s reached ludicrous proportions in the 1970s, the decade that gave birth to the big-collared leisure suit. The jumbo jet Boeing 747 made its debut in 1970, and soccer's biggest star, Pele, led the Brazilian soccer team to World Cup victory after a four-year retirement due to injury.*

PIECE OF ART *Because of its straightforward, form-follows-function design, Range Rover is the only vehicle ever to be displayed at the Louvre as a work of art.*

Suspension
This is one of the most outstanding features of a truly outstanding vehicle. It is strong and reliable, and its flexibility is such that it produces an uncannily smooth ride over really rough country whilst providing excellent handling qualities and saloon car comfort on the road. Robust beam axles front and rear give a near-constant ground clearance and they are suspended on coil springs which allow big up and down movements of the wheels. Suspension travel is controlled by long-stroke telescopic hydraulic dampers.

OFF-ROADING *Range Rover used a clever coil spring suspension to combine great off-road capability with a soft ride.*

FIRST PRODUCTION LAND ROVER *Great Britain's answer to the jeep was introduced in 1948 at the Amsterdam Auto Show.*

SPECIFICATIONS
1970 Range Rover

ENGINE	V-8, 213 cu. in., 115 h.p.
WHEE_BASE	100 in.
WEIGHT	4,400 lbs.
ORIGINAL PRICE	£1,529.00

ENGINE *The aluminum V-8 engine was based on a design originally built for Pontiac and Oldsmobile compact cars of the early 1960s.*

ANNIVERSARY EDITION *The 2003 Range Rover thirtieth anniversary limited edition sported an engine that was the most powerful, most economical, and quietest ever used in a Range Rover.*

DESIGN *An extremely strong box-section ladder-type frame provides a firm foundation for the Range Rover's mechanical components.*

1971 MERCURY CAPRI

Mercury called the Capri "the car you've always promised yourself." Its appeal was similar to the Mustang's: kicky styling, a wide array of options, and the ability to make the driver look good. A variety of four- and six-cylinder engines let Capri buyers choose between mild and wild. American sales stopped after 1977, but European production continued for another ten years.

CAPRI ID *European Capris had a pair of rectangular headlights, while those imported to the U.S. got four round lamps.*

REASON TO SMILE *While car chase fans were smiling through* The French Connection, *featuring detective "Popeye" Doyle (Gene Hackman) busting up an international heroin ring, the ubiquitous Smiley Face beamed from car bumper stickers and teenagers' notebooks. And the release of soft contact lenses in 1971 was a welcome breakthrough for lens wearers everywhere.*

WHEELS *Capri's sporty appearance was enhanced by styled steel wheels as standard equipment.*

Capri. The Sexy European
Imported for
Lincoln-Mercury

AMERICAN BROCHURE *In America, the Capri was sold at Lincoln-Mercury dealers even though it never carried either brand on its body.*

SPECIFICATIONS
1971 Mercury Capri

ENGINE	V-6, 155 cu. in., 107 h.p.
WHEELBASE	100.8 in.
WEIGHT	2,330 lbs.
ORIGINAL PRICE	$2,821.00

DESIGN *Capri styling carried the long-hood, short-deck look to an extreme. The rear seats were best suited to people of compact dimensions.*

2000

BODY *Capris were always coupes, but a hatchback style was added to the lineup in 1975.*

SPORTY STYLE *Capri's cockpit had all the sporty touches—bucket seats, console-mounted shifter, and wood-grain dash with round gauges.*

DESIGN *Simulated brake cooling scoops in front of the rear wheels were a Capri hallmark.*

1986 FORD TAURUS

The Taurus's aerodynamic styling was controversial when it was introduced. Critics called the cars "flying potatoes." But the car was a sales success and Motor Trend *named it the Car of the Year. Within a few years, most cars borrowed the smooth look of the Taurus.*

WINDOWS *Details like flush glass all the way around gave the Taurus a very low drag coefficient of 0.33.*

HANDS TOGETHER *Tom Cruise took to the skies in* Top Gun *while Jack Nicklaus proved he still had what it took to win the Masters, becoming at age forty-six the oldest player to win the tournament. Top musical performers gathered to promote peace, racial harmony, environmental stewardship, and other planetary issues, clasping hands and singing "We Are the World."*

A NEW APPROACH *A first for Ford, the manufacturer used a team approach to design the Taurus, bringing together individuals from every area of the company at the very beginning of this $3 billion project.*

STATION WAGON
The Taurus station wagon was functional and versatile, but its new look made it stylish as well.

ENGINE	V-6, 183 cu. in., 140 h.p.
WHEELBASE	106 in.
WEIGHT	2,909 lbs.
ORIGINAL PRICE	$11,322.00

INTERIOR *The easy-to-use instrument panel was the result of many long hours of ergonomic studies by Taurus designers.*

ENGINE *Taurus buyers had a choice of two engines: a 2.5-liter, four-cylinder and a 3-liter V-6. Both had electronic fuel injection.*

DESIGN *Taurus's most striking visual feature was its lack of a grille. Air for the radiator flowed through an opening below the bumper.*

BODY *Taurus was available in only two body styles: a four-door sedan and a four-door station wagon.*

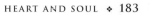

1990 MAZDA MIATA

The Miata had some characteristics that sports-car lovers thought they would never see in one car—good looks, good performance, and affordable price, plus a top that kept out the rain, a reliable electrical system, and mechanical components that didn't leak oil. It was an instant hit.

CRY FREEDOM *The first year of the 1990s was rife with symbols of unification: The World Wide Web was invented and East and West Germany had been successfully reunited following the tearing down of the Berlin Wall. In a unification of high-brow and low-brow humor,* The Simpsons *launched its tenure on the Fox Television Network. Here, actress Nancy Cartwright embraces Bart Simpson, the character she gives voice to.*

ENGINE *The appearance of the Miata's 1.6-liter engine was crafted to recall the twin-cam fours used in sports cars of the 1950s and 1960s.*

ACCOLADES *The Miata was named the Automobile of the Year by* Automobile *magazine when the sports car was released in 1990.*

DESIGN *The Miata's styling recalled that of the much more expensive Lotus Elan, left, from the 1960s.*

SPECIFICATIONS
1990 Mazda Miata

ENGINE	in-line 4, 97 cu. in., 116 h.p.
WHEELBASE	89.2 in.
WEIGHT	2,093 lbs.
ORIGINAL PRICE	$13,800.00

WEIGHT DISTRIBUTION *To help keep the weight of the car within the wheel base, the Miata's lightweight battery was installed in the trunk.*

EXHAUST *Mazda engineers spent a great deal of time tuning the car's exhaust system to get just the right sound.*

SPECIAL EDITION *In 2002, Mazda introduced the Miata SE in Blazing Yellow Mica with black leather interior. It was the first time a black leather interior was available for the Miata.*

FEATURES *The Miata was a sports car without the rough edges. The top operated easily and buyers could order air conditioning and a CD player.*

THE MIATA COCKPIT IS WHERE IT ALL COMES TOGETHER TO FEEL JUST RIGHT.

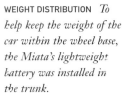

1991 FORD EXPLORER

Sport utility vehicles were once driven only by hunters, farmers, or park rangers. But in the 1980s, people began buying them to replace the family sedan and station wagon. Ford's off-road vehicles, the Bronco and Bronco II, were too rugged for this market. The more civilized Explorer arrived in 1991 and soon outsold all other SUVs.

THOSE FABULOUS PHILLIES

All The Rage

Angry young rockers like PEARL JAM give voice to the passions and fears of a generation

Pearl Jam's lead singer Eddie Vedder

FEATURES *With optional leather upholstery, AM/FM stereo, and air conditioning, Explorers could be as comfortable as any Taurus but could still offer six feet of cargo space.*

NO SILENCE *In 1991, Garth Brooks dominated the Country Music Awards while the thriller* Silence of the Lambs *swept the top Oscar categories, garnering best acting awards for Jodie Foster and Anthony Hopkins. Meanwhile, a hard-edged style of music known as "grunge" captured flannel-clad fans of such bands as Pearl Jam and Nirvana.*

DESIGN *Flush glass and an overall clean design gave the Explorer a drag coefficient of 0.43—surprisingly low for a tall, boxy vehicle.*

BODY *Unlike its predecessor, the Bronco II, the Explorer offered a four-door model that appealed to customers who made more trips to the mall than to mountain trails.*

SPECIFICATIONS
1991 Ford Explorer XLT two-door

ENGINE	V-6, 244 cu. in., 155 h.p.
WHEELBASE	102.1 in.
WEIGHT	3,681 lbs.
ORIGINAL PRICE	$17,656

A SPARE THAT'S A STRIKE *Rather than having the spare tire take up valuable cargo space, designers positioned the full-size spare in a carrier between the frame rails.*

2002 XLT SPORT *In 2002, Ford added a sporty package to the Explorer XLT model, giving the Explorer a new look.*

DOORS *Explorer featured "limousine doors" that extended to the roof-line for easier entry and exit.*

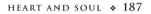

3

INNOVATIO
AND INGENU

"Imagination is the beginn
creation. You imagine what yo
you will what you imagine, a
you create what you wi

—GEORGE BERNARD SHAW

❖

*Imagining into the future characterized muc
approach to design and engineering in the twer
as this 1955 Ford Futura—the prototype
Batmobile—amply demonstrates.*

The invention of the automobile was not the "Eureka!" moment of Alexander Graham Bell's telephone in 1876 or Madame Curie's discovery of radium in 1898. Rather, the automobile evolved over several decades as the collective product of mechanics, engineers, and weekend tinkerers: Étienne Lenoir's two-cycle engine in 1859, Nikolaus Otto's four-cycle engine in 1876, Karl Benz's single-cylinder engine for a motorcar in 1885, and the Duryea brothers' first motorcar in the United States in 1893. Each built upon the trials, tribulations, and small successes of his predecessors. Henry Ford would take it to the next level.

The spirit of purposeful invention at the Ford Motor Company that began with the founder has inspired Ford employees in design, engineering, and manufacturing for the past century. Their ingenuity, craft, and skill have nurtured the development of revolutionary car styles, state-of-the-art engines, and safer, more environmentally friendly, efficient, and comfortable vehicles.

The first automobile to emerge from the Ford brain trust was the original Model A in 1903, advertised as the Fordmobile. The 8-horsepower, two-cylinder vehicle had a two-speed "planetary" transmission, twenty-eight-inch wheels with wooden spokes and three-inch tires, and a detachable "tonneau" rear-seat section. It was described in company advertisements as "positively the most

VOLVO
002185
VOLVO

VOLVO
002185
VOLVO

MODEL NAMES *The first Ford models were marketed and sold by independent dealerships like the one replicated at right. Below: Advertisement for the Ford Model F, pre-1908.*

perfect machine on the market" and "so simple that a boy of fifteen can run it."

The price was $850. "For beauty of finish," ads insisted, "it is unequaled."

Henry sold 1,808 Fordmobiles through 1905, generating enough revenue to distribute dividends to stockholders and build a three-story factory at the corner of Beaubien and Piquette Avenues. Field, Hinchman & Smith, a distinguished Detroit architectural firm, designed the modern brick plant, which was ten times the size of the original Mack Avenue facility. The building was fireproofed with sprinkler systems, fire walls, and a water tower emblazoned with the Ford trademark.

Ford production was transferred to the new Piquette Avenue plant in early 1905, spurring output. Sales averaged $365,000 a month by June, compared with $60,000 a month a year earlier. More car models were developed, as Henry and his engineers exhausted another eighteen letters of the alphabet through the Model S, from 1903 to 1908. "The popularity of our cars has created a demand for a complete line of Ford Models from which every user's individual requirements can be satisfied," advertisements declared. Others advised: "Don't experiment—Just buy a Ford."

Some Fords were experimental models that never reached the public. A few had two cylinders, some had four, and one—the gigantic Model K limousine—had six. A few cars had a chain drive, while others had a shaft drive. In some, the engine was placed beneath the driver's seat. Through constant trial and error, Henry endeavored to build the perfect automobile.

He feverishly sought an affordable car for the masses, an objective rebuked by Alexander Malcolmson and other partners, who demanded that Henry make more luxurious automobiles like the $2,800 Model K and the $2,000 four-cylinder Model B—expensive cars that reaped lucrative profits. Their heated disagreements compelled Malcolmson to form another company, Aerocar, to manufacture deluxe touring cars, a move Henry viewed as treasonous.

When the Model K failed, selling only 910 units, Malcolmson's position weakened. In 1906, he sold his stock to Henry for $175,000. After other stockholders did the same, Henry's aggregate stockholdings increased to 58.5 percent. That July, upon the death of John S. Gray, Ford's titular president and a prominent Detroit banker, Henry Ford finally became president of the company that bore his name.

Now he and his fellow engineers, Childe Harold Wills and C. J. Smith, and draftsman Joseph Galamb, could turn their attention

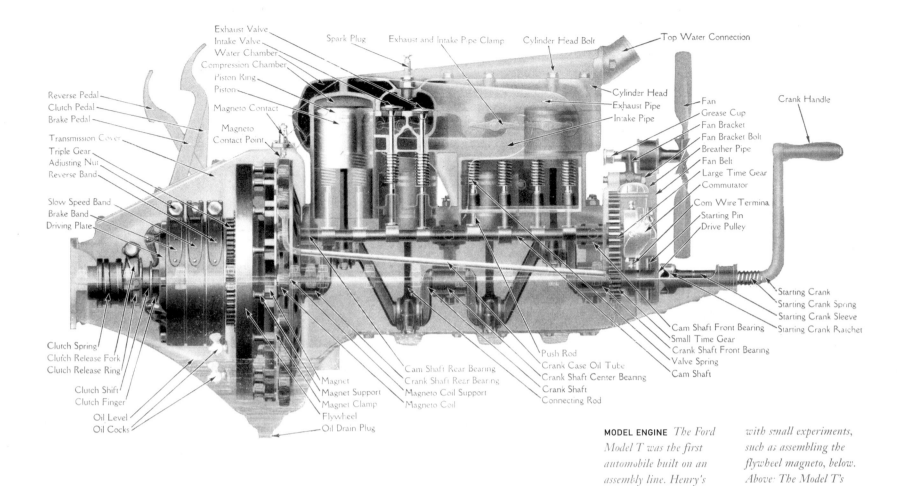

Exhaust Valve
Intake Valve
Water Chamber
Compression Chamber
Piston Ring
Piston
Magneto Contact
Magneto Contact Point

Reverse Pedal
Clutch Pedal
Brake Pedal

Transmission Cover
Triple Gear
Adjusting Nut
Reverse Band

Slow Speed Band
Brake Band
Driving Plate

Clutch Spring
Clutch Release Fork
Clutch Release Ring

Clutch Shift
Clutch Finger

Oil Level
Oil Cocks

Spark Plug
Exhaust and Intake Pipe Clamp
Cylinder Head Bolt
Top Water Connection

Cylinder Head
Exhaust Pipe
Intake Pipe

Fan
Grease Cup
Fan Bracket
Fan Bracket Bolt
Breather Pipe
Fan Belt
Large Time Gear
Commutator

Crank Handle

Com Wire Termina
Starting Pin
Drive Pulley

Starting Crank
Starting Crank Spring
Starting Crank Sleeve
Starting Crank Ratchet

Cam Shaft Front Bearing
Small Time Gear
Crank Shaft Front Bearing
Valve Spring
Cam Shaft

Push Rod
Crank Case Oil Tube
Crank Shaft Center Bearing
Crank Shaft
Connecting Rod

Magnet
Magnet Support
Magnet Clamp
Flywheel
Oil Drain Plug

Cam Shaft Rear Bearing
Crank Shaft Rear Bearing
Magneto Coil Support
Magneto Coil

MODEL ENGINE *The Ford Model T was the first automobile built on an assembly line. Henry's revolutionary approach to mass production started with small experiments, such as assembling the flywheel magneto, below. Above: The Model T's engine was light in weight with good tensile strength.*

to building plain, affordable vehicles like the Model N, a small, light four-cylinder machine marketed for $600 in 1906. The Model N was a breakthrough automobile for Ford, a highly innovative car with the first forced-feed "oiler," a unitary engine and transmission assembly, and a wire harness that replaced the tangle of wires coiling throughout the vehicle. The car also introduced a new look—a small carriage step instead of the usual footboard.

The Model N was the best car for its price in the early days of the new century, an overnight sensation that sold 6,930 units from its introduction in July 1906 through the end of 1908. This industry sales record propelled the small Detroit automobile company to the front ranks of the industry.

"The Model N was the direction Henry wanted to go," says transportation historian Bob Casey. "It was small, durable, light, and a great value for the money. But it wasn't big enough to squire four or five people; it hauled three, at best. In a way, Henry was still practicing to get it right, tinkering to find the perfect car in subsequent models."

Ford sold some 20,000 cars before Henry found his way with the Model T in 1908. The Tin Lizzie was an extremely modern car for

the times, not so much in form as in function. Henry had read reports about a new alloy, vanadium steel, reputed to be stronger and lighter than ordinary nickel steel. He and J. Kent-Smith, an English metallurgist, built a laboratory to make the Model T's crankshaft and chassis from the alloy, thus reducing the weight of the vehicle. In succeeding years, this laboratory would become an important incubator of other alloys, including tungsten steel and chromium steel.

The Model T's engine was equally novel. The four cylinders were cast with the crankcase as one block, as opposed to the traditional method of bolting four individual cylinders to separate crankcases. Casey says Henry, Charles Sorensen, and other Ford engineers had solved "an extraordinary manufacturing challenge," which resulted in engines of greater tensile strength, less weight, and less expense.

Henry also developed a novel flywheel magneto to replace the dry batteries then used by U.S. carmakers. The magneto produced a high-tension current "ingeniously distributed to the four spark plugs," *Popular Science* magazine stated in 1963. Similarly ingenious was the varnish, allegedly "cooked" in a maple syrup kettle, that Henry used to insulate the magneto.

ALPHABET CARS

The alphabet served as the basis for naming the company's models, beginning with the Model A and ending with the Model T. Then Henry decided to start all over again with his second Model A. ❖ The original 1903 Model A, seen alongside other early Ford models on the facing page, was considered a secondary means of travel compared with the horse and buggy. Many early motorists were taunted by shouts of "Get a horse!" The Farmers' Anti-Automobile Society of Pennsylvania warned that cars were dangerous and insisted drivers stop every mile at night, send up warning rockets, and then wait ten minutes before advancing. But Henry and other automakers were determined to create better automobiles, and their cars found a growing acceptance. ❖

MODEL T ON THE STREETS OF NEW YORK

1903 MODEL A

1905 MODEL B TOURING

1905 MODEL C

1906 MODEL K TOURING

1906 MODEL N RUNABOUT

1908 MODEL T

Her Personal Car

The Model T was the first production model to feature left-hand steering, a removable cylinder head that made working on the car much easier, and a closed case to house the engine, flywheel, universal joint, and transmission. To reduce the painful jerks caused by stubble fields and rutted byways, Henry mounted huge arc springs crosswise over the axles and installed a three-point engine suspension, at a time when two-point was the norm.

Several innovations, such as the three-point suspension and the detachable cylinder head, thereafter became standard throughout the industry.

Equally revolutionary was the planetary gear transmission, which reduced stripping of gears by drivers and did away with the heavy clutches that were especially vexing to women. Two gears were provided in one forward pedal, one to climb hills or overcome starting sluggishness, the other for speed. Pushing the pedal to the floor put the car in low gear, letting it out put it in high gear, and holding it halfway down put the car in neutral, which was required to crank the car or idle at intersections.

These innovations combined to produce an automobile that was not only an engineering marvel, it could fit the income limitations of most Americans. Model T advertisements were to the point—"You Can Afford a Ford."

The success of the Model T is not surprising given the depth of planning that went into it. In his reminiscences about his work in Ford's "experimental room" at the Piquette Avenue plant, draftsman Galamb said:

"For about two years, [we] worked on the design until about ten or eleven o'clock at night. Mr. Ford was there practically all the time. There was a rocking chair in the room in which he used to sit for hours and hours at a time, discussing and following out the developments of the design."

The Model T was exactly what Henry had envisioned, combining lightness with durability and power. The car weighed only 1,200 pounds, yet the engine kicked up 22.5 horsepower on a 100-inch wheelbase, enough gallop to accelerate the Model T to 45 miles per hour. Ford also made parts for repair inexpensive and easy to install. Although minor modifications were made in succeeding years, such as the addition of electric lights in 1915 and an electric starter in 1919, the basic nature of the car remained the same for nineteen years.

Credit for the Model T as a work of engineering art belongs largely to Henry. As Sorensen wrote: "In studying an old machine, and planning a new one, he had, indeed, a sixth sense."

The same could be said of Henry's rationale to leverage mass production techniques. Ford's mastery of the assembly line caught the attention of the U.S. government, which was having problems manufacturing Liberty aircraft engines during World War I. The Liberty engine's eight steel cylinders were being machined out of a solid or partially bored piece of forged metal, which slowed production. The

government's dilemma was laid before Henry and his engineers, who developed an ingenious way to make the cylinders out of steel tubing.

"By this method, a production of 2,000 rough cylinders a day was reached," Benedict Crowell, assistant secretary of war for the United States, wrote in 1919. "The final forging was so near to the shape desired that millions of pounds of scrap were saved over other methods, to say nothing of an enormous amount of labor thus done away with. The development of this cylinder-making method was one of the important contributions to the quantity production of Liberty engines."

In the 1920s, Ford did for aviation what it had done for automobiles, developing through mass production techniques the world's premier civilian aircraft manufacturing company. Ford obtained thirty-five patents in building the Tri-Motor plane, covering tail wheels, shock absorbers, wing lights, and brakes.

"Ford had built the first concrete runway in the world, which required that brakes be installed on wheels to curtail forward momentum," explains aviation historian Timothy J. O'Callaghan. Previously, planes slowed from the friction caused when the tail skidded on the ground.

To spark further development of the aviation industry, Henry offered his patents free of royalties. "Patents are silly things when they are used to hinder any industry," said Henry, still reeling from his experience with the Selden case. "We take patents on our own developments or discoveries only to prevent others from freezing us out when they may chance to make the same discovery."

The Tri-Motor was the best and safest plane in its class, designed to provide pilots with "the ability to see in every direction on both sides of the plane," a Ford press release claimed. "This is the first time the vision problem has really been solved in a big plane, the most serious problem of all in the construction of large aircraft."

Like the Model T, the Tri-Motor was built on an assembly line using interchangeable parts, a first for the aviation industry. The Tin Goose also was as versatile as the Tin Lizzie. While the Model T could haul logs and plow fields, the Tri-Motor could be reconfigured into a seaplane by attaching floats or rigged with skis to use on ice or snow.

Ford's aviation innovations soared beyond the Tri-Motor. The company invented the original navigational radio beam, which helped to guide the first flight by radio on February 10, 1927. O'Callaghan considers the radio beam to be the most important patent Ford received in the aviation field.

"It allowed planes to overcome the dangers and cancellations caused by rain, fog, and darkness, [permitting] planes to find their way from point to point in all types of weather without concern for visual observations," he writes in *The Aviation Legacy of Henry and Edsel Ford.*

FIRST CLASS *The Ford Tri-Motor is a landmark in aviation history. Praising Henry and Edsel Ford's aircraft, the* New York Times *wrote, "Reliable, scheduled air travel would have come about eventually in any case. But the Fords . . . are credited with moving the timetable ahead by several years."*

Right: The Tri-Motor's interior. Below: Edsel's cufflinks with the motto Omnium Rerum Vicissitudo— *"All Things Change." Indeed, Ford abandoned the aviation business after the 1929 stock market crash, and replaced the venerable Model T with the Model A, opposite, in 1927.*

Although the 1929 stock market crash ended Ford's commercial aviation interests, the company's adroit designers and engineers proved their skill was not confined to purely earthbound vehicles. On July 29, 1971, in a forty-fifth anniversary tribute to the Tri-Motor, the U.S. House of Representatives passed a resolution honoring Henry Ford as an aviation pioneer. It reads:

"It truly can be said that he took the airplane out of the cow pasture, put it in the hangar, obtained for aviation prestige and public confidence, and, in so doing, launched the air age. The Ford Tri-Motor, by virtue of its metallic construction, its three great engines, its commodious interior, and broad wingspan, had the look of safety and security. With the Ford name emblazoned on its side, public acceptance came inevitably."

Public acceptance of the Model T, however, was petering out.  The Tin Lizzie looked like Grandma's car next to the stylish, comfortable vehicles sold by General Motors and Chrysler in the late 1920s. Edsel remonstrated that Ford must grow with the times (his cufflinks were engraved with the motto *Omnium Rerum Vicissitudo*— "All Things Change"). Henry finally capitulated to discontinuing his revered Model T and locked himself behind closed doors to develop a successor.

What the competition did not know was that Ford engineers had been working for eight years at the Fair Lane experimental laboratory on a new "X-Engine." Two engineers, Allen Horton and E. J. Farkas, worked with Henry to create a compact, light, and powerful engine that would be as revolutionary as the Model T before it. Despite Henry's tenacity and his engineers' constant revisions, the X-Engine was a failure.

"Ultimately they were forced to reject the X-Engine because it could not achieve the stated objective of durability," says Ford historian Donn Werling. "Not all was lost, however. The experiments were extremely useful in the design and engineering of Ford's breakthrough single-cast V-8 engine in 1932."

While Ford did not invent a radically new engine in the 1920s, it did introduce a radically new car. The 1928 Model A, with its standard transmission, four-wheel brakes, hydraulic shock absorbers, windshield wiper, and laminated safety glass windshield, was in stark contrast to the outmoded Model T. The safety windshield, a Ford innovation, soon became standard equipment on all U.S. automobiles.

The Model A's appearance also was modern, thanks to the aesthetic influences of Edsel and E. T. Gregorie. Their styling treatment, with just the right accent of nickel trim, nicely turned door handles, and a well-appointed interior, transformed the public's notion of a Ford from plain utility to serviceable beauty.

The Model A did share one facet with the Model T—price. At $500, it was a veritable steal. People lined up three-deep in New York

CASTING WIDE *The Ford V-8 was the third in a series of startlingly new automobiles coming out of the Ford brain trust, following the Model T and the Model A. Like its predecessors, the car boasted a new engine, in this case a single engine block cast as one piece—an engineering breakthrough. Right: Edsel and Henry marvel at the V-8 engine. Below: A button that commemorates the V-8 engine.*

City in 1931 to glimpse Eleanor Roosevelt driving the milestone twenty millionth Ford, a Model A Fordor, on the first leg of its transcontinental tour. Traveling west, the car received the checkered flag at the Indianapolis Speedway, was inducted into the Sioux tribe, and became the first privately owned automobile to descend to the bottom of Hoover Dam. At the finale in Los Angeles, film star Douglas Fairbanks drove the Fordor in the city's 150th anniversary parade.

The Model A was an instant success, helping Ford preserve the lion's share of the car market in 1930: 40 percent compared to GM's 34 percent. But Henry's resistance to improving the automobile, coupled with a dearth of demand for cars during the Depression, decimated sales. Ford's share of the market dwindled to 28 percent in 1931, compared with GM's 43 percent share.

Henry fought back with another new car, the pioneering Ford V-8, introduced in 1932. Other carmakers had made eight-cylinder engines before, but they were heavy and expensive, causing many to focus instead on six-cylinder engines. Henry disliked six-cylinder motors and always insisted that engines should be made only with four, eight, or sixteen cylinders. Once, upon hearing that

his engineers had devised a six-cylinder engine without his knowledge, he was so infuriated that he took an axe to it.

Henry had a better idea—a one-piece V-8 engine block that would be lighter in weight and less expensive to make. There was only one hitch: the casting technology to manufacture a single V-8 engine did not exist. That didn't stop Henry. He and a group of handpicked engineers set up shop in 1931 in Thomas Edison's old Fort Myers laboratory, which had been moved to the grounds of Greenfield Village in Dearborn, to find the solution.

"Mr. Ford kept everybody away from [the project]," Emil Zoerlein, an electrical engineer on the project, said in his reminiscences. "As far as I know, Charlie Sorensen didn't know about it, [and] I don't know whether Edsel was aware. The original concept of the V-8 was Mr. Ford's. [He] came in two or three times a day [and] was vitally interested in a one-piece casting of the cylinder block. It had to be one piece, definitely. At that time the casting practices were rather young, and a lot of development had to be done. We lost an awful lot of castings . . . before we got some good ones."

Henry ordered an end to Model A production, closed his plants, and put his entire resources at the disposal of his foundry

men. On March 9, 1932, after millions of dollars in bad castings and lost sales during the shutdown, the first production V-8 came off the assembly line. Ford had worked an industry miracle. Against all odds, Henry, his able engineers, and Ford's foundry men had cast a single V-8 engine block, a major engineering milestone.

In subsequent years, Ford's foundry men would further revolutionize engine production methods. The foundry developed the first rustproof steel used in automotive production, a breakthrough adding years to a car's life. It also made the first alloyed steel-cast crankshafts; previous crankshafts were universally forged. This discovery led the way for other automobile parts to be cast instead of forged.

The V-8 also sported a new clutch design, improved suspension, and better distribution of passenger weight, making it drive more efficiently and faster than competing models. Like the Model A, it was a bargain, "The only car in the low-price field with a V-8 cylinder engine," Ford advertisements noted. The car seized the market its debut year, selling some 825,000 units, more than Chevrolet and Plymouth.

The Fordor's remarkable speed also attracted a rather disreputable following. In a letter to Henry, bank robber John Dillinger enthused:

"Hello Old Pal. You have a wonderful car. It's a treat to drive one. Your slogan should be Drive a Ford and Watch The Other Cars Fall Behind You. I can make any other car take Ford's dust. Bye-bye."

Clyde Barrow, of "Bonnie and Clyde" notoriety, worshiped his stolen V-8. In a handwritten letter to Henry, from Tulsa, Oklahoma, in 1934, he extends similar heartfelt congratulations, albeit with less proficient spelling and grammar:

"Dear Sir. While I still have got breath in my lungs, I will tell you what a dandy car you make. I have drove Fords exclusively when I could get away with one. For sustained speed and freedom from trouble the Ford has got every other car skinned, and even if my business hasn't been strickly legal it don't hurt anything to tell you what a fine car you got in the V8. Yours truly, Clyde Champion Barrow."

Bank robbers may have loved the Fords of the mid-1930s, but dealers were having increasing difficulty selling against the competition. A particular beef was Henry's insistence on using mechanical brakes. General Motors and Chrysler, on the other hand, utilized more modern, smoother-operating hydraulic brakes in their units. Dealers continually griped to

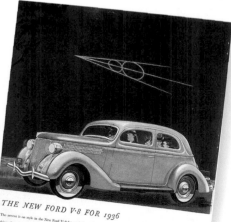

THE NEW FORD V-8 FOR 1936

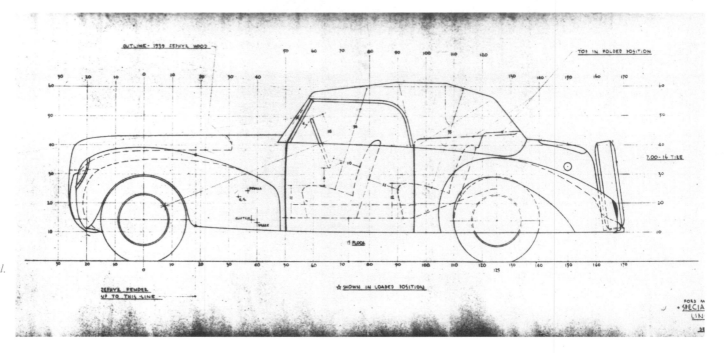

Ford, and especially to Edsel, that they were at a disadvantage and that a change in brake design was not only necessary, it was critical for them to maintain sales volumes. Finally, Henry yielded to their demands. Beginning in 1937, all Fords sported smooth hydraulic braking systems.

While Ford engineers received praise for their speedy V-8 engine, company stylists got their due for the elegant Lincoln Zephyr. The futuristic automobile, designed by Edsel and Gregorie, was one of the first American cars to have a so-called "alligator" hood and, in later models, a low, horizontal radiator grille. At $1,200, the 1936 Lincoln Zephyr was lower priced (and smaller) than the standard Lincoln, enticing a new Ford market, the upper-middle-class demographic.

The Zephyr was merely a design warm-up for Edsel and Gregorie. In 1939, they raised the curtain on the Lincoln Continental, considered one of the most exquisite cars ever made.

The Continental's origins are colorful. Edsel had requested that a "special car" be created for him to drive on vacation in Florida. In his reminiscences, Ed Martin, who worked with Gregorie, said, "I remember the day the car came over from the Lincoln plant. It was quite an event at the styling department, then called the design department. The car was painted yellow. It had special hubcaps. It was a beauty."

The prototype received such an enthusiastic reception that a decision was reached on the spot to put it into production. The Lincoln Continental became Ford's top-line car, aimed at "a person of culture with very refined good taste," company literature explained. The car's styling was so lush that *Fortune* magazine in 1950 called it "One of the most striking United States automobile designs in the past twenty years." The Continental later had the honor of being displayed at the Museum of Modern Art in New York City.

While the Continental was sumptuous, its overseas cousins were unpretentious vehicles manufactured to meet foreign laws, needs, and preferences. The Model Y, which made its European debut in 1932, was a small automobile with a four-cylinder engine, ninety-inch wheelbase, and rather stingy 22 horsepower. The price for the little car, however, was lower than for other British automobiles, such as the Morris and the Austin, and it sold well there and in Latin America, where it was exported to Argentina and Brazil.

EDSEL FORD: CAR DESIGNER

The son of Henry Ford was as interested in automobile styling as his father was in efficient automobile production. Edsel Ford and his design partner, E. T. Gregorie, collaborated on some of the most beautiful cars ever to roll off an assembly line, including the second Model A, the first Mercury, the Lincoln Zephyr, and the car many consider a design icon, the Lincoln Continental.

Known and admired by workers as "Mr. Edsel," to distinguish him from his father, "Mr. Ford," Edsel had a keen flair for the arts and, despite a privileged upbringing,

a down-to-earth demeanor. "He was very artistically inclined," his son Henry Ford II said in 1980. "He had a great feeling for the arts and was interested in them all his life."

Edsel had transformed the dour Lincoln line into a modernist sensation. The elegant yet understated 1936 Lincoln Zephyr was smaller than the standard Lincoln, featuring a 110-horsepower engine and 122-inch wheelbase, compared with the standard Lincoln's 150 horsepower and 145-inch wheelbase. Yet, it was far more dramatic in appearance, with a long, low look, and less expensive. The back of the cabin was enclosed

and seemingly very private, giving the illusion of a two-passenger car. The hood and fenders integrated smoothly and were offset by the graphic vertical blades of the grille. The car revived the dormant Lincoln line and continues today to represent luxury and style.

The 1939 Lincoln Continental further advanced the art of automobile design. The car that architect Frank Lloyd Wright called the most beautiful automobile ever made sealed Edsel's reputation as a great stylist, "ahead of his time in his understanding of . . . aesthetic values," wrote the Detroit *Free Press* in 1965. Edsel "was exceptionally

perceptive and artistically gifted," the newspaper stated. Walter Teague, a foremost artist in the art deco movement, wrote that Edsel was "a great soul . . . wise, generous, strong and simple [and] a great designer."

Edsel was much admired for his streamlined, lower-slung auto bodies and had urged the curved windshield of the Model A and the wind resistant contours of the Zephyr and Continental. "He wanted to be advised of the air friction on all [car] models," recalled Ford engineer Emil Zoerlein. "Henry Ford had very little interest in styling. He was more of an engineer. Mr. Edsel was a stylist [and]

was very ingenious about ironing out things between the styling department and [Ford's engineers]."

The Mexican muralist Diego Rivera painted Edsel in 1932, depicting him with drafting tools and pencils as he prepared to execute the design of the 1932 Ford coupe, sketched in chalk on a blackboard in the background. The impressive portrait today hangs in the second-floor hall of the Edsel and Eleanor Ford House in Grosse Pointe Shores, Michigan. The painting is a fitting tribute to someone whose influence in the automobile industry extended beyond his surname. ❖

DIFFERENT STROKES *While the Rouge plant in the painting at right pumped out American cars for the American market, overseas factories made automobiles suiting local tastes, budgets, and roadways. Ford advertised their Ford V-8 in the French market, below, and built the small Ford Model Y, below right, at the Dagenham plant, selling it in England and Latin America.*

The Dagenham plant in England unveiled three additional models in 1925: the Popular, Anglia, and Prefect. The Popular (a reconfigured Model Y) was extolled by advertisements as "not only roomy and comfortable but exceptionally economical."

Elsewhere, Ford had merged in 1934 with an old-line French automaker, E. E. C. Mathis, to become Matford. The company produced two Matford models, including a V-8. Ford-Werke AG in Germany was producing the four-cylinder Köln, which was replaced in 1934 by the four-cylinder Eifel (another variation of the Model Y). Each of these automobiles was designed for indigenous tastes, as well as the narrower streets and low-overhead bridges and tunnels of Europe.

Some foreign models, such as the 1938 Matford Cabriolet, were given unique body styles and headlamp treatments to distinguish them from their Dearborn counterparts. Indeed, an American traveling abroad in the late-1930s would be hard-pressed to recognize the cars as "Fords." But, the company's foreign assembly plants looked just like those in the U.S., accompanied by water towers or tall stacks adorned with the familiar Ford logo.

Back in Dearborn, the Rouge plant evolved into the nexus of vertically integrated manufacturing envisioned by the founder, and diverse experiments abounded in all facets of automobile production. Ford engineers produced different types of plastics and enamel paints, including a synthetic resin-based enamel finish in 1933, later duplicated by the industry. Engineers also patented a rear-engine automobile, while the foundry cast crankshafts of high-strength iron alloy that vastly reduced automobile vibration and noise.

On the manufacturing front, Ford built a tire plant at the Rouge in 1937 that produced 5,000 Ford tires a day, causing the price of tires to plunge to about $2.50 each. Some of this rubber came from Ford's own rubber plantation in Brazil.

Henry had purchased 2.5 million acres in the mid-1920s on the east bank of the Tapajos River, a tributary of the Amazon, to plant rubber trees to offset high rubber prices. Workers dammed the river and cleared native trees, using the timber to build railroads, airports, schools, banks, houses, and a hospital. Henry called his vast Brazilian holdings Fordlandia.

Unfortunately, the Depression pared

government. When the war ended and automobile production resumed, the pent-up need for new cars was overwhelming. Making cars quickly without sacrificing quality was a challenge. Thanks to Ernest Breech and the Whiz Kids, Ford's new decentralized "profit center" structure created greater accountability to ensure quality control production methods were being observed.

Most Fords after the war were nothing special, looking and performing much like their prewar predecessors. A startling exception was the 1949 Ford, the company's most important car since the V-8. The 1949 Ford was impressive, with twenty square feet of windows revealing a roomy interior of "soft-wide" seats, while the exterior sported "extra heavy, massive front and rear bumpers—a real help in tight-spot parking," one company advertisement noted.

"The '49 Ford was a turnaround car, an extraordinary vehicle," says Casey. "It was the most modern car Ford had built— that's how far the company was behind the times in the 1940s."

Ford engineers were in high gear, introducing several innovations in 1950, such as the first overhead conveyor for carrying

demand for cars, which reduced demand for tires and rubber. Fordlandia ultimately racked up a $20 million aggregate loss through late 1945, when Henry Ford II sold it to the government of Brazil for $250,000. Synthetic rubber had now become common. Moreover, the plantation could never produce enough rubber to satisfy the company's needs.

"There wasn't enough rubber coming from Brazil in a year to keep the plant going one day," says author and Ford family friend Ford Bryan. "Most of the rubber had to be imported from the East Indies."

During World War II, Ford engineers concentrated on supplying the armaments and war matériel needed by the U.S.

CAR SHOWS

In the automobile industry, few things are more exciting than the Detroit Auto Show (now the North American International Auto Show), one of many similar car shows dotting the American landscape. Here is where the world's best designers and engineers introduce their latest creations to the admiring public, who gush and guffaw at the astonishing output. Each year there is sure to be a single car that captures the imagination with its radical styling, high-tech engine features, and breakthrough color scheme. Nowadays, alternative fuel vehicles using ethanol or electricity command notice, as do novel three-wheeled vehicles out of a Robert Heinlein sci-fi novel. Children and teenagers not yet old enough to drive will be found at the steering wheel of the "coolest" car on the floor, eyes ablaze in daydreams of driving, shrieking "Vroooooom!" and advising parents, "Someday I'm gonna drive that car."

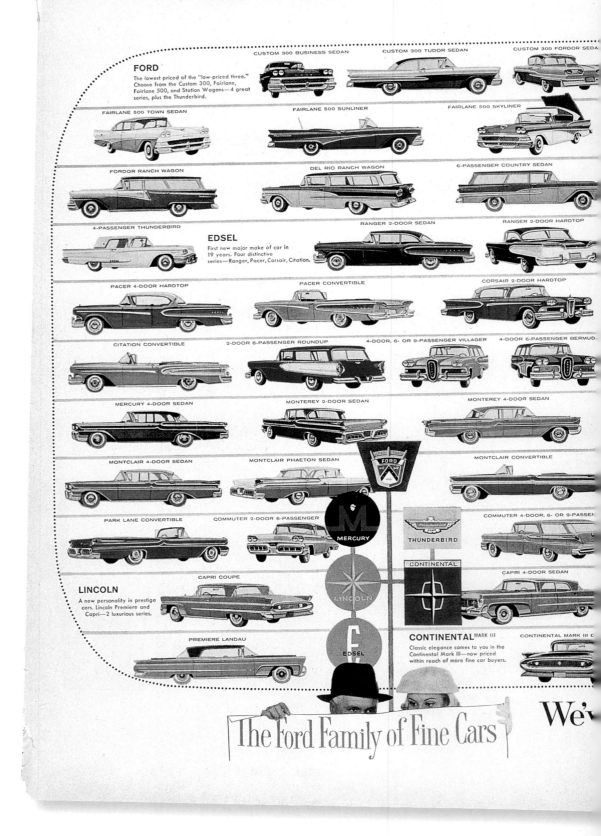

engines through the assembly process. The company's new advertising slogan extolled its initiatory role: "Ford's Out Front."

Ford's overhead conveyor marked a new direction in automobile assembly—the use of automation, the moving of a procession of parts in and out of machines without human intervention. Ford led the industry in automation research and applications. The company developed the first completely automated stamping presses and welding-machine lines for making body parts in 1950 and the first assembly plant robot in the United States, installed at the Kansas City assembly plant in 1958.

The 1950s were a period of startling discoveries and inventions. Ford debuted the industry's first torque converter automatic transmission with three-gear forward speeds (the smooth-performing Merc-O-Matic and Fordomatic), the first ball-joint front suspension in America, the first completely automated

FAIRLANE CLUB SEDAN | FAIRLANE TOWN SEDAN | FAIRLANE CLUB VICTORIA | FAIRLANE 500 CLUB SEDAN

FAIRLANE 500 CLUB VICTORIA | FAIRLANE 500 TOWN VICTORIA | RANCH WAGON

9-PASSENGER COUNTRY SEDAN | 9-PASSENGER COUNTRY SQUIRE | 4-PASSENGER THUNDERBIRD CONVERTIBLE

RANGER 4-DOOR SEDAN | RANGER 4-DOOR HARDTOP | PACER 2-DOOR HARDTOP | PACER 4-DOOR SEDAN

CORSAIR 4-DOOR HARDTOP | CITATION 2-DOOR HARDTOP | CITATION 4-DOOR HARDTOP

4-DOOR 9-PASSENGER BERMUDA

MERCURY
Performance Champion for 1958—available in 3 big series: Monterey, Montclair, Park Lane and the new low-priced Mercury.

MERCURY 2-DOOR SEDAN

MONTEREY PHAETON COUPE | MONTEREY PHAETON SEDAN | MONTEREY CONVERTIBLE | MONTCLAIR PHAETON COUPE

MONTCLAIR 2-DOOR TURNPIKE CRUISER | MONTCLAIR 4-DOOR TURNPIKE CRUISER | PARK LANE PHAETON COUPE | PARK LANE PHAETON SEDAN

VOYAGER 2-DOOR 6-PASSENGER | VOYAGER 4-DOOR, 6- OR 9-PASSENGER | COLONY PARK 4-DOOR, 9-PASSENGER

CAPRI LANDAU | PREMIERE COUPE | PREMIERE 4-DOOR SEDAN

CONTINENTAL MARK III 4-DOOR SEDAN | CONTINENTAL MARK III CONVERTIBLE | CONTINENTAL MARK III LANDAU

car for YOU
(at the price you have in mind)

Here they are—all the models of the Ford Motor Company. And every one is made of YOU ideas. Ideas that give you what you want at the price you have in mind. Go ahead. Choose the one for you, then drive it at your nearest dealer. Ford Motor Company, American Road, Dearborn, Michigan.

FORD FAMILY OF FINE CARS

The 1950s had a flair for fine ads (and alliteration), as this 1958 spread, left, demonstrates. Ford has a car for all tastes and wallets. There are Continentals, Mercurys, Thunderbirds, and Edsels; convertibles, station wagons, and sedans; even a car that seats nine passengers. Overseas lines were more limited, though still inventive. Above: The German Taunus.

steering, which company advertisements promised would "take the drive out of driving." Nor was Ford ingenuity confined to Dearborn: in England, Ford unveiled two new cars—the Consul and the Zephyr—in 1950.

For the fiftieth anniversary of the company in 1953, the voluminous Ford Archives were dedicated at Fair Lane, Henry and Clara Ford's former home. President Dwight D. Eisenhower christened the new Ford Research and Engineering Center via closed-circuit television from the White House.

cylinder block machining line, and the first full-flow oil filter built into the engine.

Not every brainchild was predicated on automobile performance. In 1953 and 1954, Ford installed four-way, power-operated front seats, power-lift windows, and "master-guide" power

The $50 million research center in Dearborn was a milestone in the history of the company's dedication to automotive science. It housed the most modern facilities at the time for practical automotive research and "pure research" in such fields as new materials and new power sources.

Winning World War II fostered an "anything is possible spirit," an insurmountable optimism that infused the designers in Ford's Styling Building, right. Below: Car interior stylist F. Beamish (left) discusses car designs with William Clay Ford.

The research center also accommodated a new Styling Building with twelve design studios. Cars had become status symbols and design was critical to public acceptance. Ford artists and engineers experimented to invent the cars of tomorrow, beginning their pilgrimage in the "Dream Room," an advanced styling studio where designers drew sketches of any kind of idea for a new car that happened to pop into their heads.

In the design studios at Ford, a magazine picture of a tropical fish might inspire a fender, or the nose of a jet fighter would spur a hood contour. Promising sketches were transferred into blueprints, engine specifications, and master body drafts to produce facsimiles—full-size and smaller-scaled clay and plastic models. From these, an original prototype automobile was developed, at a cost of $50,000.

To test the prototype's performance and durability, engineers battered it with hurricane-force winds, subjected it to subzero temperatures, and submerged it in water. Passing these tests, the experimental car was driven for thousands of miles on all manner of road, from the sand, mud, cobblestones, and steep grades of the Dearborn Proving Grounds to actual mountains, hot deserts, and snow-encrusted fields.

Assuming the prototype made the grade, it was displayed to the public at automobile shows. The final analysis was theirs.

Many futuristic Fords in the late 1950s and early 1960s started as sketches in the Styling Building: the sporty 1955 Thunderbird with its novel hood intake and pastel color scheme; the handsome 1954 Skyliner with the fashionable tinted glass sunroof; and the 1955 Lincoln Continental Mark II, in passionate hues and stunning horizontal lines.

STYLING FOR TOMORROW

In 1953, Ford completed a
new Styling Building,
which was well equipped
with the most modern
facilities for the creative
work performed by the
company's car designers,
below. The building

contained studios for the
styling of automotive trim
schemes, instrument panels,
and other interior
appointments, as well as
twelve separate studios in
which full-size clay models
were created for study before
final decisions were made on
the styling characteristics of
future models. Also in
1953, the company opened
a new Body Engineering
Building, where die models,
prototype bodies, and
assembly fixtures for cars
and trucks were developed
and tested for quality, left.
Designers and engineers
worked side-by-side drafting
the production drawings
required for each car and
truck line.

CONCEPT CARS

Ford's heralded concept cars of the 1950s and '60s combined bright or pastel hues with futuristic design. Even to the contemporary eye, the cars on these two pages are futuristic, with their radical shapes and features. But that's the point: car stylists must continually think ahead of their time. It may appear to the marketplace that automobiles change but subtly over time, yet stylists are constantly exercising their imaginations to create the next design breakthrough. Most ideas stay on the drafting table, some make it into clay models, and a few are actually built—like the cars featured here. And despite their five-decade age, these concept cars share something uniquely in common—the ability to startle viewers and produce what designers call simply the "Wow!" factor. ❖

WILLIAM CLAY FORD WITH A MODEL OF THE 1957 NUCLEON

1955 LA TOSCA

1959 LEVICAR MACH I

1962 SEATTLE-ITE XXI

1985 PROBE V

2001 JAGUAR F-TYPE

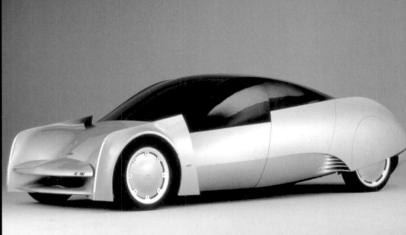

2010 SYNERGY ELECTRIC HYBRID

The latter would not have been possible were it not for Henry II's youngest brother, William Clay Ford. The Lincoln Continental had been abandoned in 1948 because of poor sales. William Clay Ford lobbied for its reintroduction and was given charge of the design. The car credited as one of the most stylish in automotive history was back, classy and swank as ever.

The Fords of the 1950s were cars that echoed the enthusiasm of the era. They were also the safest cars made by Ford up to that time, with padded dashboards, deep-dish steering wheels, optional safety belts, safety-lock doors, and swing-away mirrors.

Ford's Research and Engineering Center generated many new vehicles in the 1960s and '70s, like the Ford Econoline series, a van, pickup, and station wagon bus introduced in 1960. Ford actually was the first auto manufacturer to

build a mass-produced station wagon, in 1929. The company billed itself then as "America's Wagon Specialists."

New compact automobiles like the Ford Falcon and the Mercury Comet also made their debut, pushing Ford to the front of the industry in the nascent compact car market in the early 1960s. Despite their small size, the cars had ample interiors. "Honest-to-goodness six-passenger comfort . . . and all their luggage!" Ford advertisements extolled.

The "anything is possible" spirit was evident in a burst of innovations in the 1960s. To enhance safety, engineers introduced safety-belt warning lights and a power-window master lockout switch. Other safety features that became standard on many models were intermittent windshield wipers, front power sunroofs, and turn-signal-activated side-marker lamps.

Ford installed the industry's first stereo/tape entertainment system, high-back bucket seats, and "wall-to-wall," plush, deep-pile nylon carpeting in the 1960 Galaxie, "dyed to harmonize with the luxurious color-keyed interior," advertisements gushed, noting that the powerful automobile "is as hot as it is fine."

As baby boomers reached driving age in the mid-1960s, they sought cars with performance and pizzazz, characteristics they could not find in many Fords. The

RIDE 'EM COWBOY *Although the Ford Mustang was introduced in 1964 at the New York World's Fair, the car many consider a design icon actually predates that year. The original Mustang I was a 1962 concept car, left and bottom left (being built), and was named for the fighter aircraft of World War II—and not a bronco. The Mustang I made its debut at the U.S. Grand Prix in October 1962, where race car driver Dan Gurney revved it up to a speed of 120 mph. Below: A 1965 Mustang brochure.*

company's image had grown stuffy. To rev things up, Lee Iacocca, Ford division general manager in 1960, unveiled Total Performance, an engineering and marketing strategy aimed at this burgeoning demographic.

To conjure an image of speed and performance, Ford made a far-reaching assault on auto racing, ending the decade with victories and championships in virtually every major race and series in the world. In 1967, for example, a Ford GT40 became the first American car

piloted by American drivers to win the famed Le Mans road race in France.

The company then introduced a series of high-performance sports cars, beginning with the Mustang I. This 1962 car was an experimental vehicle created in secret as a successor to the two-seater Thunderbird, which had evolved into more of a luxury automobile. *Car and Driver* magazine called the Mustang I "the first true sports car to come out of Detroit." And the normally reserved *Sunday Times* in London praised it as "the most exciting vehicle of its class to have appeared for years."

Although the experimental car was not intended for production, it served as the basis for the historic 1964½ Mustang, the car that transformed Ford's image to a company with its finger on the pulse of a new generation.

"It was the first car designed specifically with the baby boomers in mind," says Casey. "Yet it was also a car for everyone, with huge appeal across the board. You could get it as an economy car with a six-cylinder engine and a standard transmission, a sports car with a high-performance engine, four-speed transmission and heavy-duty suspension, or you could dress it up as a luxury car. But no matter how you chose, the car was cool, emblematic of the mid-1960s in the way the Beatles were."

KEEP ON TRUCKING

Ford's famed F-Series truck line made its debut with the 1948 F-1 pickup truck. Ford's F-Series have been the best-selling trucks in America for over two decades. In 1953, Ford replaced the F-1 line with the F-100 line, and introduced a naming convention that signified the truck's curbside weight: F-100 for the half-ton trucks, F-250 for the three-quarter-ton trucks, and F-350 for the one-ton trucks. ❖ In 1984, the naming convention was tweaked again, knocking out the F-100 series in favor of a new F-150 line, which is still available today. The Ford F-Series has a strong history of trucks used for personal and commercial use, today ranging from the F-150 through the 33,000-pound F-750. ❖

FORD F-SERIES TRUCK IN THE 1997 BAJA 100

1953 F-8 BIG JOB

1955 F-100

1974 F-100 SUPERCAB

1991 F-150 XL 4X4 SPORT CABARNET

2001 F-150 SUPER CREW

2002 F-750 SUPER DUTY TRACTOR

The Mustang was performance personified, with a 108-inch wheelbase, a weight of 2,500 pounds, and, in the 289-cubic-inch V-8 version, more than 250 horsepower. It also had dazzling looks, with the widest selection of accessories ever offered on a Ford, including a Rally Pac with a tachometer and clock on the steering wheel and special wheel covers. Yet it sold for a base price of $2,368, when comparable sports cars sold for $3,000 and more.

The 1967 Cougar was Lincoln-Mercury's entrée in the Total Performance series, marketed as "America's first luxury/sports car at a popular price," thereby filling the void between the sporty fastback 1967 Mustang and the increasingly opulent Thunderbird. The Cougar sported a protuberant front grille with disappearing headlights that gave the impression of "pouncing," in keeping with the apt brand name. It also featured wraparound front and rear fenders and a memorable trio of taillight turn signals that flickered sequentially.

Ford leveraged the automobile's distinctive personality in a series of creative print and television advertisements—the "Sign of the

Cat" ad theme featuring a cougar perched on top of the automobile. Later TV commercials draped a purring Farrah Fawcett and her feline mane of blond hair on the car's roof. As a publicity stunt, Lincoln-Mercury even sent car writers a pound of "Cougar-burgers" (really raw ground beef). Overkill or not, Cougar won *Motor Trend* magazine's Car of the Year for 1967.

Another turning point that year was Ford's rise to first place in the North American retail sale of trucks, up from a 30.8 percent share in 1960 to 35 percent in 1967. The company offered 750 truck models in the medium and heavy classes alone in 1968, incorporating numerous engineering advances to improve durability and operational performance.

Ford's F-Series truck line, born in 1947, came to maturity in the 1960s. Many Ford light trucks and Econoline wagons and vans were built with twin I-beam suspension, introduced in 1965 to give rough-riding trucks more of a carlike ride. The Ford Ranchero pickup truck was upgraded to a top-of-the-line GT model with bucket seats, while the versatile Ford Bronco incorporated such enhancements as an optional swing-away spare-tire carrier. The F-Series trucks have been Ford's best-selling trucks in the U.S. market since 1981 and its best-selling vehicles of any kind since 1986.

Ford ingenuity also flowered overseas. The Escort, a new small car manufactured by Ford in Britain, was introduced to world

markets in early 1968. The new entry offered buyers "big car comfort and performance at a modest price" and was Ford's best-selling European car line until the introduction of the Fiesta minicar in 1976. When the 500,000th Fiesta was assembled the following year, it represented the "fastest first half-million" ever produced by a European carmaker. The first-year sales for the Fiesta also set a record.

In Latin America, Ford's subsidiaries posted more sales of cars and trucks in 1969 than in any prior year, up some 20 percent from 1968. Ford of Brazil added a car line to its truck manufacturing operations in early 1967, producing the new Brazilian Ford Galaxie, a car that would account for nearly 6 percent of all cars sold in the country that year.

Ford of Australia boomed, as factory sales of cars and trucks shot up 50 percent in 1967 alone, lifting Ford's market share from 18.8 percent to 20.7 percent. The Australian-built Falcon and Fairlane cars were particularly big sellers. In 1969, a new research center was opened at Broadmeadows, Australia, and a new assembly plant, equipped with the most modern machinery and tools, was completed in Saarlouis, Germany.

Ford Philippines burgeoned upon the 1972 introduction of the Fiera, a low-cost multipurpose vehicle designed to meet the transportation requirements of developing nations. The Fiera was based on a simple cab-and-chassis format, with components produced by local suppliers on a modest investment, using relatively simple manufacturing processes and tooling. This was a shrewd strategy since many emerging economies simply could not support full-scale automotive production.

Back home, Ford opened the industry's first Service Research Center in 1967 to provide more efficient and reliable vehicle repair. Among the electronic equipment used to diagnose service problems was an electronic "stethoscope" that compared the "heartbeat" of a "sick" engine with the vibration patterns of a "healthy" one.

Automotive safety efforts intensified in the late 1960s. Ford engineers created a new automobile frame in 1968 to give added protection to passengers in the event of a front-end collision. The frame featured S-shaped front side-rails that, in a severe frontal impact, absorbed much of the energy. Steel guardrails in side doors became standard on many models, as did the new computerized Sure-Track braking system, which inhibited rear wheel locking during a panic stop.

seat restraint system, copied by other carmakers. Other engineering breakthroughs included power-assisted rack-and-pinion steering, wiper-mounted windshield washer jets, and forged aluminum wheels.

During the 1970s, Ford scientists and engineers worked with their counterparts at eleven other U.S. automobile and oil companies to develop advanced emission control systems. Two systems, in particular, showed great promise: thermal reactors, special oversized engine manifolds that consumed exhaust emissions; and catalytic converters, containers of chemical compounds that transformed pollutants into harmless substances as they passed through the exhaust system. Ford scientists invented the monolithic catalytic converter in 1973. Today, that same catalytic converter remains the industry standard.

The company's creative imagination extended beyond its automotive operations. Ford Aerospace & Communications Corporation, which evolved out of the old Philco subsidiary, was awarded a $235 million contract to build seven INTELSAT V satellites for the ninety-five-nation International Telecommunications Satellite Organization in 1976. Many live television transmissions between continents, and many telephone calls, are relayed today by these geo-stationary satellites.

In the 1980s and 1990s, Ford research paced the industry in three increasingly important fields—alternative fuels, aerodynamics, and electronics. Since 1981,

Government regulations prompted many additional safety enhancements, such as improved windshield glass and energy-absorbing steering wheel columns. By 1970, these features and others combined to help reduce the death toll on U.S. highways for the first time since 1958, even though Americans drove 5 percent more miles.

Ford led the automotive industry in research on passive restraint devices, mandated by the National Highway Traffic Safety Administration for all occupants by 1975. The company's research culminated in the 1976 introduction of the continuous loop front-

VOLVO FOR SAFETY

Few if any automobile brands are more clearly associated with safety in the public consciousness than Volvo. The automobile line, which Ford purchased in 1999, was founded in Gothenburg, Sweden, in 1927. Over the years, it has built a strong following in Europe and the United States, where its station wagon model enjoyed near-cult status in the 1980s and 1990s—a car synonymous with the "thirty-something, upwardly mobile people" of the time. Volvo's reputation for high quality and safety continue to make it a favored brand, particularly among women, who account for 51 percent of its market, compared to 26 percent for Lincoln. Many Volvo drivers—male and female—rarely switch to another brand, explaining the brand's marketing maxim: "Volvo for Life."

Ford has maintained a fleet of experimental vehicles that operate on ethanol, methanol, compressed natural gas, propane, electricity, and selected combinations of fuels. Some of these saw commercial production, such as the 40,000 ethanol-fueled Fords sold in Brazil.

The company's research into aerodynamics guided the development of the first modern aerodynamic automobile, the Probe III, a strikingly dramatic experimental concept car that was displayed at the 1981 Frankfurt International Motor Show.

Ford's initial commercially available aerodynamic vehicle was the 1983 Thunderbird, followed by the breakthrough 1986 Taurus and the Sable cars. To educate the public about the radically rounded body design, Ford marketing conducted a road show on wind resistance and aerodynamics.

"It was the company's design experiments in aerodynamics that turned Ford around in the mid-'80s," says Michael Skinner, president of the Henry Ford Heritage Association. "They went out on a limb with the Taurus-Sable and didn't fall off."

Ford also invested research efforts into sophisticated new technologies like lasers, computers, and robotics. Electronic applications were designed for engine controls, driving operation, instrumentation, entertainment systems, and shock absorbers. Ford also continued the advances in metals casting that were the pride of the founder, using evaporative casting of aluminum manifolds at its Essex plant in Windsor, Ontario.

These new aluminum casting technologies conspired to make modern automobile engines so dauntingly complex that if Henry Ford popped the hood of a Ford in the 1990s, he'd be hard-pressed to tune the engine.

Henry would certainly applaud the company's modernization of the assembly line in 1985. Ford introduced modular assembly, a novel system whereby subassemblies or modules of a vehicle are produced on automated ancillary lines that then feed the main assembly line. The new system was put to the test with the production of the rear-wheel-drive Aerostar minivan at the St. Louis, Missouri, assembly plant in 1985. The trial run was a success, guiding use of modular assembly at most Ford plants today.

consumers (small engine and high fuel economy) with the desires of American buyers (larger engine and more optional equipment).

Finally, on March 5, 1993, with the introduction of the midsize Mondeo in Europe, Ford produced a viable world car. Eighteen months later, the Mondeo's North American counterparts, the Ford Contour and Mercury Mystique, made their debut.

On a global scale, Ford developed a far-reaching strategy to manufacture a "world car"—an automobile engineered on one continent using common components and the same basic platforms but built and sold throughout the world, thus making the most of costly engineering resources and development costs. The 1981 Ford Escort was the company's original world car, engineered by Mazda Motor Corporation in Japan and built by Ford in North America using mostly Japanese parts.

The plan backfired, however, when U.S. regulations mandated that the Escort would have to contain 75 percent U.S. parts. The endeavor also lacked an infrastructure within Ford to link North American and European efforts. Consequently, two different Escorts were produced. Despite nearly identical dimensions, the cars each featured a unique design, supply base, and manufacturing process.

Three years later, the 1989 Ford Probe stepped into the spotlight as Ford's next world car. The Probe was designed and manufactured by Ford, engineered by Mazda, and aimed at the sports car market in Asia, Europe, and North America. Unfortunately, this effort also foundered because of difficulties marrying the demands of European

The cars were truly a global effort: A 180-member team, including forty Ford engineers from England and Germany, moved to Kansas City to supervise the launch of the cars from the prototype stage through Job 1. The automatic transmissions were built at Ford's Batavia, Ohio, transmission plant, the steering components came from Ford's Indianapolis facility, and the four-cylinder Zetec engine was the product of Ford's European automotive operations.

"We learned that a single-platform team can develop a car that is essentially the same on both sides of the Atlantic," Ford's 1993 annual report declared.

Ford ceased production of the Mystique and Contour in the United States beginning in 2000, deferring to changing North American preferences for sport utility vehicles of all sizes over midsize sedans. However, a new kind of world vehicle was born with the debut of the 2000 Focus.

"The Focus was the first world car to capture large segments of the market in both Europe and America," says Casey. "The car was versatile, available as a hatchback, station wagon, or sedan, with enough variation to appeal to market niches on both sides of the Atlantic. It wasn't too small or too big, was well constructed, and also economical."

ON THE SIDE *After conducting extensive research into injuries caused by side-impact crashes, Ford announced plans to phase in a new kind of seat-mounted air bag protecting the head and chest in such collisions. Right: A 1996 Ford Taurus is side-impacted at the company's testing facility in Dearborn.*

Ford's focus on automobile safety sharpened in the 1980s with the building of the 1986 Ford Scorpio in Germany, the world's first volume production car to be equipped with anti-lock brakes as standard equipment. Like the Mondeo, the Scorpio won European Car of the Year, racking up an additional seventeen international honors.

Other Ford firsts in the 1980s and '90s included the first passenger-side air bags, and the first CFC (chlorofluorocarbon)-free air conditioner used in American vehicles. For luxury and comfort, Ford offered an electronic message center and keyless entry system in their luxury cars in 1980. The company's cars had come a long way from the notorious sideways shimmy of the Model T.

Ford also was the first U.S. carmaker to make dual air bags standard in some of its vehicles in 1993 and the first to provide voice-activated telematics systems on some of its models in 1996, comprising advanced security features like navigational assistance and hands-free cell phone use. It also developed specially

encoded SecuriLock keys that prevent an engine from being started, even by hot-wiring. John Dillinger and Clyde Barrow would need a different getaway car.

In researching alternative fuel vehicles, the company took another page from its past—the manufacturing of alternative fuel vehicles. Henry had designed a Fordson tractor that would burn alcohol as well as fossil fuel but never manufactured it because of high distillation costs. In 1913, he successfully built an alternative fuel vehicle, an electric automobile. He also met with Thomas Edison to discuss using the inventor's electric batteries in a line of electric cars that would be called the "Edison-Ford." Henry invested $1.5 million in the venture, which never blossomed.

"They couldn't run the car at all with the Edison battery," said engineer E. J. Farkas in his reminiscences. "So they finally had to put in lead batteries which were twice as heavy. It was finally abandoned."

"Henry was close to buying 100,000 Edison batteries for the experimental vehicle," says Werling, "but, when he realized an electric vehicle could not be competitive with gasoline-powered automobiles, he had to turn down the offer. This must have been a disappointment for Henry, given his and Edison's burgeoning friendship."

Electric power figured into the research and development being done by Ford in the late twentieth century. Several electric car prototypes, such as the Comuta vehicle manufactured by Ford of Britain and Ford U.S. in 1967, paved the way for full commercial development in the 1990s. In 1996, the company brought to market the first zero-emission electric vehicle to be developed for

FORD'S ALTERNATIVE FUEL SOURCE

From 1932 to 1942 Ford Motor Company produced its own brand of alternative fuel—Benzol. During the Depression, Henry Ford looked for ways to not only recycle the waste created by the Ford factories but to also relieve the burden on the average

worker at his plants. This resulted in Ford's mixing one part light oil, a by-product from the coal in coke ovens, and three parts gasoline to form a fuel to run automobiles. Though extremely popular, Ford Benzol was never made available beyond the

Detroit area. Ford discontinued all fuel production with the start of World War II when the light oil by-product stopped being formed because of the halt in civilian car manufacturing.

sale by an auto manufacturer, an electric-powered version of the Ford Ranger, the best-selling pickup in its class.

Today, Ford sells the widest variety of alternative fuel vehicles in the world. They run the gamut, from a natural gas–powered Econoline van to a flexible fuel (gasoline and methanol) Taurus. The company also markets dedicated natural gas vehicles, such as the more than 150 Crown Victoria cabs used by New York City's taxi fleet.

In foreign markets, Ford offers a natural gas–powered Fiesta in Europe, an electric Ranger pickup truck in Canada, and bi-fuel Falcons and Fairmonts in Australia that accelerate by burning gasoline or liquefied petroleum gas. Ford also launched a new enterprise, TH!NK, to develop one- and two-passenger, plastic-body, electric-powered vehicles. In 2000, the first of these environmentally friendly small cars and bicycles came rolling off the assembly line in Norway.

More than 90 percent of the alternative fuel vehicles sold in the world today are Fords. In 1998, the company secured a $206.5 million contract to manufacture ten thousand alternative fuel vehicles for the U.S. Postal Service. And it recently raised the curtain on a hybrid-electric vehicle, the 2005 Ford Escape, the first such sport utility vehicle in the world. These vehicles are designed to be durable, and reliable, with as close to zero emissions as possible. What seemed impossible for Henry Ford and Thomas Edison was possible after all.

Ford also leads the industry in the use of recycled materials in its automobiles. The Ford Focus is made with an array of recycled materials—recycled denim jeans to deaden sound, recycled plastic bottles in the heater body, and recycled carpeting in the fan module. The Focus has an 85 percent "recyclability potential" by weight, meaning that much of the car itself can be easily recycled.

Ford also rejuvenated its approach to automobile styling, when J Mays, among the most imaginative car designers in the world, joined Ford as vice president of design in 1997. Mays is responsible for the styling of all Ford cars and vehicles, as well as those produced under the brands Mazda, Lincoln, and Mercury. Before Ford tagged him to revitalize its design aesthetic, Mays had captured worldwide notice for his snappy Volkswagen Beetle, a car that took the curves of the famed "bug" and reimagined them for a new generation. His dazzling automobiles arrest one's attention and tug at the emotions. Even the "seen it all" spectators at the 1999 North American International Auto Show were staggered by his eye-catching concept for the new Ford Thunderbird, an automobile that evokes an era when cars were more than modes of transport—they were a form of art. Edsel Ford and E. T. Gregorie would understand.

*Designer J Mays is the
design brains behind the
Ford Thunderbird, Motor
Trend magazine's 2002
Car of the Year. Mays has
a profound attachment to
the designs of the past,
particularly the spirited
cars of the 1950s.
Opposite: Chief designer
in Ford's Living Legends
Studio, Camilo Pardo
works on a drawing of the
GT40 concept.*

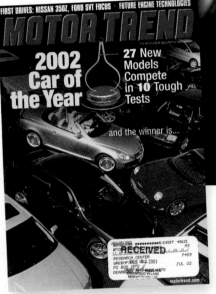

As the Information Age beckoned at the end of the twentieth century, Ford engaged a new marketplace—the online world. A medley of Web sites, including Ford.com, Volvo.com, Jaguar.com, and so on, each hyperlinked to the others, was created. And a new company formed with Ford dealers to bring direct online sales to customers made its auspicious debut—FordDirect.com.

Ford and its two primary competitors, General Motors and DaimlerChrysler, joined forces at the front lines of the B2B (business-to-business) revolution, creating the world's largest virtual marketplace, Covisint. Today, billions of dollars in transactions routinely travel on this Internet-enabled global exchange, electronically connecting Ford with the universe of suppliers that feed parts and components to its assembly plants.

Some suppliers have been with the company since its beginnings, a heritage that runs deep. Many provide added services, including design expertise, enhanced customer service, and value chain management, a network-based system for managing supplier inventory that offers a level of teamwork that did not exist a generation ago.

At the dawn of the new millennium, the ingenuity and innovation behind the creation of automobiles remained as it was a century ago, a collaborative effort spanning continents. There is but one difference—the active participation of the consumer in the process.

This consumer-oriented strategy harks back to the "purposeful inventions" of Henry Ford—the formulation of ingenious methods of manufacturing to create products that the public truly needs and wants. Ford's startling originality these last hundred years was predicated upon that promise. As Henry David Thoreau wrote: "This world is but a canvas to our imaginations."

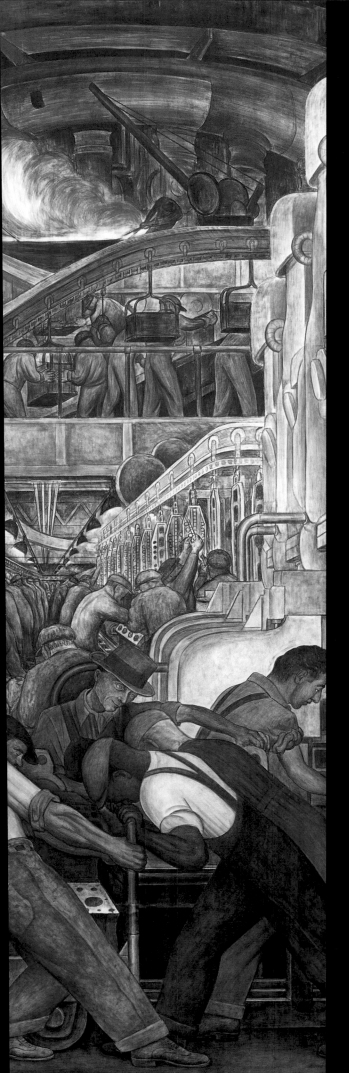

4

CHAPTER FOUR

CITIZEN O[...]
THE WORL[...]

"People are the common deno[...]
progress. So . . . no improvement i[...]
unimproved people, and advance is [...]
people are liberated and educated [...]
wrong to dismiss the importanc[...]
railroads, power plants, mills, an[...]
familiar furniture of economic dev[...]
But we are coming to realize . . . [...]
certain sterility in economic mon[...]
stand alone in a sea of illite[...]

—JOHN KENNETH GALBRAITH

❖

Henry Ford's profound impact on industry a[...]
was captured in Diego Rivera's masterpiece Detroit[...]
left, on display at Detroit Institute of Arts. Ford[...]
of the assembly line and mass manufacturing[...]
captivated the Mexican muralist, who, though a[...]
had deep interest in the capitalist syst[...]

RESPONSIBILITY *From concern for employees to keeping an eye on the environment as well as the bottom line, Ford Motor Company has attempted to be a good corporate citizen. Opposite: Postwar rationing of gasoline made fuel-efficient Fords an attractive commodity in Britain.*

Most companies are founded solely for profit purposes, capitalizing on an opportunity in a market to charge high prices and reap a windfall. Very few companies, however, originate to serve the betterment of mankind. When Henry Ford founded Ford Motor Company on June 16, 1903, he wanted to make the average person's life fuller, easier, and happier by selling affordable automobiles, tractors, and trucks—despite the objections of his more profit-minded partners.

"Purpose first, then profit" was Henry's maxim. This moral code is deeply ingrained in the business ethic at Ford, a company cognizant of its unique position to effect positive change for society. The roots go back to Henry's determination to put personal mobility and good pay within the reach of the masses. His success at achieving that vision is perhaps his greatest contribution to society. In the process, he created a vast global enterprise and generated, directly and indirectly, enormous wealth for millions of people. Ford Motor Company's efforts on behalf of education, human rights, and environmental conservation are evident throughout its history.

This enduring creed of corporate citizenship was conceived on an American farm in the nineteenth century. Henry knew from firsthand experience that farming was backbreaking, toilsome work and that machinery could ease its burdens.

LAND OF OUR FATHERS *Born and bred on a farm, Henry knew the rigors of the field. "It is no wonder that, doing everything slowly and by hand, the average farmer has not been able to earn more than a bare living while farm products are never as plentiful and cheap as they ought to be," he wrote. With his "automobile plow," he sought to make the farmer's work less toilsome. Right: Henry sowing seeds on his farm. Below: A Ford tractor radiator plate marking the golden anniversary of Ford.*

"I have followed many a weary mile behind a plough, and I know all the drudgery of it," he once said. "What a waste it is for a human being to spend hours and days behind a slowly moving team of horses when in the same time a tractor could do six times the work!"

Years before he founded Ford Motor Company or even built his first automotive buggy, Henry had constructed a steam-powered "farm locomotive"—a crude tractor built in 1882 from an old mowing machine, using a small foot-powered lathe. His chief objective was to build a machine capable of assisting the average farmer—the family man in the field from sunup to sundown. "The manufacturing of a big tractor, which only a few wealthy farmers could buy, did not seem to me worthwhile," he explained.

"Henry always wanted to relieve the travail of farming," says archivist Terry Hoover. "All his life he believed that hard work could be mechanized in some way so that horsepower could replace manpower. He had an altruistic sense of his own purpose. More pecuniary objectives were secondary."

Ford's first gasoline-powered farming vehicle was his experimental "automobile plow," built in 1906. The tractor utilized an engine from Ford's Model B automobile. A later version, in 1907, used the engine from Ford's best-selling Model N, the precursor to the Model T. Basically, Henry pursued the same course with the tractor that he sought with the automobile—the making of affordable, utilitarian vehicles.

"The only kind of tractor that I thought worth working on was one that would be light, strong, and so simple that anyone could run it," Henry said. "Also it had to be so cheap that anyone could buy it."

Henry concocted a versatile tractor that could be used either as a stationary engine or hitched to some type of machinery to perform a multitude of arduous farming tasks—plowing, cultivating, reaping, milling, threshing, and so on. It would pull stumps, plow snow, haul and saw wood, and perform even non-farming assignments. When Detroit's printing shops were shut down by a coal shortage, Henry printed the *Dearborn Independent* by hitching a tractor to the printing presses.

His first commercially produced tractor was the Fordson, manufactured by another company, Henry Ford & Son, Inc. When Henry's backers at Ford Motor Company did not approve of his plans to make inexpensive tractors, he simply formed another business concern to manufacture them.

The new company operated strictly in an experimental capacity until

HENRY FORD & SON *When Henry's original backers balked at the sale of tractors, he formed another company to manufacture them. Like the Model T, the Fordson tractor, in assembly at left, was rugged, dependable, and inexpensive. Henry wrote:* "It had to be so cheap that any one could buy it." *Above. This 1920 postcard cartoon sums up Henry's creativity. Below: An original (repainted) Fordson tractor sales sign. Overleaf: The Fordson's cousin, a 1916 Model T touring car.*

the advent of World War I. A shortage of manpower and the sinking by German submarines of freighters carrying food to England caused famine conditions. The country desperately needed tractors to till, sow, and harvest the land. As Henry recalled, "There were not enough draft animals in all England to plough and cultivate the land to raise crops in sufficient volume to make even a dent in the food imports."

At the request of the British government, Charles Sorensen delivered two experimental Fordson tractors to England. The country ultimately bought more than six thousand, at $750 each. Ford refused to accept a profit on the sale. "It was these tractors, run mostly by women, that ploughed up the old estates and golf courses and let all England be planted and cultivated," Henry beamed.

Henry Ford & Son, Inc. was absorbed into Ford Motor Company in 1919, following Henry's purchase of his fellow stockholders' shares. The distinctive blue tractor that helped Britain ward off famine soon appeared in dealers' showrooms and in the fields of America to do a hundred jobs a team of horses could not.

The four-cylinder Ford tractor, as it now was called, was dispatched to farmers worldwide. In 1922, more than 750 were sent to France and more than 1,000 to Argentina, Brazil, and Uruguay. Ford tractors built roads in Colombia, towed sugar cane in the Philippines, and cultivated farms in Norway and New Zealand. The tractor's price, like the price of the Model T, kept falling—from $790 in 1920 to $395 in 1922.

Henry had fulfilled his ambition to "lift farm drudgery off flesh and blood and lay it on steel and motors." He was the farmer's friend, regarded not as a rich man with a hobby but as someone sincere in his efforts to ease their toil. "Within a few years a farm depending solely on horse and hand power will be as much of a curiosity as a factory run by a treadmill," he predicted.

Henry was right about the tractor. But it was not the greatest innovation to affect America. That honor belonged to the Model T. At the time of its introduction in 1908, more than half the people of the United States lived on 6 million farms or in towns of fewer than 2,500 inhabitants. There were 200,000 automobiles in the country, but less than 2 percent of farm families owned a car.

Chimney Rock

FREEDOM FOR ALL *The Model T brought mobility to the average family. The advertisement, right,* *underscores this change. Above: A Model T at Chimney Rock in 1910.*

The Model T arrived at a propitious time to meet their needs. Average people used to horses made an easy transition to this motorized form of transport. "It homogenized the nation, tearing down cultural and physical barriers," says Henry Ford historian Donn Werling.

"For the rural public," Werling continues, "the Model T was a once-in-a-lifetime experience. Their labors eased and they could suddenly and quite easily travel well beyond their small spheres. In a very real sense, the Model T represented a social revolution. It liberated women who, generally speaking, weren't physically capable of handling the rigors of horse and buggy. That was something their fathers or husbands typically did."

The Model T also empowered a fuller life. With new leisure time, people began to take motor trips. As a system of roads developed in the 1920s, the country unfolded just beyond the windshield: Yellowstone National Park, the coast of Maine, the shores of the Pacific, the prairies of Kansas, the palms of Florida all became accessible in a way that was not possible before.

In bringing the farmer to the city and enabling the city dweller to enjoy the country, the Model T produced another change. The two migrations met head-on to create that bastion of modern living—the suburb.

Henry continually pared the price of the car so everyone could, in effect, have one. But to create an affordable automobile, Ford required greater worker productivity. Henry achieved this

OPENING   THE   HIGH-

Back of all the activities of the Ford Motor Company is this Universal idea—a wholehearted belief that riding on the people's highway should be within easy reach of all the people.

An organization, to render any service so widely useful, must be large in scope as well as great in purpose. To conquer the high cost of motoring and to stabilize the factors of production—this is a great purpose. Naturally it requires a large program to carry it out.

It is this thought that has been the stimulus and inspiration to the Ford organization's growth; that has been the incentive in developing inexhaustible resources, boundless facilities and an industrial organization which is the greatest the world has ever known.

In accomplishing its aims the Ford institution has never been daunted by the size or difficulty of any task. It has spared no toil in finding the way of doing each task best. It has dared to try out the untried—with conspicuous success.

objective through a combination of mass production techniques and higher wages.

Times were desperate in 1914—the average day's pay in all U.S. industry was $1.75 and many industries were in recession. In 1913, when the company attempted to offer Christmas bonuses to

WITHIN REACH *Prior to the introduction of the Model T, average Americans found it difficult if not impossible to own an automobile. As this paperwork for the purchase of a Model T Tudor Sedan indicates, a down payment of only $193 was all it took to get one's hands on the wheel of a car, within reach of the average pocketbook.*

Hence, Henry's radical decision was to double wages to $5 a day. For years Henry had figured out sums and sketched engines on wood shingles that he had picked up in the shop. Now there was a big improvement—a large blackboard. On it, Henry wrote the automobile industry wage standard, $2.34 for a nine-hour day. Observers recall he then tossed down the chalk and demanded, "Figure out how much more we can give our men."

The executives worked all day, cautiously adding twenty-five cents an hour, and then another twenty-five cents. Every so often Henry walked back in, barked, "Not enough," and walked out. Finally, one man snapped, "Why don't you just make it $5 a day for eight hours work and bust the company?" "Fine," said Henry. "We'll do that."

workers with more than three year's duty, only 640 of 14,000 workers at Ford qualified—the turnover was constant. Henry reasoned higher-paid employees would work harder to retain their jobs and, thus, create more and better automobiles that they could then afford. "If you cut wages, you just cut the number of your customers," he explained.

Whether or not this exchange was apocryphal—there are several accounts of the birth of this great idea—there is no doubt that Henry Ford was its most important champion. The news hit like a thunderbolt. Many newspaper editors thought Henry had undermined the foundations of capitalism and would certainly sink Ford. The *Wall*

THE FORDS *After Henry doubled the average wage for automotive workers, job seekers descended upon Ford Motor Company. Those working for Henry and Edsel at Highland Park, shown in a stereoscope card at right, wore badges like the one below and when asked what they did for a living would say simply, "I work for the Fords." Below right: Unskilled young men and boys attend the Henry Ford Trade School at the Rouge plant in 1938.*

Street Journal scoffed, "Economic blunders if not crimes." Cartoonists had a field day, depicting factory sweepers in fur coats and cigars, descending majestically from chauffeur-driven limousines to pick up their brooms.

Ford employees, however, felt fortunate to be working for "the Fords," the familial name they gave the company. On Friday nights, many workers would wear their company badges on their best suits, as they and their wives or girlfriends danced the night away in downtown Detroit. Families were proud to have a "Ford man" as the breadwinner.

"If you expect a man to give his time and energy, fix his wages so that he will have no financial worries," Henry said. "There's something sacred about wages—they represent homes and families and domestic destinies."

Henry later considered the $5 workday the finest cost-cutting move he ever made. In 1914, when the $5 workday began, the company had been hiring 53,000 people a year just to maintain a constant workforce of 14,000 employees. After doubling wages, Ford hired only 6,508 men in 1915. By enhancing worker productivity through higher wages, Henry had proved that management could afford to cut prices while making a better product. The beneficiary of his wisdom was the general public, able at last to afford the cost of an automobile.

"Ford succeeded in showing that industrial production can be production for the masses—instead of production for the benefit of the monopolist or banker," wrote economist Peter F. Drucker. "Indeed, he showed that the most profitable production is production for the masses."

Ford would do more for its workers than provide a living wage. Henry made the Highland Park and Rouge facilities the safest, cleanest, most modern and well-lighted plants on the planet. State-of-the-art ventilators and dust-collecting apparatus cleaned the air, first-aid stations were located throughout, and constant improvements were made to reduce worker injuries.

Henry had a profound interest in the social welfare of his workers and their families. Many employees were immigrants unschooled in American customs, language, and values. Henry formed an English school in 1914 for foreign-born employees and a trade school in 1916 for poorer boys who wanted a technical education.

When enrollment at the trade school stood at four hundred with a waiting list of six thousand in 1920, Henry told the school principal, "Reverse those figures. Let four hundred wait." The school began admitting four hundred students a month, thousands graduating into promising careers in the auto industry. Detroit newspapers often

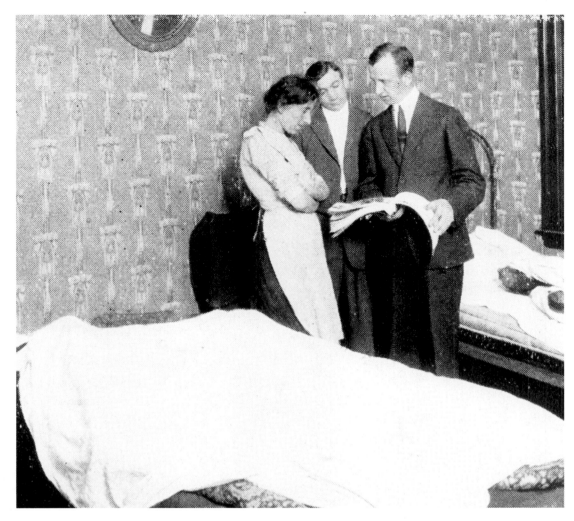

HELPING HANDS *Ford's Sociological Department was guided by Henry's belief that a "man and his home had to come up to certain standards of cleanliness and citizenship," as he wrote in his autobiography. Ford gave employees financial incentives to live up to these ideals, which were assessed by the department's fifty employees, one of whom is pictured at left. Below: A report card and school badge from the Ford Trade School.*

carried want ads seeking "Expert Mechanics—Graduates of Henry Ford Trade School Preferred."

For someone with an elementary education, Henry was exceptionally devoted to scholarship. He gave both his time and money to the Berry Schools, founded by Martha Berry in 1902 to teach indigent boys and girls, and had a passion for the six McGuffey Eclectic Readers used in the grade schools of his youth. Ultimately, he accumulated a collection of the primers second only to that of the University of Virginia, where the author of the reader had taught.

A favorite pastime was to test his memory with a fellow McGuffey collector. Henry would recite a line, then the other person would follow with the next line, and so on, until one of them was stumped.

Some of Henry Ford's programs have been criticized for being patronizing. To enhance the quality of life for employees, Henry created the Ford Sociological Department, hiring fifty employees whose mission was "to extend help and protection, not charity." Each worker was provided a Model T to travel to employees' homes to observe their health practices, living conditions, and diet and whether or not they were saving money, improving their hygiene, and resisting the temptations of alcohol and tobacco. The employees who passed the grade—investing their wages to maintain healthful living conditions for themselves and their families—would qualify for the top $5-a-day wage.

The Sociological Department also furnished emergency loans, helped workers obtain low-cost mortgages, and arranged free dental examinations. After workers' compensation laws were passed in the late 1910s, Henry instructed that the department care for injured employees according to their needs, even if that meant giving them more financial assistance than required by the new laws.

Although the Sociological Department was disparaged for infringing upon people's privacy, Ford was one of the few companies in America with an enlightened labor policy of any kind in the 1910s and early '20s. Industrial welfare activities at most companies were little more than an annual gift of a turkey on Thanksgiving and a free picnic in the summer.

"When my father worked at the Highland Park plant in 1917, the Sociological Department investigators came to the house to check up on how my folks were doing," Ford historian Ford Bryan recalls. "If there was a medical or legal problem, they wanted to know about it, if for no other reason than to help out. They didn't mean to bother people; they always meant to help them. Maybe I'm biased, but that's how my folks always saw it."

"With one foot on the land and one in industry, America is safe."
— HENRY FORD

FACTORY IN A MEADOW

FORD MOTOR COMPANY

FORD'S VILLAGE INDUSTRIES: RURAL AND URBAN AMERICA COMBINE

Henry Ford always said he never liked the livelihood of his forebears, and as a boy he would do virtually anything to get out of his chores. But after Henry turned the American economy upside down with his assembly line approach to building automobiles, offering high wages for the work involved, he felt deep responsibility for the procession of young men who fled the homestead for the city. To give something back to the communities he'd grown up in, he unveiled his Village Industries program.

The idea was profound—building small factories to make parts and other components for Ford vehicles and utilizing hardworking craftsmen from area farms as the labor supply and hydroelectric river power as the energy source. As Henry explained his decision, "With one foot in industry and one foot in agriculture, America is safe."

Since farming traditionally is a spring to autumn endeavor, the work provided by the program would augment and stabilize the income flow during winter doldrums. "Henry

ANKIN-MILLS.

other states, all of them on the banks of rivers and many, in fact, on the sites of abandoned gristmills, which had used river power to move their waterwheels.

Each plant employed about one hundred workers, although some, such as the Green Island, New York, plant on the Hudson River, offered employment to close to a thousand. Plants made copper welding rods, lamp assemblies, wheels, and even parts for tractors. A few, such as the Saline Village Industries plant in Saline, Michigan, were involved in another of Henry's interests—soybeans—using the plant's gristmills to process the beans into solvents for automobile paints and plastics.

"If you go to any of these communities today, from the upper peninsula of Georgia to the Hudson Valley of New York, and ask people about the Village Industries, they will tell you they regard Henry Ford as a hero," says Donn Werling. "Their forefathers recognized that what he was trying to do represented progress of a scale not seen previously in these small rural communities. He offered them paradise—now lost." ❖

wanted to bring the factory to the countryside, because he felt some guilt for having caused the exodus to the cities," says Bryan, who has written extensively on Henry's Village Industries and other company subjects.

Henry had long propounded the virtues of clean hydroelectric power. His and Clara's home at Fair Lane received its electricity from their nearby powerhouse on the banks of the Rouge River, dedicated by his friend Thomas Alva Edison in October

1914. An eight-foot dam on the river powered twin 55-kilowatt generators that continue to function today.

The first Village Industries site (also on the banks of the Rouge) was a small plant built in 1919–20, in Northville, Michigan. An old gristmill stood on the site, and it was reconfigured into a factory to manufacture valves for Ford automobile engines. Over the next twenty years, more than thirty Village Industries plants sprouted throughout Michigan, Ohio, Mississippi, New York, and

Henry set up a subsidiary to build affordable houses for workers. At a time when employee health plans were unheard of, he built and supported the Henry Ford Hospital in Detroit, which offered inexpensive medical care and clinical treatment and was the first general hospital in the United States to treat psychiatric patients.

Certainly, Ford was unlike any other company in America in terms of its labor policies. The workforce was a veritable cross-section of society, spanning employees from diverse cultures, creeds, and colors, as well as a large number of disabled individuals. One in four Ford employees had a physical handicap of some kind in 1930, a time when many employers didn't even consider these individuals for jobs.

Ford believed otherwise. "There are hundreds of [occupations] which a handicapped man can fill to the utmost satisfaction," company literature stated in 1930. "No man is discriminated against because of his age or physical condition, unless he has a contagious disease. [And] no man is ever discharged from Ford employ merely because he is physically unable to do his work. Instead, a new job, where he can acquit himself satisfactorily, is found."

Each disabled person received the exact same pay as able-bodied employees. Henry also hired hundreds of ex-convicts as workers, believing an honest day's work and pay would curb recidivism, for the good of society.

Ford's enlightened policies went well beyond employee welfare. The company was an early advocate of materials recycling, reusing shipping crates or turning them into running boards and the sides of "Woodie" wagons. It was against plant rules to open crates with a crowbar, which would damage their integrity for further use.

Ford also turned sawdust and scraps from the factory floor into fuel for its own needs or into charcoal briquettes that were sold commercially. Workers were directed to saw logs into parallel planks instead of "squaring" them, thereby producing 35 percent more usable wood. By Henry's count, 100 million feet of wood was salvaged each year by the company's conservation strategies.

Henry preferred harnessing nature as an energy source and used zero-emission hydroelectric energy to power dozens of Village Industries.

IDEALISM, OR PATERNALISM?

Few employers of his day and age were as involved in the lives of their employees, or had such strong opinions about the importance of work in one's life, as Henry Ford. "The natural thing to do is to work—to recognize that prosperity and happiness can be obtained only through honest effort," he said. "Human ills flow largely from attempting to escape from this natural course." To implement his views, Henry effected rules and activities at Ford that were unique—and criticized. Henry was labeled an "ignorant idealist," someone whose heart was in the right place but whose tactics were controversial. Some programs he instituted, like the Sociological Department, were called invasive and paternalistic. Others would certainly raise eyebrows today. At left is a photo of the graduation ceremony at Ford's English School. Students would enter a "Melting Pot" in the traditional garb of their country of origin and exit in American clothing.

Menu

OF

Dinner Served at Ford Exhibit

CENTURY OF PROGRESS

August 17, 1934

TOMATO JUICE SEASONED WITH SOY BEAN SAUCE

SALTED SOY BEANS — CELERY STUFFED WITH SOY BEAN CHEESE

PUREE OF SOY BEAN — SOY BEAN CRACKER

SOY BEAN CROQUETTES WITH TOMATO SAUCE

BUTTERED GREEN SOY BEANS

PINEAPPLE RING WITH SOY BEAN CHEESE AND SOY BEAN DRESSING

SOY BEAN BREAD WITH SOY BEAN RELISH

SOY BEAN BISCUIT WITH SOY BEAN BUTTER

APPLE PIE (SOY BEAN CRUST)

COCOA WITH SOY BEAN MILK — SOY BEAN COFFEE

ASSORTED SOY BEAN COOKIES — SOY BEAN CAKES

ASSORTED SOY BEAN CANDY

Henry further promoted manufacturing processes using nontoxic natural materials like wheat and soybeans. Coil cases on the Model T were partially made from wheat gluten, and the oil extracted from soybeans was refined to make enamel for paints and fluid for shock absorbers. What was left from this process (the meal) was molded into plastic horn buttons, gear shift balls, distributor cases, and window-trim strips. Ford scientists later developed a fiber from soybean protein for use in making fabric for car seats.

"I foresee the time when industry shall no longer denude the forest, nor use up the mines, but shall draw its material from the annual produce of the field," Henry said. "The part that has food value will be separated and made into a perfect food for man, and the rest of the plant will find its use in industry."

In 1941, the Rouge plant processed some 1,600 bushels of soybeans a day. Company engineers invented, designed, and built four giant "flakers" that year to grind 4,800 pounds of beans an hour, the first stage in the oil extraction process. More than two bushels of soybeans went into each Ford automobile in the 1940s.

While one couldn't actually eat Ford cars, one could digest Ford Soy Milk, the first commercially viable soy milk. Other soy milk products were on the market in the 1940s, but most people disliked the flavor, which was nothing like cow's milk. Ford scientists had a better idea. Instead of grinding soybeans to make the milk, they dissolved the protein out of the soybean, then purified it. After drinking the soy milk, Henry wrote a note: "First good milk. No [more need for the] cow."

Henry eventually did for soybeans what his friend, the eminent scientist Dr. George Washington Carver, did for the peanut. The company even developed an all-vegetable whipping cream derived from Ford soy milk, called Presto Whip. Bill Ford recalls that his father, William Clay Ford, often ate at Fair Lane and was confounded by the variety of soy products.

"Virtually the whole meal would be made from soybeans," Bill said. "Henry thought it was great. I'm not sure my father thought it was so wonderful."

A laboratory dedicated to Carver was established in the abandoned Dearborn waterworks, and was named the Nutritional Laboratory of the Ford Motor Company. The fact that Carver was African American didn't seem to diminish Henry's appreciation, which made Henry rather unique for his time. "All Ford plants in America were completely integrated," says Bryan. "The plants didn't pay any attention to color or nationality."

THE PEACE SHIP *Henry hoped to stop World War I by sailing to Europe and promoting a "continuous mediation committee." The Oscar II, "the Peace Ship," sets off in 1915, left. Above: A Peace Flag from 1918. Today's United Nations embodies the "continuous mediation committee" Henry sought. Opposite: African American workers at Ford during World War II.*

The founder had earned his employees' respect and the admiration of many other African Americans. One time Henry offered his hand to a black farmer to shake in introduction, but the farmer declined it because his hands were dirty. "Henry bent down and picked up a handful of dirt, rubbed it together in his palms, and proffered his hand again," Werling says. "This time, the other man shook it. And he never forgot the gesture."

After Henry's death, *The Journal of Negro History* wrote that he "had endeavored to help humanity by offering men work at living wages and making it comfortable for them in his employment. In this respect he was a great benefactor of the Negro race, probably the greatest that ever lived."

Today, we expect such forthrightness in our business leaders, but in Henry's day most businessmen kept their opinions to themselves. Henry, of course, was as blunt as a ball peen hammer when it came to expressing his views, even if those opinions went against the grain.

"Mr. Ford felt the colored people were oppressed," engineer Emil Zoerlein said in his reminiscences. "He felt they should be helped and educated. It was part of his feeling for them that led him to the various things he did do around here for them."

Another example of Henry's doing what he felt was right, irrespective of the impact on company profits, was his opposition to the war in Europe. When World War I broke out in August 1914, Henry vehemently denounced it, insisting he would close his factories before he would contribute one cent to the war effort. James Couzens, Ford's business manager, was perturbed that Henry's pronounced view would hurt sales. Couzens finally quit after Henry refused to throw out an antiwar article scheduled for publication in *Ford Times*.

"Henry sincerely believed that war was morally wrong and World War I would be the war to lose all wars," says Werling. "So he set out to stop it."

In 1915, Henry chartered the *Oscar II*, the Peace Ship, which would sail to Europe with Henry and other like-minded individuals on board to preach an end to the war. Their specific goal was to create a "continuous mediation committee" to hasten the peace process. "I believed . . . that some of the nations were anxious for peace and would welcome a demonstration for peace," Henry later said.

Fifteen thousand people lined the docks in New York City as the Peace Ship and its delegates set sail for Norway, navigating submarine-infested waters. Newspapers all around the world covered the journey, many

GEORGE WASHINGTON CARVER

The distinguished African American chemist and botanist Dr. George Washington Carver

became Henry's close friend following the death of Thomas Edison in 1931. The two men shared the same lofty principles of easing the plight of the American farmer and the rural poor, yet they came from radically different backgrounds. Carver was born into a slave family in Missouri, in about 1861. He later earned his M.A.—difficult since many colleges rejected the

application of the brilliant student. In 1896, Booker T. Washington invited him to come to Tuskegee Institute in Alabama, where Carver would teach and work for the next forty-seven years. He conducted many experiments to find new uses for a wide range of crops, most notably the peanut. This research is credited with inspiring an agricultural revolution in the South. Henry and Carver

often walked together in the fields of Henry's farm, discussing agriculture and each other's research and, afterwards, sampling a variety of culinary fare, such as dandelion sandwiches. Henry was so impressed by his friend's work that he dedicated a laboratory in Dearborn to the scientist.

crediting the sincerity of the "peace pilgrims," others vilifying the odyssey as a harebrained, wasteful exercise. The *New York World* commented that it was the "foolish exploit of an ultra-rich idealist."

Although Henry was in ill health for much of the voyage and returned home early, his fellow delegates continued their pilgrimage, traveling to Sweden, Denmark, and Holland to urge creation of their continuous mediation committee. Ultimately, it was apparent that peace was impossible and the effort failed.

While some newspapers harangued Henry for funding the effort, others extolled his integrity. In a January 1916 editorial titled "Henry Ford Deserves Respect, Not Ridicule," the *New York American* commented:

"He at least tried. Had every citizen of the United States, including the president and his cabinet and the members of Congress, put forth one-tenth the individual effort that Henry Ford put forth, the boys would have been out of the trenches by Christmas."

Henry never regretted his involvement. "The mere fact that it failed is not, to me, conclusive proof that it was not worth trying," he said in 1922. "We learn more from our failures than our successes. . . . I think everyone will agree that if it had been possible to end the war in 1916 the world would be better off than it is today."

When troubles brewed for America, the country often sought assistance from its most inventive native son. In the early 1920s, after more than 600,000 U.S. farms went bankrupt, the nation again turned to Henry, and he offered a solution.

He would buy a government-owned nitrate plant at Muscle Shoals, Alabama, to sell nitrate to farmers for use as fertilizer, charging vastly lower prices than those being levied by British and Chilean producers, which had commandeered the nitrate market. One newspaper estimated Henry would save farmers $100 million a year in fertilizer costs.

The nitrate plant was in disrepair and unutilized, having been built by the government on the banks of the Tennessee River during World War I to make synthetic nitrate explosives. The plant was powered by the current of the Tennessee River and its major

BLACK MONDAY *The Great Depression took a toll on Detroit, forcing the closure of many banks, including the National Bank of Detroit, left, seen here at its temporary quarters in* *1930. Above: A postcard depicting Detroit in the heyday of the Roaring Twenties, before the stock market wrought havoc on the city's financial institutions.*

tributaries, among the most powerful rivers in America. But the dams that had been built were incomplete. Henry offered $5 million for a ninety-nine-year lease on the dams and outright ownership of the plant.

Farmers were ecstatic. Henry Ford was in their corner again. Some newspapers predicted Henry eventually would harness the power of the Tennessee River to provide cheap electricity to the nation. The press was mostly favorable, inadvertently launching the ill-fated "Henry Ford for president" campaign.

As time wore on, however, the Ford proposal met resistance on Wall Street and in certain corridors of Congress, prompting Henry to withdraw his offer in 1921. The plan to harness the Tennessee River bogged down for another twelve years, until President Franklin D. Roosevelt signed the historic Tennessee Valley Authority Act in 1933.

The federal government accomplished with the TVA what Henry had sought, building dams, power plants, and transmission lines to sell inexpensive fertilizers and electricity to individuals and local communities. Henry had lit the fire, kindling the interest of private and public groups to bring industry, agriculture, and recreation to the South, consequently improving the standard of living for millions of Americans.

After the Depression forced the closure of many banks in the 1930s, the nation again turned to Henry. In February 1933, Henry and Edsel offered to take over the assets and liabilities of two troubled Detroit banks, Guardian National and First National, forming two new banks using $8.25 million of their own capital. The banks declined. Their directors and officers were concerned that Henry would terminate their employ and put the banks into receivership, thus exposing them to liability claims from depositors.

Undaunted, Henry persisted in his attempts to help Detroit during the banking crisis, finally capitalizing (for $3 million) a new bank, the Manufacturers National Bank of Detroit, in August 1933. The new bank acquired the assets of five failing financial institutions in Dearborn and Highland Park to serve depositors in those communities.

Henry's wide-ranging efforts to help the country through difficult times won the admiration of millions of Americans. It was no surprise, then, in 1937, when *Fortune* magazine surveyed its readers, "Will you name one manufacturer or manufacturing company whose policies you approve of in the main?" that the overwhelming response was Ford Motor Company.

What was astonishing was the percentage—47.2 percent. Lagging in second place was Procter & Gamble with a comparatively paltry 3.3 percent.

Property of --
Mr Edsel B. Ford

European Address:

C/o Automobiles Ford
225 Quai Aulagnier, Asnieres
Paris. France

United States Address:

C/o Ford Motor Company
Detroit, Michigan
U.S.A.

ART APPRECIATION *Edsel and Eleanor Ford, shown at home in 1937, were noted art collectors. Their collection ranged from American folk art, like the 1880 wood carving by Wilhelm Schimmel, right, to works by Gauguin and Titian. Above: Edsel's travel itinerary book, the pocket crammed with notes on art he'd seen abroad.*

EDSEL AND ELEANOR FORD: ART PATRONS

They were a couple whose names were synonymous with philanthropic and charitable endeavors, particularly in the field of the arts. Edsel and Eleanor Clay Ford were urbane, sophisticated, and intelligent collectors of fine and decorative arts. They also were beneficent givers, donating many great works to the Detroit Institute of Arts, the world-class museum in the Motor City.

Edsel, renowned for his daring, luxurious automobile designs in the 1920s and '30s, and Eleanor, whose uncle, Joseph L. Hudson, founded the thriving department store bearing his surname, were Detroit's "first

couple." They had become acquainted with Dr. Wilhelm R. Valentiner, director of the Detroit Institute of Arts—locals call it the DIA—from 1925 to 1943. Edsel served on the Arts Commission of the City of Detroit from 1925 to 1943 and Eleanor from 1943 to 1976.

The Fords' Cotswold-style home at Grosse Pointe Shores, Michigan, was filled with impressionist and postimpressionist paintings by Van Gogh, Renoir, Cezanne, Matisse, and Degas, as well as works by Italian Renaissance artists such as Fra Angelico and Titian and eighteenth-century English portraits painted by Sir Joshua Reynolds and Sir Henry

Raeburn. The couple's eclectic taste was reflected by the different periods of furnishings at their estate, from French Louis XV and Louis XVI armchairs and settees to American William and Mary wing chairs to English oak stools and exquisite Elizabethan-era carved paneling in Edsel's study.

Then there was the art deco–styled "Modern Room," designed by Walter Teague, a founding father of the art deco movement in the 1930s. Although the room was built for the children of Edsel and Eleanor, Edsel—always the modernist—liked it so much and was so inspired by its streamlined contours that he incorporated this look in the startling 1936 Lincoln Zephyr automobile that he and E. T. Gregorie designed.

Valentiner advised Edsel and Eleanor on their artwork acquisitions and conducted classes on artists and art history at the estate in Grosse Pointe Shores. Not only did the Fords later bequeath many works they had collected over the decades to the museum, particularly after Edsel's untimely death in 1943 and Eleanor's passing in 1976, they also contributed financially, giving large sums of money with which to buy other artworks, endow exhibitions and educational activities, and expand the museum.

And, when times were tough for the museum financially, the Fords could be counted on to provide relief. When the museum was forced by the Depression to cut its budget from $400,000 in 1928 to $40,000 in 1933, Edsel and Eleanor provided their own personal money to support the museum's activities and help keep it afloat during the bleak period.

Edsel and Eleanor were also the chief artistic and financial backers of one of the museum's proudest holdings—the famed frescoes (water-based pigments painted on damp plaster) executed by the great Mexican muralist Diego Rivera in the DIA's Garden Court. Edsel shared Rivera's interest in industrial design, though not the muralist's Marxist leanings. Ford Motor Company also had a major assembly plant outside Mexico City, hub of its Latin American automotive enterprises.

A decision was reached for Rivera to base the mural on Detroit's position as an industrial nexus, using Ford's Rouge Complex, then the world's largest industrial facility, as the subject matter. Rivera spent a month making sketches at the Rouge, where Ford controlled virtually the entire process of automobile manufacturing, bringing in raw materials on its own fleet of ships and gradually transforming them into vehicles. Rivera's masterwork detailed this highly complex, mechanized process.

When completed in 1933, the *Detroit Industry* murals created uproar. Many viewers were affronted by what they considered sacrilegious and even pornographic imagery. Today, the mural's nudes, symbolizing the fruitfulness of the earth, barely raise an eyebrow. Others were perturbed by Rivera's political and propagandistic metaphors, including obvious references to socialism, race relations, and environmental destruction. One panel, for instance, features workers in gas masks creating chemicals, below which a smaller panel depicts microscopic human cells engulfed by poisonous gas. The *Detroit News* criticized the murals as "a slander to Detroit workingmen."

Despite protests, the museum—with Edsel's backing—held firm. That was not the case in New York City, where Rivera was commissioned by the Rockefellers to paint a mural for the massive Rockefeller Center complex. After finding the work objectionable—it contained a portrait of the Communist leader Lenin—Rockefeller had it destroyed in 1933. ❖

MUCH TO CHEER *Workers at the Willow Run Plant applaud President Franklin Delano Roosevelt during his visit in 1942. Below: A commemorative fiftieth-anniversary horn button. Opposite: Henry II at ease with Ford workers. Like his grandfather and father, Henry II was progressive in his views about race. After the 1967 riots in Detroit, Henry II issued a corporate directive elevating affirmative action to a top priority.*

Ford's visionary policies continued uninterrupted during the thirty-four-year tenure of Henry's grandson. Henry Ford II was a new breed business leader—an "industrialist-statesman." He was as highly regarded for his business acumen as for his championing of civil rights and improved labor-management relations.

In an oft-quoted 1946 speech titled "The Challenge of Human Engineering," Henry II called for a "new frontier [in] industrial human relations." To achieve it, "management and labor must accept their share of responsibility to the public welfare and live up to their commitments," he said. The common goal was "to raise the standard of living by reducing costs, thereby bringing more and better products within the budgets of more and more people."

The stirring address won the praise of business leaders and labor officials, quelling union unrest and culminating in a generous Ford contract agreement with the UAW in 1946. In it, Ford granted workers a 15.1 percent wage increase, costing the company an additional $41 million. Some called it the best contract since the $5-a-day wage.

Labor relations improved further when Ford added adjusted cost-of-living benefits for both hourly and salaried employees in 1950, and supplemental employee benefits for out-of-work employees in 1955.

The latter was the first such program in the automobile industry. It recognized that sporadic unemployment caused by the cyclical nature of the automobile business wreaked a grievous financial and emotional toll on workers. Henry II earmarked $55 million to provide income to workers during periods of unemployment, representing five cents an hour for each paid hour of employment. In 1955, some 3,700 Ford employees availed themselves of this additional unemployment compensation.

Although Ford and the UAW have locked horns on occasion over the years, for the most part they have worked in harmony to ensure continually improving working conditions.

Like his grandfather before him, Henry II took sides on issues that went against popular business opinion. He often protested the imposition of protective tariffs on U.S. automobile imports, even though these cars would compete against Ford products. Henry II believed the competitive playing field must be even to achieve global free trade parity. "In order for others to buy from us, they must be able to sell to us," he explained.

DELEGATES AT LARGE *As Henry II broadened his interests to address global concerns, he delegated more responsibility to top lieutenants like Philip Caldwell, below, president*

of Ford of Europe and, later, of Ford Motor Company. Right: Henry II, in top row, in his capacity as alternate delegate to the United Nations.

Other orations touched on grander themes. In an address to the nation for Ford's fiftieth birthday in 1953, broadcast to more than 55 million television viewers, Henry II commented:

"We're the strongest nation in the world, but we haven't found the best way to use all our strength. We're the richest nation in the world, but we still haven't enough good homes, good schools, and good hospitals. We have the greatest technical know-how, but we've been slow to teach other nations how to use it."

He concluded by asking that the U.S. "accept the responsibility the world expects of us." The remarks reminded Americans in the midst of the 1950s economic boom that great power and wealth must be deployed for the good of humanity, not just the individual.

President Dwight Eisenhower had watched the address at the White House. Seizing on the moment, he offered Henry II the post of alternate delegate to the United Nations. Honored to have been asked, Henry accepted, and would make several memorable speeches to the UN assembly. In one address espousing global free trade, Henry II stated:

"We are interested in the mutual advantage which flows from an unfettered exchange of skills, goods, and ideas with other peoples. This is neither altruism nor imperialism—it is simply enlightened self-interest."

Continuing his grandfather's legacy of giving to benefit society, Henry II helped establish the United Foundation in 1949, joining with the heads of Chrysler, General Motors, and the UAW. The foundation provides monetary support to fight cancer, heart disease, blindness, arthritis, and other illnesses and also addresses societal and family needs.

That same year, Henry II also created the Ford Motor Company Fund, a nonprofit organization supported primarily by contributions from the company. In announcing the establishment of the fund, he said:

"The purpose [is] the alleviation of want and human suffering and the betterment and improvement of mankind through the making of contributions to organizations operating exclusively for charitable, scientific, literary, or educational purposes. This action is an attempt to organize ourselves to discharge to the best of our ability our obligations as an industrial citizen."

AMERICA'S HOMETOWN

Henry Ford Museum & Greenfield Village is the founder's tribute to "real" history, the way Henry

believed it should be experienced and taught. Dedicated to the memory of Thomas Edison, the village and museum constitute the largest living history museum in the world, with many famed edifices, dismantled and rebuilt on the grounds. There's Edison's Menlo Park laboratory, where he invented the

lightbulb, the Wright Brothers' bicycle shop, and even Ford's first automobile workshop at 58 Bagley Avenue. In the museum is a world-class collection of antique cars (such as Henry's 999 racecar), tractors, and aircraft, among them a Ford Tri-Motor plane. Walking outside (or motoring by in a vintage Model T), visitors

are transported to the nineteenth and early twentieth centuries. Henry's birthplace is lovingly restored and re-created, as is the one-room schoolhouse he attended as a child. "He founded this remarkable museum to inspire others," a placard states.

Ford Motor Company Fund seeks to build better communities and a better quality of life in the places where Ford conducts business. The fund has five "giving priorities"—education, environment, health and welfare, civic affairs, and the arts and humanities. Ford Fund grants totaled more than $105 million for 2001, a 25 percent increase over 2000 and a stunning 6000-percent-plus increase since the fund's inception. Education was the fund's top priority in 2001, receiving 50 percent of the grants donated.

Honoring his grandfather's instinctive interest in education, in 1956 Henry II donated Henry's 210-acre Fair Lane estate to the University of Michigan to establish a campus in Dearborn. This gift was accompanied by a $6.5 million grant from the Ford Fund to aid in the development of a new educational center on the site.

Henry also would have endorsed his grandson's efforts on behalf of disadvantaged young people and the long-term unemployed. Henry II had an idea for an organization that would help these individuals find meaningful summer jobs. He presented his concept to President Lyndon Johnson, who in 1968 approved it as the National Alliance of Business Leaders and named Henry II chairman. Now called the JOBS program, for Job Opportunities in the Business Sector, the organization continues to find work for those most in need.

These progressive activities were complemented by efforts to make automobiles safer. Ford had introduced the first safety glass in the 1920s, the first all-steel bodies in the 1930s, and a plethora of occupant protection features in the 1950s—including padded instrument panels and visors; deep-dish, energy-absorbing steering wheels; safety door latches; rearview mirrors; and safety belts.

In the 1960s, Ford's reputation for safety burgeoned upon the dedication of the Ford Automotive Safety Research Center—a first in the industry. Launched in 1967, the research center embarked upon the new "accident prevention approach" to automotive safety. Ford scientists introduced various simulators to evaluate accurately and quickly the quality and performance of brake linings, tires, steering systems, and so on.

These manifold efforts to improve safety fostered crashworthy, safer automobiles. Indeed, Ford today has more vehicles with five-star crash test safety ratings from the U.S. National Highway Traffic Safety Administration than any other carmaker. A five-star rating is the highest awarded.

Ford's workforce during the latter half of the century remained as diverse as in the days of Henry Ford. However, this was not the case at many of its independently owned Ford dealerships and suppliers. Henry II decided to make a difference, launching Ford-funded minority dealership and supplier programs. In 1967, Ford signed a historic contract with Ernie Banks, the great Chicago Cubs ballplayer, making him the first African American to own a Ford dealership. It was located in Chicago. Since then, minority dealerships have sprouted nationwide and, today, have their own separate trade association. Similarly, a Minority Supplier Development Committee has helped swell the ranks of minority suppliers.

RENAISSANCE REVIVAL *The Renaissance Center was conceived to revitalize the city of Detroit. Henry II was such a huge supporter of these efforts that he moved Ford Division corporate offices to the cluster of majestic spires. (Ford Division returned to* *Dearborn in the late 1990s.) This civic venture received political backing by Detroit's first African American mayor Coleman Young (second from right) and financial support and cheerleading by Henry II (right) and Ford Motor Company.*

As the civil rights tensions of the 1960s and the recession of the 1970s conspired to decimate the economies of Detroit and other U.S. cities, Henry II took action to save his hometown. With political backing from Detroit's first African American mayor, Coleman Young—who liked to call Henry II "Hank the Deuce" (much to Henry's amusement)—he led the charge to build the historic Renaissance Center in downtown Detroit. The $350 million hotel and office development on the city's riverfront was financed largely by Ford and other Detroit-area companies whose support Henry II enlisted.

In June 1975, topping-out ceremonies were held for the first of four thirty-nine-story towers with one seventy-seven story center tower designed by architect John Portman. Two years later, on April 15, 1977, Henry II presided at the dedication. Today, this unmistakable cluster of glass and steel towers—the RenCen, as locals call it—is the gleaming center of Detroit's skyline and a symbol of its ongoing revitalization. It is now the world headquarters of General Motors Corporation. Henry II's civic venture enticed many citizens and businesses that had fled Detroit for the suburbs to return. It also serves as a beacon guiding companies to reconsider Detroit as a commercial nexus.

Ford has undertaken similar programs across the world to improve the economic prospects of other cities and their citizens. For nearly twenty years, Ford of Europe has funded diverse conservation, cultural, and environmental programs in dozens of countries. They run the gamut, from funding the reconstruction of Shakespeare's famous Globe Theater in London to supporting an organization to protect in Poland the white stork and wetlands.

The School Construction Program sponsored by Ford Mexico and its Mexico dealerships helped create more than 150 schools in Mexico during the 1980s and '90s, attended by some 100,000 students. In Vietnam, Ford made the largest American investment ever in this emerging economy, erecting a manufacturing facility and sales and service infrastructure for trucks, minibuses, passenger cars, and TH!NK electric cars. The company also built a "safety village" in Hanoi to promote road safety among children, teenagers, and young adults.

Ford has assisted disaster relief efforts throughout the world, helped build dozens of Habitat for Humanity homes in America, and remains the largest single donor to the United Way. The company also offers every salaried employee sixteen hours of paid time off per year to volunteer for community projects. In southeast Michigan alone, 18,000 volunteers contributed 144,000 hours to 1,143 projects in 2000.

Ford's workforce today is a snapshot of the world. The company's human rights agenda calls for eradication of prejudices toward people of different ethnicities, religions, sexual orientations, and nationalities. Ford's Employee Resource Groups are a microcosm of our unique differences—"differences to be valued," Bill Ford has said. They include the Ford-employees African-Ancestry Network; Ford Asian Indian Association; Ford Chinese Association; Ford Employees Dealing with disAbilities; Ford Interfaith Network; Ford Parenting Network; Ford Gay, Lesbian, or Bisexual Employees; Ford Hispanic Network Group; Middle Eastern Community; and Professional Women's Network.

When Bill Ford assumed chairmanship of Ford in 1999, he elevated Ford's environmental stewardship to a top company priority. Bill has led the charge at Ford to preserve the environment, a passion for nature he inherited from his great-grandfather. Henry had built a hydroelectric dam to supply power to his house, had put up bat houses to control mosquitoes organically, and could stand endlessly, hour after hour, promoting the potential of soybeans, gleefully pointing out his two-piece suit made of soybean fabric. He was an industrialist and a conservationist.

This birthright lives on. Bill believes firmly that industry and nature can coexist in harmony to better serve humanity. And he

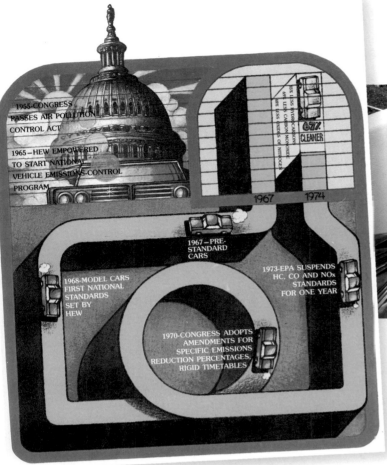

is adamant about proving it. "Ford has to be a leader in social issues, whether it's education, the environment, or any other social issue," Bill said.

"We have some of the best people and some of the best players. We are such a large player on the world scene and have access to resources, both monetary and educational. We must lead in this regard."

Ford's environmental leadership is exemplified by its continuing efforts to remove toxic agents from many of its manufacturing processes, the company's impressive fleet of alternative fuel vehicles, and its tenacious commitment to materials recycling.

Ford uses more recycled material in its cars and trucks than any other carmaker, and it was the first vehicle manufacturer to implement Recycling Design Guidelines for "maximum recoverability" of a vehicle. Thanks to the ingenuity of Ford engineers, who developed a handheld identifier that can distinguish between four basic types of plastic, more than 50 million recycled plastic soda pop bottles have found new life as luggage racks and door padding. Old computers and telephones have been recycled into grilles, and obsolete steel containers have become the raw materials for engine blocks and cylinder heads.

Ford's North American assembly plants recycle more than 380 million pounds of waste each year. Similar efforts are under way at all Ford plants around the world. In the mid-1990s, the company created a

network of 120 certified vehicle dismantlers in Germany to ensure environmentally sound recycling of old vehicles. Owners of vehicles without catalytic converters were given financial incentives to purchase or lease a new Ford. The incentive program was a huge success—more than 300,000 vehicles have been taken off the road and recycled, generating enough recycled metal to build twenty Eiffel Towers.

Ford has won many awards for its efforts to preserve, conserve, or clean up the environment, including the Keep America Beautiful Award for Excellence, the highest honor presented by the organization. Ford also has been lauded by the U.S. Environmental Protection Agency as a "Champion of the World" for its efforts to protect the ozone layer of the atmosphere.

Curtailing global warming is a high priority for Ford. The company is a charter member of the International Cooperative for Ozone Layer Protection, whose mission is to eliminate the use of ozone-depleting substances years ahead of government mandates. Ford stopped using chlorofluorocarbon (CFC) in its air-conditioning systems on cars and trucks on 1994 models, two years before federal regulations were passed, and it no longer uses CFC solvents to clean electronic circuit boards, using inert gas wave technologies instead.

The company also was one of the first auto companies to provide CFC retrofit kits.

Ford is spreading the gospel of environmentalism throughout the countries where it conducts business. It has successfully campaigned to eliminate leaded fuel in India, treated wastewater to serve as a source of irrigation water for rice farmers in Vietnam, and created special incinerators to eliminate emissions from paint areas at the Setúbal, Portugal, plant. That facility now has the lowest environmental emissions of any similar plant currently in operation in Europe.

Ford also is spearheading efforts to protect endangered species and preserve wildlife habitats. At the company's Cuautitlán Assembly Plant outside Mexico City, the Ford Wetland Enhancement Project provides reptiles and amphibians with habitat and cover, a garden for desert flora, and a raptor management area for hawks, owls, and shrikes. This is the first project of its kind in Mexico, where Ford's roots stretch back to 1925.

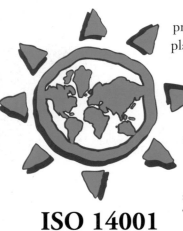

ISO 14001

As Ford builds for today, it is preserving resources for tomorrow. Older plants like the Rouge Complex and the Windsor plant in Ontario, Canada, are being rebuilt into the most environmentally responsible automotive manufacturing facilities in the world. At the Windsor plant, built in the 1920s, Ford has built an on-site wastewater treatment plant to intercept any inadvertent release of oil or chemicals. There is no connection from anywhere in the plant to the municipal storm sewer except for rainwater drainage from roads and the plant roof. Consequently, runoff to the Detroit River is managed carefully. Today, the rebuilt plant is a model of environmental efficiency.

This massive reconstruction effort, and the one currently being undertaken at the Rouge, proves that so-called brownfield redevelopment can give new life to old manufacturing facilities without harming the environment or reducing employment. These projects are guided by a subsidiary, Ford Motor Land Services Corporation, whose responsibility it is to negotiate and process the sale of Ford real estate holdings around the world. Ford Land's mission is to turn vacant land tracts into thriving retail centers, quality office space, and shopping malls.

"Enlightened corporations understand that environmental and social issues are business issues," says Bill Ford. "They realize that, ultimately, they can only be as successful as the world in which they exist. That has always been our belief at Ford Motor Company. We are in this together."

Bill Ford sees Ford Motor Company as more than an institution. It is a living, breathing "family" made up of hundreds of thousands of employees, dealers, and suppliers and millions of consumers who buy its products and services. Independent business

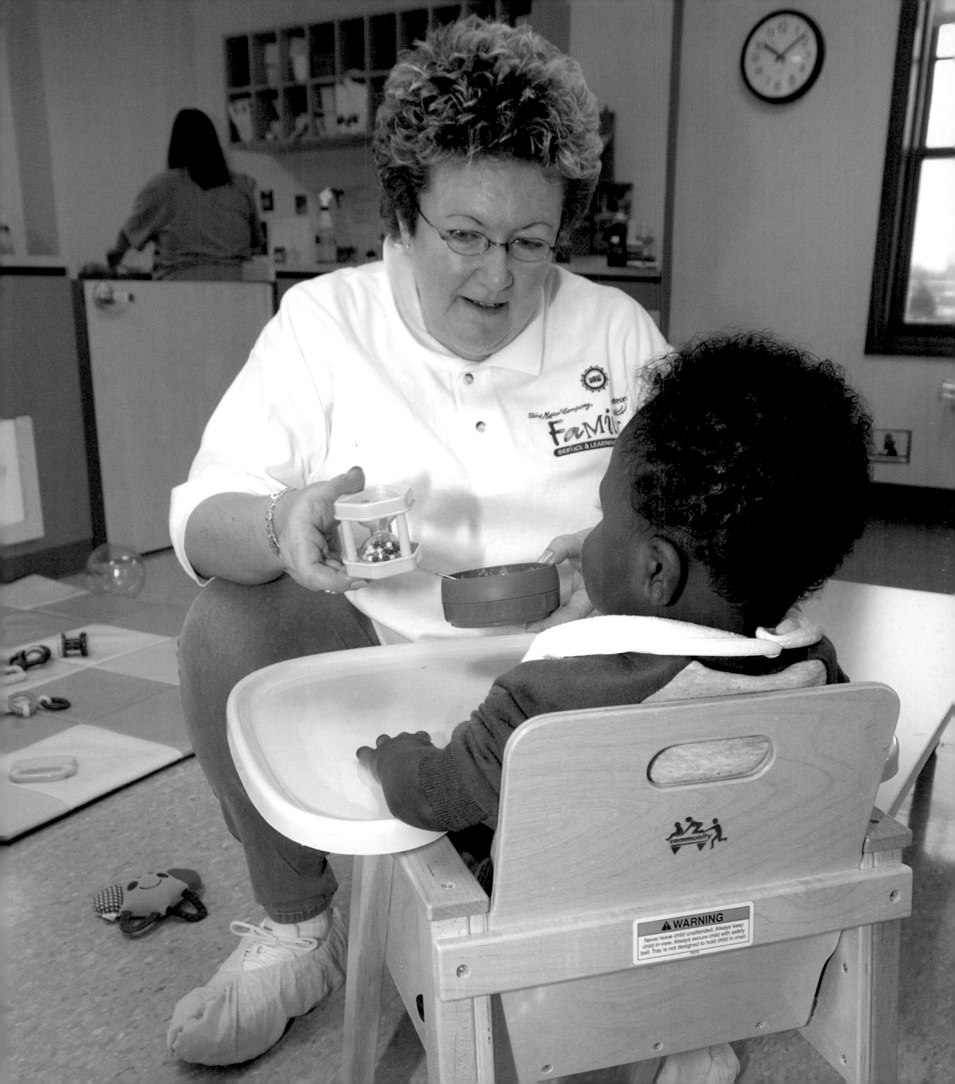

INDUSTRIAL EVOLUTION *The Rouge Complex, a symbol of America's industrial might in the twentieth century, has been reimagined and is being revitalized as a model of sustainable manufacturing for the future. Above:*

Ironworkers building the new Dearborn Truck Plant in 2001. Right: From asphalt and concrete to an oasis of green, the Rouge Complex of tomorrow in an artist's rendering.

ROUGE HERITAGE PROJECT

Henry Ford built the largest industrial facility in the world, the Rouge Complex, in order to exert as much control as possible over the entire process of manufacturing an automobile. Beginning in 1917 on the banks of the Rouge River, the plant was the manifestation of Henry's vision of Ford as a vertically integrated company, taking raw materials and processing them at Ford foundries and factories into cars.

Henry's self-reliance, his desire to "own" the entire automobile manufacturing process, is perhaps best described by an inscription by noted naturalist and author

Henry David Thoreau. The inscription, in the oak mantel of a fireplace at Henry's home at Fair Lane, reads: "Chop your own wood and it will warm you twice."

Today, 550 acres of Ford-owned Rouge Complex property are being reborn to serve the interests not of a vertical process but of a virtual one. Ford Motor Company purchases many of the parts and materials that go into its vehicles from a legion of global automotive suppliers, and needs for the old Rouge factories have changed. Bill Ford led the board in making the decision to redevelop the Rouge into a model of

GROWING GREEN *Mustangs ready for shipment, below, line up at the site of the Dearborn Assembly Plant, site of the Rouge Heritage project.*

sustainable manufacturing, incorporating a number of flexible manufacturing and environmental features intended to make the Rouge a healthier, more productive, and more supportive work environment.

The new Dearborn Truck Plant is designed to be flexible—giving Ford the ability to quickly respond to market conditions by switching from one vehicle platform to another. Workers are separated from machinery by overhead walkways, and Web-enabled computer terminals are located on the assembly floor so workers can contact suppliers in real time about

The plant also boasts a 454,000-square-foot "living roof," covered with an innovative carbohydrate-based surface, supporting live plants and soil to reduce storm water runoff and invite several species of indigenous birds to the area. Climbing plants also help shade and cool buildings, and runoff from streets, buildings, and parking lots is directed to culverts planted with native species to filter water before it enters the Rouge River. The $2 billion redevelopment project also provides ample natural light and ventilation and relies on solar panels to provide energy to a visitor center.

Ford believes that substantial cost savings will result from the environmental

save approximately $35 million in construction costs. The roof also lowers costs by keeping the factory cooler. The thirty-five large skylights in the Dearborn Truck Plant will enable the company to turn off half the interior lights during the day.

The design and architectural work was done in conjunction with William McDonough + Partners, a world-renowned design firm specializing in creative and environmentally sustainable buildings. When completed, the reborn Rouge is likely to attract the same attention it captured eight decades ago, when the Albert Kahn–designed plants were unveiled to the world. ❖

people own and manage the more than twenty-thousand Ford dealerships in more than 150 markets around the world. These individuals are the face of Ford to the public, conveying what Ford stands for as a global company and community member.

More than two hundred independent automobile supply companies provide nearly 90 percent of the components and materials used in the production of Ford vehicles, while another ten thousand provide the company with all the other products and services needed to run the company's business, from advertising to capital equipment. Suppliers are so integrated into Ford's product development process that they now have direct responsibility for the design and engineering of many components and systems.

Ford has provided employment over the past century to literally millions of people. Many generations of the same family have given their talents and efforts to the company. As they were when working for "the Fords" in the early days of the twentieth century, Ford's more than 300,000 employees today are proud to be part of their company's singular heritage.

They are "all members of the Ford family." This is the frequent mantra of Bill Ford, who believes that all employees are as much "Fords" as are he, his father, uncles, cousins, grandfather, and great-grandfather, the indomitable Henry Ford, and all of their spouses and children. The relationships that these employees build and nurture with each other and with all Ford stakeholders, from investors to customers, are Ford Motor Company.

As Ford celebrates its extraordinary history in 2003, the world celebrates with it. Ford made possible our forefathers' first automobiles, their children's first voyage on an airplane, the geostationary satellites that broadcast television to their grandchildren, and the alternative fuel vehicles driven today by their great-grandchildren. Ford built the armaments that helped win two world wars and contributed countless innovations, making our lives much easier, happier, and more prosperous. By its one-hundredth birthday on June 16, 2003, Ford Motor Company will have produced approximately 300 million vehicles and will end its century as it began—a company focused on succeeding in business and doing the right thing.

"A good company delivers excellent products and services," says Bill Ford. "A great one does all that and strives to make the world a better place."

From Henry to Bill, Fords have built a great company whose greatest achievements are perhaps yet to come.

INDEX

Boldface indicates pages with photos.

PHOTO CREDITS